Brownell, Blaine A

The urban ethos in the South, 1920-1930

DATE DUE			

THE URBAN ETHOS IN THE SOUTH, 1920–1930

The Urban Ethos
in the South
1920-1930

BLAINE A. BROWNELL

Louisiana State University Press
BATON ROUGE

ISBN 0–8071–0157–5
Library of Congress Catalog Card Number 74–82003
Copyright © 1975 by Louisiana State University Press
Manufactured in the United States of America

This book was designed by Dwight Agner. It was
composed in VIP Electra by The Composing Room of
Michigan, Inc., Grand Rapids, Michigan, and printed and
bound by Colonial Press, Inc., Clinton, Massachusetts.

for MARDI

Contents

Tables

Acknowledgments

HISTORICAL RESEARCH demands the facilities of libraries, and I have enjoyed throughout the course of my labors an unusual degree of eager, capable assistance and friendly cooperation. I especially want to thank the staffs of the Louis Round Wilson Library at the University of North Carolina at Chapel Hill, the Milton Eisenhower Library at The Johns Hopkins University, and the Purdue University Library. George R. Stewart of the Birmingham Public Library, Harriet C. Owsley of the Tennessee State Archives, and Elizabeth Hughey of the Methodist Publishing House Library in Nashville went far beyond the call of duty in answering my inquiries and directing me to useful sources. I am also grateful to the staffs of the following libraries for their assistance: the Georgia State Library, the Virginia State Archives, the Alabama Department of Archives and History, the City Archives in the New Orleans Public Library, the Atlanta Historical Society; the public libraries in Atlanta, Memphis, and Nashville; and the libraries at the University of Alabama, Atlanta University, the University of Georgia, Emory University, Fisk University, Louisiana State University, Memphis

State University, Samford University, the University of South Carolina, the University of Tennessee, Vanderbilt University, and Winthrop College in Charleston. The city clerks and their staffs in Atlanta, Birmingham, Memphis, and Nashville were most helpful in directing me to relevant city-council minutes, planning-commission records, and other municipal documents.

A grant from the Penrose Fund of the American Philosophical Society and a Faculty X-L Grant from the Purdue Research Foundation supported two summers of research in southern cities. A Senior Fellowship at the Institute of Southern History at The Johns Hopkins University in 1971–1972, funded by the Ford Foundation, provided an invaluable year for writing and reflection, uninterrupted by the usual academic duties.

I also wish to thank the editors of the *Journal of Southern History*, the *American Quarterly*, and the *Mississippi Quarterly* for permission to include portions of previously published articles.

Anne Marie O'Malley, a graduate research assistant at Purdue University, prepared most of the tables and handled a variety of other chores capably and promptly. The secretarial staff of Purdue's History Department and Evia D. Wilson of the University of Alabama in Birmingham typed various drafts of the book with a minimum of errors. Leslie E. Phillabaum and Ruth Laney guided the manuscript through the stages of editing and production with the skill and good judgment that distinguish the Louisiana State University Press.

This book has benefited, more than anything else, from wise counsel and informed criticism. I am indebted to Charles N. Glaab, Louis P. Galambos, Walter B. Weare, Donald J. Berthrong, Philip R. Muller, Ronald Walters, Elisha P. Douglass, Robert M. Miller, Hugh Davis Graham, Harold D. Woodman, Robert E. May, Joseph L. Arnold, Edward S. LaMonte, and James N. Duffy for their written and oral comments on various parts of the project. Two Fellows at the Institute of Southern History—Peter Kolchin and David M. Katzman—read portions of the manuscript and provided detailed and especially helpful suggestions and criticism. And all those persons who attended an Institute seminar at which a chapter of this project was presented helped me to rethink crucial questions and tackle unresolved problems.

This book is the product of an idea originally suggested by George E. Mowry, who patiently guided me through the initial stages and helped shape the principal conceptual directions of the work. I am also greatly indebted to George B. Tindall, who generously shared with me his immense knowledge of twentieth-century southern history at virtually every phase of the writing, and to David Herbert Donald, who read a substantial portion of the manuscript, offered numerous perceptive comments, and helped to make my year at the Institute of Southern History both intellectually exciting and productive.

Because of the assistance of these capable scholars, this book is much better than it otherwise would have been. I have been continually impressed by their insight and deeply flattered by their friendship. Many of them will doubtless take exception to some of the things I have written, and none of them should be held responsible for any errors of fact or judgment which I have made.

My wife Mardi—to whom this book is affectionately dedicated—shared my research labors, suffered through my various moods, read the manuscript, penetrated my efforts at pretense, and bore us a son and a daughter in the course of my work on the project. Most of all, she made life worth living and this book worth writing.

Introduction

Whoever sets out to analyze the mind of a city faces a difficult task.
—*Atlanta Life*, November 27, 1926

WRITTEN HISTORY is, inevitably, the imposition of order on chaos. Or so it sometimes appears to the historian dealing with popular thought. Scholars who concern themselves with images of the city are perhaps especially prone to think of history as a stream of consciousness rather than a logical or rational development in time. For such images have generally been diffuse, nebulous, and extremely difficult to interpret except in the most superficial way.

This book began some years ago as a survey of images of the city held by urban dwellers in the American South during the 1920s. The mass of material containing such views is enormous and largely uncatalogued. Much of it has never before been taken seriously by scholars. And the variety of individual urban views and notions is equally imposing. I soon came to the conclusion that urban images were obviously related to historical reality—that they might help explain why our cities have developed as they have—and that these images would remain disjointed and nebulous unless they were related to the socioeconomic groups which espoused them and to larger patterns of social thought. The key to understanding such images, in other words, was to see them as products of and responses to a historical situation. I was interested in knowing who put forth such images, why the images took the form that they did, and how they might have influenced urban development.

The principal goals of this study are, first, to demonstrate that a more or less consistent conception of the city, a guiding complex of beliefs concerning the nature and role of the urban community—an *urban ethos*—was maintained and expressed by spokesmen of the leading white commercial and civic groups in the major "circulating media" in southern cities during the 1920s—newspapers, chamber of commerce publications, church periodicals, promotional tracts, and official city documents. Secondly, I hope to show that this ethos was shared in some degree by large numbers of city dwellers—and found in labor union publications, novels, and black newspapers—and that it was one major conceptual context within which urban policy was formulated.

The study differs from previous examinations of "urban imagery" in that it deals with random visions of the city in terms of larger "concepts of community" (which involve not only visual representations but notions about the city's history and future, its role within regional and national patterns, and its relationship to the individual and to various social groups). It is, in short, an effort to examine urban imagery, urban boosterism, and concepts of the urban community in the context of a relatively specific historical and regional situation, and to relate them to general patterns of social thought and municipal policy.

Since the large mass of urban citizens simply did not leave their attitudes as part of the historical record and, in any event, were far less likely either to concern themselves with the formulation of abstract concepts of the city or to direct urban policy, this study is limited to the attitudes of what can be generally designated the "business-oriented middle class." More precisely, it concentrates on the concepts held by members of the white commercial-civic elite—those business and civic leaders whose principal focus of attention was the downtown business district, and whose views were most often reflected in the major urban newspapers and in many other printed sources.

This book is therefore not an examination of urban opinions "from the bottom," but of those enunciated by a conscious urban elite. This delimitation is unfortunate since there are doubtless a variety of other urban views that are not represented (though many of these have probably been lost to the historical record in any case). But it is fortuitous in the sense that upper socioeconomic groups possessed the requisite power and resources, and the greater opportunity, to determine urban policy and translate their thinking into action.

Neither is the book a thorough study of black urban opinions, though a good deal of attention is given to the attitudes of the southern black middle class. Black commercial and civic spokesmen expressed many of the major themes of urban boosterism and the urban ethos, but their views in this respect, as in most others, were clearly secondary in importance to their overweening concern with problems of race. Blacks constituted a substantial proportion of southern urban populations in this period. The attitudes of black leaders reflect, I think, the degree to which they shared concepts of the urban community prevailing among white commercial-civic spokesmen and interpreted these concepts in the light of Afro-American aspirations and experience.

In the study of popular thought or "community ideology" it is important that the sources employed reflect, as much as possible, the attitudes of groups rather than individuals, that the views expressed have a primarily "public" rather than "private" dimension. I have therefore relied principally on printed materials rather than on manuscript sources (which are, in any event, very poorly catalogued for the purposes of such an investigation). The use of printed sources was not particularly selective. Virtually all available publications—from major urban dailies to church bulletins, labor papers, and chamber of commerce periodicals—were examined. (The major sources employed in the study are discussed in the Bibliographical Essay.) At least one major daily for each city was examined intensively for the entire decade, and in most cases two papers were analyzed. A wide range of other publications was also consulted in detail. The research net was cast over as wide an area as possible. The concentration of my research, however, and the relevance of my conclusions concern the views of the white commercial-civic elite. The great bulk of the sources is taken from the 1920s, though the paucity of black publications for these cities during the decade necessitated the use of some material from earlier years (as in the case of the Nashville *Globe*).

It should be obvious to any historian that printed urban materials are never fully representative of the views of all groups in the city, especially those lower on the socioeconomic scale. Most urban citizens are "spoken for" in the public prints. It is impossible to know precisely how much the circulating media influenced the opinions of the city populace, but it is probably accurate to say that the majority of printed materials both shaped and reflected public opinion, in varying degrees. It seems to me that many of the elements of what I have termed the urban ethos were shared by many groups in the city, but given the difficulties of proof I offer this observation as a possibility rather than a fact.

There were exceptions to every general pattern of thought encountered in urban publications during the decade, and the disagreements on aspects of specific city policies were particularly pronounced. Consequently, I have focused on those conceptions of the urban community which seemed to have broad acceptance—at least among members of the white commercial-civic elite—that were found in a variety of different publications, with different editors, political opinions, and audiences. I have made no systematic effort to demonstrate the representativeness of my sources, though I have not employed any single concept of the city unless it also appeared in a variety of other publications. I have quoted extensively from the sources to give the reader some basis for judgment in this respect and also to convey in the best possible manner the style and spirit of contemporary discussion.

The focus is on southern cities because they have been largely ignored by other urban historians, and because the South has traditionally been the least urban section of the country and, presumably, the most anti-urban in its opinions. If patterns of thought in most American cities were also present in the urban South, then this should illuminate our understanding of national urbanism. Similarly, the differences between southern and nonsouthern cities in this respect can tell us a great deal about the diversity of the American urban experience. Principal attention is devoted to major cities of the "central South"—Atlanta, Birmingham, Memphis, Nashville, and New Orleans— with secondary attention to the smaller cities of Charleston and Knoxville. Cities in Texas and Florida have been excluded from the study because their development during the 1920s was atypical of the prevailing patterns of southern urbanization: in both states cities grew at an exceptionally rapid pace, due largely to the petroleum industry and interior railroad trade in Texas and to land speculation and tourism in Florida. Most of the cities included in my analysis (with the notable exception of Charleston) experienced considerable growth in the early twentieth century, but had reached a stage of relative urban "maturity" by the 1920s. Cities in the "border" states—Maryland, Virginia, Kentucky, Oklahoma, and Arkansas—have also been generally excluded from the study, mostly because their development was influenced considerably by patterns of urbanization in the middle Atlantic, midwest, and southwest regions. Some attention has been devoted to Norfolk and Richmond but not to Louisville, Baltimore, or Little Rock. The major goal was to achieve a sample with sufficient diversity *and* regional integrity.

Most of the book is devoted to an examination of the sources, elements, and functions of the urban "ethos." Regrettably, this word has many religious associations that are not intended here. What I mean by the term is a general overarching conception of the city which stressed the desirability—indeed, the necessity—of both urban growth and social order in such a way that they would be mutually reinforcing. The urban community was seen as corporate and interdependent, a delicate balance of various groups and institutions. The greatest challenge to the metropolis was its ability to contend with the consequences and implications of expansion while at the same time preserving the existing socioeconomic order and retaining commercial-civic leadership. The kind of city envisioned in the urban ethos—which I have described as "corporate-expansive" in form—could be attained, according to most commercial-civic spokesmen, not by basic changes in institutions or the urban class structure, but by an emphasis on "responsible" citizenship, social control, and regulation of the physical city through urban planning. The urban ethos was thus both a means of dealing conceptually with urban reality—of comprehending the city—and of providing conceptual guidance in the formulation of urban policy.

Urban boosterism—dismissed by most historians as supersalesmanship or mindless hoopla—was actually an expression of the urban ethos and, further, a rhetorical effort to achieve the realization of the corporate-expansive city by promoting urban unity, growth, and commercial-civic priorities. The urban ethos and the urban boosterism that expressed it were not simply rationalizations of economic interests. Rather, they reflected a complex of social views and functioned as justifications of municipal policy and social control. Certainly, they were more complex and substantive than most historians have suggested.

Like other broad conceptions, the urban ethos was not a precise or

rigorous ideology. Its ideological role—its usefulness, if you will—depended
on a certain degree of vagueness and generality. Whether it is precise enough
to be of much use in historical analysis is a question to be answered in further
research. Actually, a greater danger in a work of this kind is that the diversity
of historical experience will be veiled by a contrived interpretive uniformity.
This is certainly not my intention, and I should make clear at the outset that
the urban ethos was a *general* conception, shared by most members of the
commercial-civic elite but by no means in all its aspects and in the same
measure. On the other hand, it seems to me that it is significant precisely
because it was widely shared, because it seemed to exist on a plane above
normal political controversies and other differences of opinion within the
business-oriented middle class. I have therefore attempted what I hope is a
"constructive" imposition of order on chaos, in an effort to understand in
retrospect what, I think, few individuals fully understood at the time.

No one has ever "proven" that thought influences action, even though
most of us know that this is the case. Certainly, as rationalizations or
justifications of action, ideas have played a rather pronounced role in human
history. I proceed here on the assumption that what men think can indeed
help to explain how and why they act, even if it does not *determine* their
actions, and I have made an effort to suggest the relationships between the
urban ethos and urban reality. I have not attempted an overall history of the
urban South in the 1920s; this study is primarily devoted to images, conceptions, and *perceived* reality. And my conclusions, due to the methodological
necessities of intellectual history, are based more on illustration than on proof.
Given the dearth of scholarship on southern cities, however, I trust that this
book will serve in some small way to further general knowledge of urbanization
in the nation's most "rural" region.

The book opens with a brief survey of southern urbanization and the seven
particular cities involved and then proceeds to an analysis of relationships
between conceptions of the city and socioeconomic factors; of contemporary
comparisons between southern cities and other urban and nonurban environments (the spatial dimension of urban consciousness); of awareness of
urban problems; of varied elements of the urban ethos and reflections of that
ethos in municipal policy and in popular interpretations of local history (the
temporal dimension of urban consciousness). I have not attempted to
compare the southern urban ethos with views of the city in other regions,

though the effort to promote urban expansion while maintaining social order has been deeply rooted and perennial in the history of urban business and civic elites in the United States. Urban historians who have worked on other American cities in the late nineteenth or early twentieth century will, I think, note some significant similarities here.

The 1920s was in some respects a crucial period for many southern cities. Rapid population and territorial growth over the preceding several decades had brought with it myriad social problems and demands on municipal authorities. Most important, southern cities, perhaps even more than nonregional urban areas, experienced a confrontation for the first time between a still accelerating trend toward urban centralization and a new and growing capacity for decentralization provided by technological innovations like the telephone and the automobile. These contradictory tendencies—embodied in the skyscraper and the motor vehicle—promised unprecedented urban growth *and* social transformation, and it was most difficult for business and civic leaders to predict the future directions or character of urban development. They were, in fact, coming face-to-face with the realities and implications of the twentieth-century American metropolis. The southern urban ethos of the 1920s (regardless of what it may have been in other parts of the country or in other periods) was most definitely a conceptual response to these realities and contained preferred meanings of dealing with them.

THE URBAN ETHOS IN THE SOUTH, 1920–1930

1   Cities of the South: Crucibles of Change

> The changes Atlanta has undergone ... have been so very marked that numbers of native Atlantans are sometimes undecided about which corner to turn, right in sight of the block in which they were born.
>
> —Sarah Huff, *My 80 Years in Atlanta* (1937)

THE SOUTH was experiencing a transition by the 1920s that both contemporary observers and later historians considered momentous. A region overwhelmingly rural and agricultural was clearly becoming more urban and industrial; and new currents of thought and activity, spurred on by the domestic mobilization of World War I, swept across the southern landscape. "Skylines that once pictured ancestral trees," William J. Robertson wrote in 1927, "to-day bear the outlines of factory stacks and skyscrapers. Hills and meadows that once knew only the deer and the fox and the paths of the lonely mountain folk, support roadbeds of trunk line railroads and great highway systems." When the South passed into the third decade of the twentieth century, an essentially static society, as George Brown Tindall commented, "entered an unfamiliar terrain of diversity and change in which there lurked a thousand threats to the older orthodoxies." Indeed, "the stream of Southern history broke upon the social and economic rapids of the 1920s" with such force that it would never again be the same.[1]

1 William J. Robertson, *The Changing South* (New York, 1927), 1; George Brown Tindall, *The Emergence of the New South, 1913–1945* (Baton Rouge, 1967), 184, 285.

The city emerged repeatedly as the most appropriate symbol of regional change. "Over the whole land hung the incessant machine-gun rattle of riveting hammers," Wilbur J. Cash recalled; "in many places the streets were like those of a rebuilding war area, with the yawning walls of old buildings coming down and of new buildings going up." Similarly, Ellen Glasgow vividly described the whirlwind pace and blind rush of urbanization during the decade:

Everywhere people were pushing one another into the slums or the country. Everywhere the past was going out with the times and the future was coming on in a torrent. . . . To add more and more numbers; to build higher and higher; to push harder and harder; and particularly to improve what had already been added or built or pushed—these impulses had united at last into a frenzied activity. And while the building and the pushing and the improving went on, the village grew into the town, the town grew into the city, and the city grew into the country.[2]

The pushing and the building were evident not only in Atlanta, Memphis, and Richmond but also in the scores of small towns scattered across the region which woke—like William Faulkner's mythical Jefferson, Mississippi—from their "communal slumbers into a rash of Rotary and Lion Clubs and Chambers of Commerce and City Beautifuls." The southern small town followed an archetypal American pattern, "dubbing itself city as Napoleon dubbed himself emperor and defending the expedient by padding its census rolls—a fever, a delirium in which it would confound forever seething with motion and motion with progress."[3]

This fever of southern town-building had never been so high, but it was not entirely new. Though the region persisted for most of its existence in the ways of an agricultural economy and a predominantly rural society, the significance of its cities was always greater than their size or numbers suggested. A handful of important urban centers dotted the southern coastline by the eighteenth century; and, as settlement proceeded westward, towns appeared on the major navigable streams to connect areas of the expanding frontier with the seaport cities. Bustling river entrepots like Memphis, Natchez, New Orleans, Louisville, and St. Louis anchored a growing regional economy and

2 Wilbur J. Cash, *The Mind of the South* (Vintage Books ed.; New York, 1941), 268; Ellen Glasgow, *One Man in His Time* (Garden City, N.Y., 1922), 47.
3 William Faulkner, "The Courthouse (A Name for the City)," in Malcolm Cowley (ed.), *The Portable Faulkner* (New York, 1967), 22.

contributed much in the way of cultural flavor and recreational satisfactions. The antebellum urban network in the South was fashioned by the dictates of a cotton-dominated economy. But a number of planters and merchants nevertheless promoted urbanization, and the larger cities sought new, more diversified channels of trade in expanding hinterlands, just as did their sister cities in the North. In fact, in terms of regional increases in urban population (discounting the black slaves who could not voluntarily take up residence in urban places), city growth in the South generally paralleled the pattern in the North between 1800 and 1850.[4]

The southern urban fabric was altered, if not torn, by the Civil War. Manpower and capital were drained away, and some southern cities were left in ruins. The region's economy did not begin a significant recovery until the railroad-building boom of 1879 and the flow of northern capital which it encouraged. Even amid such circumstances, cities rebuilt themselves; over-sized small towns took on metropolitan airs; and a new, rising class of urban businessmen began to assume social and economic leadership. New South spokesmen of all varieties, from national leaders of the movement like Henry Grady to small-town businessmen, came to see the salvation of the South precisely where Thomas Jefferson had once perceived damnation for the country—in cities. But southerners paid a price for their new-found sources of capital and factories. While the "antebellum business community, long inhibited by ties to the Old Order, burst into effusions of assent and hosannas of delivery" in the postwar era, as C. Vann Woodward wrote, the region "remained essentially a raw-material economy organized and run as a colonial dependency."[5]

Southern cities expanded at record rates after the turn of the century, and a 1920 New York *Times* article hailed the "South's Giant Stride from the Pawnshop to Prosperity."[6] The availability of hydroelectric power, the advent of the Piedmont textile industry, and the commercial and industrial development of the larger cities all augured well for the fulfillment of the perennial

4 See Blaine A. Brownell, "Urbanization in the South: A Unique Experience?" *Mississippi Quarterly*, XXVI (Spring, 1973), 105–20; Leonard P. Curry, "Urbanization and Urbanism in the Old South: A Comparative View," *Journal of Southern History*, XL (February, 1974), 43–60.

5 C. Vann Woodward, "The Southern Ethic in a Puritan World," in *American Counterpoint: Slavery and Racism in the North-South Dialogue* (Boston, 1971), 42–44.

6 New York *Times*, February 15, 1920.

New South dream. But the region's economy remained on a raw-material foundation, supplying the more mature industrial plants of the Northeast and Midwest.

Howard W. Odum's monumental assessment of the region in 1936 revealed that eleven southern states were among the lowest in the nation in tangible per capita wealth in 1930. Income and wages ranged 30 to 50 percent below the national level, and the real wages of southeastern workers declined by one-third between 1914 and 1929. Even with the emphasis on industrial expansion during the 1920s, the South received less than one-fourth of its income from manufacturing by the end of the decade, and the percentage of southern workers engaged in extractive industries was far greater than that engaged in manufacturing. In 1929 the eleven southeastern states (including Kentucky) registered 20.8 percent of their wage earners in manufacturing, compared with 31.4 percent in the Northeast and 27.6 percent in the middle states.[7]

Of the seven southern cities under consideration here, only Knoxville and Charleston had higher proportions of their work forces engaged in the manufacturing and mechanical category than in commercial activity at the turn of the century (see Table 1). In 1910 and 1920, however, only Memphis maintained a higher percentage of commercial employment. Birmingham and Knoxville, especially, revealed their significant commitment to industry, while Atlanta, Nashville, and New Orleans reflected fairly balanced urban economies. By 1930, this pattern was considerably less pronounced, with Atlanta, Charleston, Memphis, and New Orleans all registering a greater percentage of their workers in commerce than in industry. Compared with the South as a whole, these cities were important industrial centers, but they were also more oriented to commerce than larger urban areas in the North and Midwest.

The southern agricultural economy staggered along during the 1920s, depressing most of the countryside and, to some degree, the economies of cities like Memphis which were particularly dependent on the transfer and processing of farm products. Even manufacturing cities like Birmingham failed to significantly expand their industrial potential during the decade; and problems of unemployment and poor working conditions continued to

7 Howard W. Odum, *Southern Regions* (Chapel Hill, 1936), 48, 49, 69, 71, 72.

TABLE 1

Percentages of Commercial and Industrial Employment in Selected Southern Cities, 1900–1930

1900	Commercial	Manufacturing and Mechanical
Atlanta	30.1%	24.2%
Birmingham	32.3	24.2
Charleston	24.5	24.9
Knoxville	29.5	30.6
Memphis	31.8	21.4
Nashville	29.9	25.8
New Orleans	28.5	23.9
1910		
Atlanta	26.1	28.4
Birmingham	26.3	33.1
Charleston	23.9	29.8
Knoxville	29.0	33.9
Memphis	29.8	25.5
Nashville	27.5	30.3
New Orleans	29.3	30.1
1920		
Atlanta	27.2	27.7
Birmingham	25.3	35.0
Charleston	25.3	32.0
Knoxville	21.9	42.9
Memphis	30.4	28.2
Nashville	27.9	32.2
New Orleans	28.7	32.0
1930		
Atlanta	25.9	24.7
Birmingham	26.5	29.7
Charleston	26.6	26.2
Knoxville	25.4	39.6
Memphis	28.4	27.7
Nashville	26.5	30.2
New Orleans	30.6	26.5

Source: *Census of the United States*, 1900, 1910, 1920, 1930.

bedevil most regional urban areas, especially in the years from 1920 to 1922. Nevertheless, a number of southern cities achieved genuine metropolitan status during the period, and many economic indicators—from bank receipts to sales—were encouraging. Urban leaders firmly believed that full prosperity was just around the corner if it was not already staring them in the face.

The Process of Southern Urbanization

That the South lagged behind the rest of the nation in urban development by about fifty years, at least until the 1940s, is a widely accepted generalization. The South had an urban population of 15.2 percent in 1900, while the national percentage was 15.3 in 1850; in 1870 the figure was 25.7, which the South did not reach until about 1920. Given this "lag" in the pace of southern city growth, and the oft-noted distinctiveness of the region, observers have been tempted to regard urbanization in the South as significantly different from that in the rest of the country.[8]

Edd W. Parks wrote in 1934 that the southern city was "governed and given character by the country immediately surrounding it" to a greater degree than was the case in other sections, and it was more inclined to value "tradition and family." Subsequent observers have contributed to this view. Gerald M. Capers argued in 1968 that the distinctiveness of the region was as attributable to its overwhelmingly rural character as it was to the presence of the Negro or the South's defeat in the Civil War. The southern urban population was thus "drastically influenced" in the postwar period by hordes of rural migrants who were poor, ill-educated, fixed in traditional ways, and enamored of "bucolic individualism." The comparatively greater significance of such rural types and their values rendered southern cities, in this view, less cosmopolitan, less prosperous, less tolerant, less interested in modern urban services and amenities, and bereft of a genuine sense of urban community. "The rural lag hurt the South," Capers concluded, "and the South hurt the rest of the nation."[9]

In a similar vein, William D. Miller attributed the social "retrogression" and violence characteristic of Memphis in the first decades of the twentieth century to the "feudal survivals" of a "romantic agrarian myth," the values of

---

8 T. Lynn Smith was the first to suggest this lag in southern urganization in his "The Emergence of Cities" in Rupert B. Vance and Nicholas J. Demerath (eds.), *The Urban South* (Chapel Hill, 1954), 32–33.
9 Edd W. Parks, "Southern Towns and Cities," in William T. Couch (ed.), *Culture in the South* (Chapel Hill, 1934), 512–14; Gerald M. Capers, "The Rural Lag on Southern Cities," *Mississippi Quarterly*, XXI (Fall, 1968), 254–55, 257–58.

which were largely shared by the substantial rural contingent that comprised "the great majority" of the city's population by 1900. Anne Firor Scott also speculated that a "southern rural culture pattern," among other things, had particularly affected regional city development. The process of urbanization in the South, she wrote, "offers peculiar challenges to the historian because it is, or seems to be, in many ways unique." [10]

In a number of respects, of course, the southern urban population was unique in composition. Urban expansion throughout the country was dependent on a large influx of native and foreign-born peoples, since the city birth rate was inadequate to support rapid growth. Urban migration in the South, unlike that in the North and Midwest, was principally from within the region, mostly of native-born southerners who had previously lived in rural areas and small towns. Rarely did the number of foreign-born residents exceed 10 percent of the population of any southern city. In addition, southern urban areas contained comparatively greater numbers of blacks than cities elsewhere in the country. This had been true during the antebellum period, and following the Civil War—though many freedmen remained on the land, often to be entrapped in the peonage of the sharecropper and tenant systems—many rural blacks sought out regional towns and cities. Between 1860 and 1900 the black proportion of the Memphis population almost tripled, from 17 to 49 percent; it rose from 20 to 40 percent in Atlanta, 14 to 21 percent in New Orleans, and 23 to 27 percent in Nashville. The bulk of this increase occurred during the Reconstruction years, but Charleston and Savannah maintained black majorities by the end of the century, and the massive northward migration of blacks during and after World War I was presaged by a large movement of Negroes into southern cities in the first decades of the twentieth century. Between 1900 and 1920 the urban black population in the South increased by some 886,000 (65 percent) and that in the North by a little over 671,000. [11]

The southern urban economy remained more commercial and service-oriented—and less industrial—than that in the North. Birmingham's almost

10 William D. Miller, "Rural Values and Urban Progress: Memphis, 1900–1917," *Mississippi Quarterly*, XXI (Fall, 1968), 263–74; Anne Firor Scott, "The Study of Southern Urganization," *Urban Affairs Quarterly*, I (March, 1966), 6, 9.

11 Reynolds Farley, "The Urbanization of Negroes in the United States," *Journal of Social History*, I (Spring, 1968), 248–58; Thomas J. Woofter, Jr., *Negro Problems in Cities* (Garden City, N.Y., 1928), 29.

purely industrial origins were genuinely unique in both regional and national terms. In addition, southern cities were generally characterized by lower population density, and the settlement pattern of black and foreign-born residents tended to be more dispersed in the urban South than in Boston, New York, Philadelphia, Chicago, and other large northern cities. And a lower per capita income level in the region reduced the potential tax base for southern municipalities, which in turn generally limited the quantity and quality of public services that cities could provide.

These more-or-less distinctive features of southern cities cannot be discounted; but they must be balanced against some of the rather pronounced similarities among cities across the country. The South has traditionally contained fewer and smaller cities than other regions, and more than its share of rural dwellers. This is hardly convincing evidence, however, that the dynamics or functions of southern cities were unique in either their character or their consequences. Though we can expect to find certain differences between cities in various regions of the country, the most distinctive feature of southern urbanization may, from at least one perspective, be the extent to which it paralleled city development in the nation as a whole.

For one thing, technology constantly operated to reduce regional urban differences, especially in the twentieth century. The process of urban decentralization which accompanied the arrival of the automobile, for example, cut across regional lines and occurred in cities across the country at about the same time. Outward population movement had begun in the largest centers like New York in the midnineteenth century; but it was not until the 1920s and the impact of the motorcar that the move to expanding suburbs began in earnest. The central cities were generally most concentrated between 1920 and 1930, after which urban fringe areas registered the greatest population growth. Cities in the South were very much a part of this national pattern.[12] Of thirty-eight regional urban areas, consistent and generally

12 York Wilbern, *The Withering Away of the City* (Tuscaloosa, 1964), 20; Leo F. Schnore, "Urban Form: The Case of the Metropolitan Community," in Werner Z. Hirsch (ed.), *Urban Life and Form* (New York, 1963), 171. That "large American cities have always grown chiefly by peripheral accretion" is demonstrated convincingly by Kenneth T. Jackson. "Urban Deconcentration in the Nineteenth Century: A Statistical Inquiry," in Leo F. Schnore (ed.), *The New Urban History: Quantitative Explorations by American Historians* (Princeton, 1975), 110–42. The decentralization of the urban population was masked—in the South as elsewhere in the country—by the periodic annexation of settled territory on the urban periphery.

uninterrupted population decentralization was apparent in eight by the 1920s and in nineteen more by the 1930s.

Furthermore, cities throughout the country were affected at roughly the same time by other technological developments of the late nineteenth and early twentieth centuries—from electricity to architectural innovations. A lexicon of "urban problems"—housing, transportation, sanitation, congestion, police protection, and a full panoply of needs requiring expanded city services—was universally applicable to all cities regardless of their size or regional location, though the degree of these problems—like the drainage difficulties in New Orleans—naturally differed from community to community as well as within particular cities.

As southern cities grew, their class structures began to assume the familiar cast of those in northeastern and midwestern municipalities, and patterns of land use and population distribution were basically the same in cities throughout the country. Indeed, one of the most common observations made about southern urban centers by visitors—with the obvious exceptions of some areas of Charleston and New Orleans—was that they essentially resembled most other American cities.

The influence of rural migration on the development of southern urban areas has doubtless been significant, but the extent to which this migration set the South apart from the experience of other sections is quite another matter. The fact is, all larger American cities drew substantial portions of their expanding populations from rural areas in the years between 1880 and 1920, and rural natives comprised a larger proportion of the urban migration even in the years of peak foreign immigration. In addition, large numbers of rural southerners found their way into cities bordering on the region, especially in the Midwest. Social dislocation, adherence to older—possibly preurban— values, economic distress, and violent conflict were by no means unique to the South but were characteristic of cities all over the United States. And the qualitative differences that did exist between cities in the South and the non-South were probably eroded over time.

The history and tradition peculiar to the region, the comparatively greater number of rural people and the greater reliance on an agricultural and commercial economy, and the large concentration of blacks with their distinctive subculture—all had an impact on southern cities, but one that was not sufficient to produce a genuinely "unique" urban experience. The Civil

War slowed the pace of southern urban development in the nineteenth century, the largely internal regional migration to the cities produced a more homogeneous ethnic pattern than that which existed in the North, and the small town was relatively more significant within the southern urban configuration. But the basic dynamics of urbanization in the United States were about as predominant in the South as elsewhere in the country.

Southern cities were generally founded by the imperatives of commerce, located on major transportation routes, peopled by rural migrants, covetous of surrounding markets, and transformed by commerce, industry, and technology in the late nineteenth and twentieth centuries. The southern urban economy became more complex, and the city population was increasingly fragmented along class and racial lines and decentralized over an expanding metropolitan area. Commercial and civic leaders shared with their counterparts in northern and midwestern cities a deep concern for urban order, and southern municipalities adopted similar political forms and provided a growing array of city services. Significantly, southern cities were affected by technology, certain governmental arrangements, and demographic trends at relatively earlier stages in their development, thus distinguishing their experience somewhat from that of nonsouthern cities. While these unique features were indeed consequential, they do not mark a discernibly new or different *type* of city, nor do they suggest a unique process of urban development and pattern of urban life. The southern urban "lag" most accurately refers to temporal rather than qualitative distinctions, and it parallels Howard Odum's conclusion that "the culture of the Southeast is more regional in the sense of a time lag than it is conditioned primarily by physiography or regional culture as a separate entity." Thus, southern cities—like the regional culture—could be judged "immature rather than decadent." [13]

Gerald Capers maintained that in an "objective history of individual southern cities . . . the experience of New Orleans, Memphis, Mobile and Houston will be found to differ only in degree from that of Richmond, Nashville, and Louisville." [14] But the differences among regional cities—in size, geographic circumstances, cultural backgrounds, and economic functions—also precluded the existence of a "solid" urban South. In some

13 Odum, *Southern Regions*, 497.
14 Capers, "The Rural Lag on Southern Cities," 259.

ways, Birmingham more closely resembled Youngstown, Ohio, than New Orleans in the early twentieth century. Though southern cities certainly had more in common with each other and with nonregional cities than they did with their own rural hinterlands, the urban South was also diverse. Since cities have acted throughout history as repositories of local and regional culture, we would expect southern urban areas to reflect certain traditions, values, and mores peculiar to the local area and to the South. But regional cities had hardly existed in a state of pervasive sameness; and by the 1920s they were significantly larger, more complex, and more heterogeneous than they had ever been before.

Seven Southern Cities

The principal urban centers under consideration here—Atlanta, Birmingham, Memphis, Nashville, and New Orleans—had all experienced substantial growth following the Civil War. The Crescent City of Louisiana was, in the 1870s, a major national seaport while the Magic City of Alabama was little more than a railroad crossing—but all five cities had reached "metropolitan" size (more than 100,000 population) and a certain degree of socioeconomic maturity by the 1920s, and all thoroughly dominated their surrounding hinterlands. The smaller cities of Knoxville and Charleston were, respectively, a rapidly growing, inland university town and an older, declining, but culturally distinguished seaport—and thus both, for different reasons, did not fit the mold of the mature, expanding, central southern metropolis.

The major characteristic of most of these cities was growth, in terms of both population and land area (see Tables 2, 3, and 4). In the twenty years before 1920, the populations of Atlanta and Knoxville more than doubled, and the number of Birmingham residents increased almost fourfold. Memphis, Nashville, and New Orleans expanded less spectacularly, but together they added almost 200,000 people during the period. Only Charleston among the seven cities failed to maintain a significant pace of growth in the 1920s. Memphis more than doubled its land area in 1899, and later annexation swelled the city's territory by an additional 56 percent. Atlanta more than doubled its geographical size between 1900 and 1920, and Nashville's territory almost doubled in the same period. The most impressive expansion in municipal limits occurred in Knoxville and Birmingham, whose land areas

TABLE 2

Population Growth in Selected Southern Cities, 1900–1920

	Population: 1900	Population: 1920	% Increase
Atlanta	89,872	200,616	123
Birmingham	38,415	178,806	365
Charleston	55,807	67,957	21
Knoxville	32,637	77,818	138
Memphis	102,320	162,351	58
Nashville	80,865	118,342	46
New Orleans	287,104	387,219	34

Source: *Census of the United States,* 1900 and 1920.

TABLE 3

Percentages of Population Increase in Selected Southern Cities, 1900–1930

	1900–1910	1910–1920	1920–1930
Atlanta	72.3%	29.6%	34.8%
Birmingham	245.4	34.8	45.2
Charleston	5.4	15.5	−8.4
Knoxville	11.4	114.1	36.0
Memphis	28.1	23.8	55.9
Nashville	36.5	7.2	30.0
New Orleans	18.1	14.2	18.5

Source: *Fifteenth Census of the United States,* 1930.

TABLE 4

Territorial Expansion of Seven Selected Southern Cities, 1900–1920

	Square Miles 1900	Square Miles 1920	Percentage Increase 1900–1920
Atlanta	11.00	26.20	138.2
Birmingham	6.29	50.00	694.8
Charleston	5.50	5.85	.06
Knoxville	3.97	26.00	554.9
Memphis	16.00	25.03	56.4
Nashville	9.50	18.10	90.5
New Orleans	196.25	196.25	

Sources: R. D. McKenzie, *The Metropolitan Community* (New York, 1967), 336–38; *The World Almanac and Encyclopedia,* 1900, 395–96; *The World Almanac and Encyclopedia,* 1920, 702–704.

increased by almost 555 and 695 percent respectively in the first two decades of the twentieth century. Only Charleston and New Orleans failed to grow geographically—but the Crescent City's municipal boundaries already coincided with those of Orleans Parish, including by 1900 more than 196 square miles. This growth—translated into crowded neighborhoods, rising rents, a larger work force, congested streets, bigger industries, new businesses and residential areas, and greater and greater pressures on municipal authorities—was the central and overriding reality in the urban South during the 1920s.

Atlanta, Georgia, was foremost among those cities cited as examples of the New South. Popular literature likened the city to the ancient Phoenix, the mythical bird that rose in splendor from the ashes of its own destruction. And the theme of rebirth was not without some validity. Besieged and burned during the war, Atlanta became a political and economic center during Reconstruction and was rebuilt more rapidly than anyone would have dared to predict. Situated in the north central portion of the state, Atlanta straddled a complex of railroad lines that radiated from its center to every remote corner of the South and connected the Gate City with the major eastern metropolises to the north and with the economic development in Florida to the south.

By 1920 Atlanta contained more than 200,000 people, about a third of them black. In 1929 the city's expansion during the decade was culminated with the "Greater Atlanta Plan" that united some of the outlying communities into a borough system of administration with Atlanta as the principal borough. The city contained more than 270,000 residents in 1930, and the metropolitan area population rose during the decade from 325,688 to 440,906.[15]

Atlanta was a city of contrasts. A prosperous, cosmopolitan center, it was the favorite example to which smaller communities aspired. Its growth during the decade and the pervasive braggadocio of the "Atlanta spirit" were conversation pieces throughout the South. But the same city that thought of itself as "the metropolis of the South, and, basically, a branch of New York," that boasted annual Metropolitan Opera performances, and that was the

15 Relevant population data for all seven southern cities is contained in Tables 5 and 6. For details on the Greater Atlanta Plan and the Phoenix theme, see Franklin Garrett, *Atlanta and Environs: A Chronicle of Its People and Events* (2 vols.; New York, 1954), II, 648, and Ivan Allen, *Atlanta from the Ashes* (Atlanta, 1928). For background on the city's development before the 1890s, see James Michael Russell, "Atlanta, Gate City of the South, 1847 to 1885" (Ph.D. dissertation, Princeton University, 1972).

site of the region's most prominent interracial commission was also designated "the most religious city in the country" by Billy Sunday in 1927 and was
the Imperial City of the Ku Klux Klan. As Edd Parks observed, "Rural
Georgia had little tangible connection with it, save to supply it with food, and
the city quite evidently is not proud of Georgia." Atlanta seemed poised
between the sections and between past and future. "South of the North, yet
north of the South," W. E. B. DuBois wrote around the turn of the century,
"lies the city of a Hundred Hills, peering out from the shadows of the past into
the promise of the future." Indeed, the "seething whirl of the city seemed a
strange thing in a sleepy land." [16]

The city radiated outward along the major rail lines, with the better white
residential areas lying to the north on Peachtree Street and eastward, and in
new suburbs like West End to the southwest. Many poor whites and blacks
lived in a "railroad laced area" to the west of the central business district. The
black population was concentrated within two miles of the city core, and
Negro neighborhoods were plagued—as in other southern cities—by con-
sumption, pneumonia, inadequate sanitation, poor city services, crime, and
housing segregation. On the other hand, Atlanta contained some of the
outstanding Negro educational institutions in the country, most notably
Atlanta University; several large black businesses; a relatively sizeable black
middle class, dominated increasingly in the 1920s by a new, aggressive,
upwardly mobile, entrepreneurial elite; and active social and civic organizations like the Neighborhood Union and the Urban League. [17] The Wheat
Street Baptist Church was the second largest Negro religious institution in the
nation, and the Atlanta *Independent*, perhaps the most prominent of southern
black newspapers, was published in the city from 1903 until 1932 when its
dominance was superseded by the rising Atlanta *World*.

The city's mayor-council government was, by the charter of 1913, an
unwieldy body. The voters not only elected the mayor and thirty-three
councilmen, but also the forty-four members of the city executive committee

16 Parks, "Southern Towns and Cities," 509; *Atlanta Life*, February 19, 1927; William E. B.
  DuBois, *The Souls of Black Folk: Essays and Sketches* (Fawcett Books ed.; New York, 1961),
  65.
17. Thomas D. Deaton, "Atlanta During the Progressive Era" (Ph.D. dissertation, University of
  Georgia, 1969), 35–36, 171–75, 209; August Meier and David Lewis, "History of the Negro
  Upper Class in Atlanta, Georgia, 1890–1958," *Journal of Negro Education*, XXVIII (Spring,
  1959), 128–39.

TABLE 5

Population and Population Characteristics of Seven Selected Southern Cities, 1900–1930

1900	Atlanta	Birmingham	Charleston	Knoxville	Memphis	Nashville	New Orleans
Total Population	89,872	38,415	55,807	32,637	102,320	80,865	287,104
% Native-born White	57.5	52.2	38.9	74.7	46.2	59.1	62.4
% Foreign-born White	2.7	4.6	4.5	2.7	5.0	3.7	10.3
% Negro	39.8	43.1	56.5	22.5	48.8	37.2	27.1
1910							
Total Population	154,839	132,685	58,833	36,346	131,105	110,364	339,075
% Native-born White	63.6	56.3	43.1	76.9	55.1	64.2	65.4
% Foreign-born White	2.8	4.3	4.1	2.2	4.9	2.7	8.2
% Negro	33.5	39.4	52.8	21.0	40.0	33.1	26.3
1920							
Total Population	200,616	178,806	67,957	77,818	162,351	118,342	387,219
% Native-born White	66.3	57.3	49.2	84.0	58.7	67.9	67.1
% Foreign-born White	2.4	3.4	3.2	1.0	3.6	2.0	6.7
% Negro	31.3	39.3	47.6	14.5	37.7	30.1	26.1
1930							
Total Population	270,366	256,678	62,265	105,802	253,143	153,866	458,762
% Native-born White	64.9	59.6	52.3	83.1	59.8	71.0	67.1
% Foreign-born White	1.7	2.3	2.6	0.8	2.1	1.2	4.3
% Negro	33.3	38.2	45.1	16.2	38.1	27.8	28.3

Source: *Census of the United States*, 1900, 1910, 1920, 1930.

Note: The table does not include the small number of persons contained in the "Other" category in the census. Thus, the percentages do not always total 100.

TABLE 6

Standard Metropolitan Area Population for Seven Selected Southern Cities,
1900–1930

	1900	1910	1920	1930
Atlanta	179,420	252,124	325,688	440,906
Birmingham	140,420	226,476	310,054	431,493
Charleston	88,006	88,594	108,450	101,050
Knoxville	111,142	132,713	160,024	209,613
Memphis	153,557	191,439	223,216	306,482
Nashville	122,815	149,748	167,815	222,854
New Orleans	307,456	362,599	413,750	505,306

Source: Donald J. Bogue, *Population Growth in Standard Metropolitan Areas, 1900–1950: With
an Explanatory Analysis of Urbanized Areas* (Washington, 1953), 61–62, 65–67.

Note: Bogue's principal contribution is the collection of population statistics according to the
"Standard Metropolitan Area" designation introduced with the Census of 1950. This replaced the
older "Metropolitan District" concept in use since 1910. According to Bogue (viii), "the S. M. A.
consists of central cities, the entire county containing these cities, and any other counties having
metropolitan characteristics [as of 1950] which are integrated with the central city."

and ten independent department heads. One city primary ballot contained no
less than ninety-four candidates. The police, fire, school, and park departments were under separate boards that were largely self-perpetuating. A
number of local citizens moved to remedy the situation in the early 1920s.
"There is no graft among city officials," wrote the local secretary of the
Taxpayer's League, "but the taxpayers believe that there is criminal inefficiency.... The impression is firmly fixed in the public mind that the city
does not get more than 30 to 50 cents of value for every dollar expended."
Under these pressures, many of the separate city departments were abolished
and consolidated in 1922.[18]

Significant proportions of the city's native white and foreign immigrant
populations rose in occupational status between 1870 and 1910. Blacks,
however, experienced substantially less advancement on the socioeconomic
continuum and found it almost impossible to rise above the level of unskilled
or semiskilled employment. Furthermore, as Richard J. Hopkins has noted,
"constant movement and change dominated the occupations and habitats of
most Atlantans in the late nineteenth century." This was true for migration

18 Frank Weldon, "Atlanta Moves Toward a Modern Charter," *National Municipal Review,* IX
(March, 1920), 139, 141; Paul W. Miller, *Atlanta: Capitol of the South* (New York, 1949),
47–48.

both within and away from the city: native blue-collar whites were most likely to leave the city and blacks were most likely to remain (though both groups changed their places of residence within Atlanta quite frequently). Also prevalent was "a direct correlation between occupational rank and residential stability," with the most secure in terms of socioeconomic status being also the most stable in terms of residential mobility. The city was thus in a state of constant occupational and residential flux; neighborhoods were often transformed over the course of a few decades and thousands of families moved to take advantage of new opportunities. But these opportunities were decidedly few and less appealing where Atlanta's blacks were concerned.[19]

Atlanta seemed to typify the prospects of the new metropolitan South. Growth and flux loosened the ties of tradition, and thousands of new residents arrived to taste sweet success—or at least to avoid a penniless existence on a Georgia dirt farm. That municipal facilities and services were strained by these demands was a measure of both the problem and the solution. If only the city could keep pace with its own growth, many spokesmen reasoned, that growth might go on forever.

Birmingham, Alabama, was not founded until 1871. It was envisioned from the beginning as a major industrial city, and the rich deposits of coal, limestone, and iron ore located in the immediate vicinity and the influx of northern capital during the 1880s combined to make it the steel center of the New South. In the early days, life in Birmingham was a varied mixture: the deadly dust in the coal mines, the melting heat of the blast furnaces, rutted and pitted roads, free-flowing liquor, and the frequent violence of rugged men in an unsettled community.

From a population of under 40,000 in 1900 the city grew dramatically in the next two decades, reaching almost 179,000 residents by 1920. Between 1900 and 1910 Birmingham's central city growth rate was greater than that of any other major city in the United States except for Tulsa and Oklahoma City, and more than three times the rates of population increase in Atlanta and Houston. The city annexed many surrounding communities through the "Greater Birmingham Plan" approved by the state legislature in 1910, and the

19 See Richard J. Hopkins, "Status, Mobility, and the Dimensions of Change in a Southern City: Atlanta, 1870–1910," in Kenneth T. Jackson and Stanley K. Schultz (eds.), *Cities in American History* (New York, 1972), 216–31; and Richard J. Hopkins, "Patterns of Persistence and Occupational Mobility in a Southern City: Atlanta, 1870–1920" (Ph.D. dissertation, Emory University, 1972).

population continued to spill over into newly developed suburbs. By the 1920s Birmingham was the most striking example of urbanization in the South and one of the most impressive in the nation.[20]

In 1934 Edd Parks cast his eye over the sprawling city in Jones Valley: "The buildings are all of a kind: relatively new, with a preponderance of modern skyscrapers dwarfing the more ordinary store buildings and the semi-classical governmental and institutional structures. Situated on the slope of Red Mountain, it escapes a monotonous regularity chiefly through the natural ruggedness of the terrain. For Birmingham," he concluded, "is primarily a child of the twentieth century, and it has no old traditions that cause men to regret the passing of old landmarks." Martha C. Mitchell characterized the city as a "pushing bragging busy town with a northern and western flavor," a city "completely alien to the quiet little hamlets that lay just over the mountain." Birmingham reflected the tough, anxious spirit of the new industrial age more than any other southern urban area, and many southerners doubtless looked upon her with mixed emotions. The South Carolina poet Josephine Pinckney described the city as a town "nourished on steel with all the vigor and intensity that this diet implies."[21]

The city appeared on the surface to be dedicated to the capitalist prosperity that pervaded the rest of the country during the 1920s. "In real estate fortunes were made over night," one resident recalled. "Men rushed downtown in their pajamas to their offices to make 'rich deals,' some even slept in their offices to 'keep in touch with the market.'" Beneath the surface, however, local economic fortunes were not so bright. The iron and steel industry, as Tindall noted, advanced only slightly in some areas during the decade and actually declined in others. Birmingham's percentage of pig iron production dropped between 1905 and 1939, and the production of rolled iron and steel increased only moderately. This was primarily because the United States Steel Corporation (which acquired the Tennessee Coal and Iron Company in Birmingham in 1907) was careful that its southern subsidiary did not expand

20 For a more detailed and extended analysis of Birmingham in the 1920s, see Blaine A. Brownell, "Birmingham, Alabama: New South City in the 1920s," *Journal of Southern History,* XXXVIII (February, 1972), 21–48.

21 Parks, "Southern Towns and Cities," 508; Martha C. Mitchell, "Birmingham: Biography of a City of the New South" (Ph.D. dissertation, University of Chicago, 1946), 278; Josephine Pinckney, "Bulwarks Against Change," in William T. Couch (ed.), *Culture in the South* (Chapel Hill, 1934), 40.

at the expense of its northern plants, and the industry established prices on the basis of "Pittsburgh plus," thereby nullifying Birmingham's natural competitive advantages for most of the decade. Fortunately, the city's economy was sufficiently diversified to compensate for, or at least to conceal, this lag in the steel industry, and real estate and financial operations could be quite lucrative. But the Great Depression revealed just how weak the city's economic foundations really were.[22]

Because of its commitment to industry and mining, Birmingham had always been a blue-collar city. According to contemporary estimates, its working class was composed in 1924 of over 106,000 "industrial employees," most of whom were employed in the city's 788 manufacturing establishments. Of this number, 14,216 worked in the iron and steel plants and over 5,000 in the area's iron ore and coal mines. Largely unskilled rural natives, most workers toiled long hours for the low wages that made southern industries competitive with those in the North. Many lived in the company towns in the dingy industrial suburbs on the city's fringe, in which housing was often barely adequate at best. Organized labor suffered in Birmingham since the industrialists had crushed the miner's strike in 1908, and its complaints were muted by the general prosperity of the 1920s.[23]

Many unskilled and semiskilled white workers did achieve moderate success in the city, however, both in terms of advancement in occupational status (even into nonmanual labor) and real property holding. As in Atlanta, the working class population was highly volatile, moving from job to job, from residence to residence, and from city to city. Those who held property and a higher socioeconomic rank tended to stay longer in the area than those who did not, and—at least during the late nineteenth century—blacks were more stable than blue-collar whites. Birmingham contained a larger proportion of first- and second-generation immigrants than Atlanta, however (comprising almost half the white work force in the iron and steel industry as late as 1910). Also, black workers began to move out of the city much more frequently in the early twentieth century, as they were forced out of some occupations by whites and as the racial climate worsened. Paul Worthman concluded that "Birmingham, like other cities in the United States, provided its workingmen with oppor-

22 Florence H. W. Moss, *Building Birmingham and Jefferson County* (Birmingham, 1947), 205; Tindall, *Emergence of the New South, 1913–1945*, 80–81.
23 Birmingham *Labor Advocate*, April 26, 1924.

tunities for individual advancement." But these opportunities were usually moderate rather than spectacular, and were denied to the vast majority of the city's Afro-Americans. [24]

Blacks accounted for almost 40 percent of Birmingham's residents in 1920. But even though there were twenty thousand more Negroes in the city by 1930, the black percentage of the population declined to 38.2. The heart of the black business district lay along Eighteenth Street, in the midst of theaters, restaurants, and soft-drink emporiums. Negro residential settlements tended to be dispersed, though to a lesser degree than in most southern cities, and blacks were usually located in the least desirable sections and increasingly concentrated toward the central core. Though Negroes constituted the base of the city's industrial labor force (about three-quarters of the workers in the iron and steel industry in 1910 were black), they experienced far less upward occupational mobility, were much less successful in accumulating real property, and were "constantly pushed," as Worthman wrote, "out of various occupations toward the bottom of the occupational hierarchy." [25]

Blacks were also subjected to the stringent discipline and control of vagrancy-law enforcement, arrests for petty vice and crime, the convict-lease system, and a venal-fee system whereby sheriffs' deputies were compensated for arrests regardless of whether they resulted in convictions. Some of these measures were meliorated by the 1920s—like the county fee system and the local practice of leasing convicts to the local mines—but blacks continued to be sentenced to hard labor for petty offenses and the "wars" on vagrancy were both periodic and severe. [26]

Birmingham's neighborhoods had been, in the late nineteenth century, relatively heterogeneous, and the urban profile in some ways resembled the familiar preindustrial model—with "an affluent area surrounded," as Worthman noted, "by increasingly poorer sections near the periphery." By the early twentieth century, however, this pattern had been clearly reversed,

---

24 Paul B. Worthman, "Working Class Mobility in Birmingham, Alabama, 1880–1914," in Tamara K. Hareven (ed.), *Anonymous Americans: Explorations in Nineteenth-Century Social History* (Englewood Cliffs, N.J., 1971), 172–213.

25 *Ibid.*, 175, 196–97. Also see Paul B. Worthman, "Black Workers and Labor Unions in Birmingham, Alabama, 1897–1904," *Labor History*, X (Summer, 1969), 375–407.

26. Carl V. Harris, "Reforms in Government Control of Negroes in Birmingham, Alabama, 1890–1920," *Journal of Southern History*, XXXVIII (November, 1972), 567–600; Carl V. Harris, "Economic Power and Politics: A Study of Birmingham, Alabama, 1890–1920" (Ph.D. dissertation, University of Wisconsin, 1970).

especially with the addition of outlying communities in the annexation of 1910. Poorer neighborhoods began to ring the downtown commercial and industrial districts, and the city's more affluent citizens resided increasingly in more pleasant areas on the Southside, such as South Highlands and Mountain Brook.[27]

Birmingham would be surpassed in size and economic power by Atlanta later in the century. But the two urban centers were virtually the same size in the 1920s and, on the basis of the Magic City's almost incredible growth rate and its impressive industrial base, few leading citizens of either city would have been surprised if Birmingham became the dominant metropolis of the central South.

A major river town that claimed a proud, elegant, and scandalous history extending far back before 1860, Memphis, Tennessee, emerged from the Civil War relatively unscathed. But the scars of yellow fever were not as easily avoided as those of war: a major epidemic in 1878 virtually destroyed the city, severely reducing its population through death or the widespread emigration to escape the ravages of disease. Thus, in many respects, the "modern" history of the city began with the growth and industrial development of subsequent decades. Memphis' formative period, wrote one commentator, "was that of the 'New South,' not the 'Old,' from the era between Reconstruction and World War I, when the city was 'settled' by an ambitious country folk."[28]

The greatest single expansion of Memphis—more than doubling the city's land area—came in 1899, after the railroad had effectively sundered the older elongated pattern the city had assumed along the Mississippi River. This was followed by additional annexations of surrounding territory in 1909, 1913, 1917, and 1919. Though the city's population increased almost 25 percent between 1900 and 1910, Memphis fell from its position as the third largest city in the South to fifth place, thanks to the growth of Atlanta and Birmingham. The city's rate of growth in the 1920s was about 56 percent, reaching a population of more than 253,000 in 1930.[29]

Memphis remained the largest inland cotton and hardwood market in the world, but it apparently suffered from the economic malaise that struck its

27 Worthman, "Working Class Mobility in Birmingham, Alabama," 200, 203–204; Brownell, "Birmingham, Alabama: New South City in the 1920s," 23, 25.
28 Gerald M. Capers, "Memphis: Satrapy of a Benevolent Despot," in Robert S. Allen (ed.), *Our Fair City* (New York, 1947), 216.
29. William D. Miller, *Memphis During the Progressive Era, 1900–1917* (Memphis, 1957), 67.

agricultural hinterland during the decade. Wage levels in the city were
relatively low, even compared to those in other regional urban areas, and the
river town lacked the industrial base of Birmingham. Memphis' economy was
hardly collapsing, but the profits from local "resort industries" and downtown
commercial establishments apparently failed to offset the inability of agriculture to revive in the period.

Memphis was a city of newcomers. A 1918 survey indicated that only 2
percent of the white parents of school children had been born in the city.
About three-quarters of the population came from surrounding farms and
small towns. The city's population was also relatively unstable. As a hub for
both land and river transportation, Memphis attracted transients in search of
work or simply wandering from town to town. Located at the intersection of
three states, the city was also a haven for out-of-state criminals seeking
sanctuary from authorities in Arkansas, Mississippi, and Alabama. Memphis
had the reputation, at least partly deserved, of a wild river town. Tourists and
farm workers from a wide area came to gamble, drink, and frequent the
renowned red-light districts that inspired some of Faulkner's prose. "Perhaps
. . . the greatest evil of Memphis from a criminal standpoint," two observers
commented in 1928, "is its transient, pleasure-seeking population."[30]

About 38 percent of Memphis' residents were black. As in other regional
cities, Negro areas of settlement were scattered over the urban landscape and
living conditions were none too good. The principal concentrations of blacks
were along the riverfront, and more than half of the city's 61,000 Negroes
lived in the southeastern sections. Members of the rising black middle class
purchased large, spacious homes once owned by whites along Mississippi
Boulevard. "Many of the families own one, and some two, automobiles,"
Thomas Woofter noted, "the children go away to college, and a high standard
of social and community life is maintained." Though Robert R. Church, a
prominent Negro Republican leader, regularly delivered the black vote to the
relatively sympathetic Democratic machine, and the local Inter Racial
League attempted to meliorate the problems of the city's black communities,
the majority of Memphis whites looked with suspicion on blacks and
small-scale racial violence was a consistent feature in the downtown sections.

30 Capers, "Memphis," 216; Andrew A. Bruce and Thomas S. Fitzgerald, "A Study of Crime in
   the City of Memphis, Tennessee," *Journal of the American Institute of Criminal Law and
   Criminology*, XIX (August, 1928), 10.

In 1919, especially, a series of rumors about a black revolt brought thousands of heavily armed men of both races into the streets. Violence was somehow averted, though contemporary observers noted that one careless gunshot could have produced a bloodbath.[31]

Memphis politics in the early twentieth century were dominated by "Boss" Edward H. Crump, who successfully welded—at least for a time—the city's rising business middle class, the rural newcomers, the blacks, the Irish and Italian minorities, and the saloon interests into a potent political force. To achieve efficiency and curtail waste, Crump supported the creation of a commission form of government and various other reforms, and his proudest achievement was the reduction of the tax rate. His influence extended far beyond the boundaries of Memphis, and even into the councils of national government.[32]

From 1920 to 1928 the reins of municipal authority rested in the hands of Mayor Rowlett Paine, a wholesale grocer, who inaugurated an extensive public health program, made brave promises to clean up the city's vice warrens, secured a former army sergeant to discipline the police force, and appointed a woman as juvenile court judge. Crump had no "determinative influence" in the new administration, though he stubbornly resisted some of its policies. Because of Ku Klux Klan strength, he was obliged to support Paine for reelection in 1923. In the campaign of 1927, however, Paine decried bossism, criticized Crump's reliance on black support, and pledged never to appoint Negroes to positions in municipal government—and lost the race to the mayoral candidate Crump supported.[33]

31 Woofter, *Negro Problems in Cities*, 60–61, 104; Tindall, *Emergence of the New South, 1913–1945,* 167; Inter Racial League, Memphis and Shelby County Division, *The Inter Racial League Blue Book* (Memphis, 1926); William D. Miller, *Memphis During the Progressive Era,* 126–27; Kenneth T. Jackson, *The Ku Klux Klan in the City, 1915–1930* (New York, 1967), 49. Also see James H. Robinson, "A Social History of the Negro in Memphis and in Shelby County" (Ph.D. dissertation, Yale University, 1934).
32. William D. Miller, *Memphis During the Progressive Era,* 148–49, 178, 190. Also see William D. Miller, *Mr. Crump of Memphis* (Baton Rouge, 1964). Melvin G. Holli has argued persuasively against Miller's suggestion that Crump's regime resembled those of Tom Johnson in Cleveland and Samuel "Golden Rule" Jones in Toledo: "Although Crump occasionally employed reform rhetoric, established a few milk stations for the poor, and put screens on public school windows, he used most of the energy of his administration to enforce the laws and instill efficiency into the municipal government in the structural-reform tradition." Melvin G. Holli, *Reform in Detroit: Hazen S. Pingree and Urban Politics* (New York, 1969), 249, n 25.
33 Virginia Phillips, "Rowlett Paine, Mayor of Memphis, 1920–1924," *West Tennessee Historical Society Papers,* XIII (1959), 99–100; William D. Miller, *Mr. Crump of Memphis,* 142.

An ambitious annexation program, a particularly turbulent population, and the prevalence of low wages and a depressed hinterland all contributed to the urban chaos of Memphis during the 1920s—a chaos only partly assuaged by a relatively strong political organization, a determined commercial-civic elite, and the most impressive city-planning effort of any regional urban center. But Memphis continued to command much of the trade on the great river which she surveyed from the bluffs, and her rising skyscrapers and new highways seemed to confirm her destiny as an important commercial entrepot.

In contrast to the largest cities of the region, Nashville, Tennessee, was a small urban community. "Compared with Atlanta," Edd Parks wrote, "Nashville seems an overgrown small town, with narrow and out-moded streets, grimy old buildings, and the settled placidity of middle age." Highly conscious of its venerable traditions, the city was nevertheless by 1920 "reaching somewhat reluctantly for new commercial projects." The capital of Tennessee, the site of numerous educational institutions (including Vanderbilt University), and the center for the Southern Agrarians, Nashville was also known as the "country music capital of the world" after mountain fiddler Jimmy Thompson took the microphone at radio station WSM in 1925. It also was a city of contrasts, with Andrew Jackson's Hermitage and a full-scale replica of the Greek Parthenon within a few miles of each other and perhaps equally close in the hearts and minds of older citizens. "Like every Southern city, it lives on inconsistencies," Parks commented. "[It] allows baseball on Sundays, yet forbids movies; prides itself on culture, but has no decent theatre and is shunned even by road shows; points with pride to historical tradition while it seeks the very things that, inevitably, must destroy the value and validity of those traditions." [34]

Nashville's life and economy, even with its reputation as a cosmopolitan educational center, were primarily oriented to the middle Tennessee region. Neither a major manufacturing center nor an essential cross-country transportation link, it was a commercial focus for a relatively rich and diversified agricultural district. Unlike its sister Tennessee city to the west, Nashville

---

34 Parks, "Southern Towns and Cities," 509–10. Also see Edwin Mims, *Adventurous America: A Study of Contemporary Life and Thought* (New York, 1929), 104. (Mims was a member of the faculty at Vanderbilt University.)

seemed less affected by the rural depression during the period, and there were factories in the city and several chemical plants located along the urban periphery.

The "Athens of the South" was also an active political town, a haven for attorneys who found obvious advantages in their proximity to the nexus of state government. The town was consistently treated to feuds between "Major" Edward Bushrod Stahlman and "Colonel" Luke Lea, owners of the *Banner* and *Tennessean* respectively, and enlivened by the fact that it was, as Ralph McGill recalled, "a city with gambling houses, a sprawling red light district back of the capital, and a Western spirit somewhat like that of Chicago." But Nashville remained rather insular until the coming of the Great War and its domestic mobilization. One local historian concluded that World War I "marked the beginning of a time when wider currents . . . flowed through Nashville's climate, for the first time, to any degree, since the War Between the States." [35]

The city's population grew by 30 percent during the 1920s, from more than 118,000 to almost 154,000. The growth rate for the metropolitan area (Davidson County) was slightly greater—32.8 percent—as Nashville, like other regional urban areas, experienced considerable growth on the city's fringe. This also represented the largest expansion of the city in a single decade in the first half of the twentieth century. Between 1910 and 1920 the number of blacks in Nashville dropped about 25,000, bringing the percentage of Negroes in the population to less than fifteen at the outset of the 1920s. During the decade, however, the number of blacks increased by more than 31,000, raising their proportion of the population to 28 percent.

Nashville had a city commission form of government from 1913 until 1921. A brief experiment with a city manager system ended in 1923 with the creation of a mayor-council government and the election of the mayor by the city's voters rather than by the council. The number of wards and councilmen rose from fifteen in 1921 to twenty-five in 1928. Hilary E. Howse, who had been mayor from 1909 to 1915, was reelected in 1924 and served until 1938—providing an important continuity of leadership in the highest municipal office. One observer noted a "revived interest in civic righteousness" in

35 Ralph McGill, *The South and the Southerner* (Boston, 1963), 91; Jesse Clifton Burt, *Nashville: Its Life and Times* (Nashville, 1959), 103.

the first years of the decade but lamented that the changes in city administration had not produced "the radical reforms hoped for by many voters."[36]

Nashville's neighborhoods, like those of Birmingham, became increasingly homogeneous in the early twentieth century; but members of both races were found in significant numbers in almost half of the city's census tracts. Many foreign-born whites, or those of immigrant stock, were found in a section along West End Avenue—"one of the better conservative white residential areas of the entire city." A contemporary observer isolated only one small strictly black section, and "considerable numbers" of white residents were found in all other areas which contained a majority of blacks. But some areas were experiencing substantial racial turnover. The Ninth Ward, for instance, lost 1,247 whites and gained 424 blacks during the 1920s. Black residential patterns were becoming more segregated and concentrated near the central business district and in East Nashville, just across the river. The data from the 1920 and 1930 census reports demonstrated the movement of blacks into increasingly restricted areas, many of which were located along the Cumberland River in the least desirable sections of the city.[37]

Contemporary studies confirmed that local social service expenditures were extremely low in Negro sections, and that racial violence was widespread, especially in "mixed" areas. But Nashville Negroes justifiably boasted of Fisk University, Meharry College (where over half the black physicians in the nation were trained), and an active business and civic leadership. Two of the most prominent black citizens were James Carroll Napier, who served on the city council before the turn of the century, became president of the National Negro Business League in 1903, and was register of the U.S. Treasury under President Taft, and Henry Allen Boyd, secretary of the National Baptist Publishing Board, publisher of the Nashville *Globe*, and president of the oldest black bank in the country.[38]

36 For information on city government, see the city charters of Nashville for 1921, 1923, and 1928. Also see Irby Roland Hudson, "Nashville's Experience with Commission Government," *National Municipal Review*, X (March, 1921), 160; Arthur B. Mays, "Nashville: A Study in Political Pathology," *ibid.*, XII (January, 1923), 12–15; and Burt, *Nashville*, 136.

37 J. Paul McConnell, "Population Problems in Nashville, Tennessee, Based on United States Census Reports for 1920 and 1930 and Other Related Local Data" (MS in YMCA Graduate School, Nashville, Tennessee, 1933), 2–3, 8–9, 11–12, 66–68. (A copy of this manuscript is available in the Tennessee State Library and Archives, Nashville.)

38 *Ibid.*, 11–12, 36, 42–44, 77; Harlan Welch Gilmore, *Racial Disorganization in a Southern City* (Nashville, 1931); Burt, *Nashville*, 106; August Meier, *Negro Thought in America*,

New Orleans, Louisiana, was the largest urban area in the South and one of the major seaports in the nation, rivaling New York and San Francisco in the bulk of its river and ocean commerce. Located in the flat lowlands near the mouth of the Mississippi River, it had always been a crucial commercial outlet for the nation's broad midsection, especially in the heyday of the steamboat. By the twentieth century the railroad had tapped much of the midwestern trade that had previously followed the course of the river, though the railroad also served to expand New Orleans' trading radius in other areas and in new directons. The city remained in the twentieth century a major seaport for South American imports and a clearing house for the agricultural produce of the lower South, and its sustenance still depended on the great river that had formed and shaped it from the beginning.

New Orleans was without question the most cosmopolitan city in the South, the product of a multiplicity of ethnic and cultural traditions. It contained the largest proportion of foreign immigrants of any regional urban area—6.7 percent in 1920—and Italians were particularly prominent. By 1930 over 28 percent of the city's residents were black, and the African cultural influence blended with those of French, Spanish, English, and Italian derivation. But one is tempted to say that it was not so much a melting pot concoction as a hearty Creole gumbo. The older core city retained a pervasive Old World atmosphere, a certain bohemian air and Creole character that attracted artists, writers, and bon vivants from all over the world. As one moved westward from Canal Street, however, the Anglo-American influence of the nineteenth century grew more apparent: large mansions with spacious lawns lay along St. Charles Avenue and business buildings rendered the newer downtown sections hardly distinguishable from the commercial cores of other large American cities.

The tale of New Orleans was thus a tale of two cities, each seeming to pay homage to different gods. Contrasts in the city—temporal, spatial, spiritual—abounded, and were of endless fascination to residents and transients alike. As one visitor to the city remarked in 1924, "with all its modernism, it is like some

---

1880–1915: Racial Ideologies in the Age of Booker T. Washington (Ann Arbor, 1963), 253–54. According to Meier (152–53), "In Nashville at the turn of the century, a light-skinned elite of barbers, contractors, and merchants in the city market was gradually giving way to a darker-skinned group consisting chiefly of physicians and dentists associated with the Meharry Medical School along with some businessmen and professors."

of the cities of Italy and Spain—Bologna, Madrid, Pisa, and other historical and interesting landmarks of the Old World. The traffic of a twentieth century city flows by, and beneath the aged buildings of another world and another age." In the more able literary hands of Sherwood Anderson and William Faulkner New Orleans became a "dear city of Latins and hot nights," and "a courtesan whose hold is strong upon the mature, to whose charms the young must respond."[39]

In 1920 New Orleans contained more than 387,000 people. Relatively old and established, the city's population growth was not proportionately as great as the expansion of inland cities like Atlanta and Birmingham. Even so, the number of New Orleans' inhabitants grew by more than 18 percent during the decade, to a population of almost 459,000 in 1930. The metropolitan area expanded by 22.1 percent in the same period, to a population in excess of 500,000. This was sufficient to rank New Orleans as one of the largest cities in the country.

Ever since the nineteenth century New Orleans had expanded westward from the downtown district along the Mississippi River, primarily because large areas of the city were uninhabitable until the development of effective drainage systems in the years between 1910 and 1930. As a consequence of this unusual topography, New Orleans' urban profile looked like "a crazy-quilt to sociologists acquainted with the ecology of conventional American cities." Whites moving to new residential areas invaded the once-solid black districts, leaving in their wake pockets of Negroes scattered throughout the city. As late as 1920 only 6 of the 272 census districts were completely white and none was solidly black. Significant Negro settlement along the urban "fringe" was disrupted, however, by the streetcar, which enabled blacks to live nearer the central business district "in the formerly swampy areas between the white residential sections" and still travel to their places of work. The largest regions of black settlement in the 1920s were located near the heart of New Orleans, between Broad and Bourbon streets and St. Charles Avenue and Broadway, and along the riverfront. Black Creoles, descended from the city's antebellum "free people of color," dominated a number of trades in the

---

39 Oliver S. Arata, "New Orleans: The City of Romance," *Southern Literary Magazine*, I (April, 1924), 44; Sherwood Anderson, "A Meeting South," in Etolia S. Basso (ed.) *The World from Jackson Square: A New Orleans Reader* (New York, 1948), 343; William Faulkner, *New Orleans Sketches*, ed. Carvel Collins (New York, 1958), 14.

nineteenth century, but members of the rising, non-Creole, non-Catholic black middle class developed the newer Negro business enterprises and professional groups in the twentieth century.[40]

The leading figure in Crescent City politics in the early twentieth century was Martin Behrman, born in New York City of German Jewish parents. Adopting the Roman Catholic faith in New Orleans, he worked his way up through ward politics, easily defeated a "silk stocking" opponent in the mayoralty election of 1904, and assumed leadership of the Choctaw Club— the dominant faction of the city Democratic party and "a good cross-section of the citizenry," including bankers, merchants, realtors, lawyers, gamblers, and professional politicians. Supported by contributions from major business elements and from gambling, liquor, racing, and prostitution interests, Behrman and the Choctaws tolerated much open vice, ignored the Sunday closing laws, manipulated assessments, regulated utilities, and retained their power until John M. Parker—the vice-presidential nominee on the national Progressive party ticket in 1916—was elected governor of Louisiana in 1920. Parker cut off state patronage to the Choctaw machine and Andrew J. McShane, owner of a hide export business, was narrowly elected mayor. But Behrman quickly regained his power. His support of Henry L. Fuqua, who defeated Huey P. Long for governor in 1924, restored good relations with Baton Rouge, and Behrman was reelected in 1925 by over two thousand votes. He died in office in January, 1926. Arthur O'Keefe, a prominent businessman and Behrman's commissioner of public finance, assumed the highest city office in a special election and continued to serve for the remainder of the decade. Throughout Behrman's regime, a tradition of cooperation between municipal government and the leading business interests grew and extended into subsequent administrations.[41]

A commission form of government replaced a seventeen-member aldermanic council elected by the wards in 1912, although the Choctaw machine

40 Harlan W. Gilmore, "The Old New Orleans and the New: A Case for Ecology," *American Sociological Review*, IX (August, 1944), 385–94; Woofter, *Negro Problems in Cities*, 62–63, 70–71; Meier, *Negro Thought in America*, 152.
41 George M. McReynolds, *Machine Politics in New Orleans, 1897–1926* (New York, 1936), 92–93, 99–101, 109, 133–35, 138, 149, 173–74, 185–86, 208–12, 217–23; Herman B. Deutsch, "New Orleans Politics—The Greatest Free Show on Earth," in Hodding Carter *et al.* (eds.), *The Past As Prelude: New Orleans, 1718–1968* (New Orleans, 1968), 319–20; Works Progress Administration, "Biographies of the Mayors of New Orleans" (MS in New Orleans City Archives, New Orleans Public Library, 1939), 155–58, 162, 172–73.

was able to promptly assume domination of the new body. The Commission Council in the 1920s was composed of the mayor and four commission-councilmen elected at large for terms of five years.[42]

New Orleans took decisive action during the 1920s to preserve the old Creole city—the Vieux Carré—from the commercial exploitation and architectural innovation that had thoroughly transformed the ancient sections of other large cities. This policy insured the continued existence of a uniquely authentic urban culture, to be sure, but it also preserved the city's most valuable natural resource in the true spirit of "enlightened" business practice. The spirit of the twentieth century, however, was given free rein in the "American" city west of Canal Street, an area, according to one visitor, "bristling with energy and ambition, noise and electric lights, shops, Movie theatres, banks, tourist offices, skyscrapers and street cars."[43] It was this district of New Orleans that symbolized for civic and commercial leaders the promise of a city that, on the basis of geographical location, had never had a right to survive in the first place.

Charleston, South Carolina, had roots that reached even more deeply into the loam of southern history. Comparing it to New Orleans, Josephine Pinckney wrote, "Charleston seems a trifle more austere in spite of its sunny climate and sub-tropical flowers; the English culture [having] absorbed the French to a surprising degree."[44] And Charleston was hardly a major national seaport. Between 1870 and 1910 its population remained virtually stationary, and though the city grew by 21 percent between 1900 and 1920—to a population of almost 68,000—it actually lost residents during the 1920s.

One visitor speculated in 1917 that "Charleston is perhaps the only city in America that has slammed its front door in Progress' face and resisted the modern with fiery determination. There are no skyscrapers, no blighting factory chimneys, no glaring electric signs. . . . Everything is leisurely and sleepy and mysteriously reminiscent." Even Edd Parks likened the city to a museum: "Although it has an extremely fine port and is an important commercial city," he observed, "this phase of its life has been rather largely neglected."[45]

These portraits of Charleston were, however, a bit overdrawn. Fertilizer

42 *Charter of the City of New Orleans* (New Orleans, 1922), 1–11; Deutsch, "New Orleans Politics," 315–16.
43 Mildred Cram, *Old Seaport Towns of the South* (New York, 1917), 289.
44 Pinckney, "Bulwarks Against Change," 48.
45 Cram, *Old Seaport Towns of the South*, 125; Parks, "Southern Towns and Cities," 508.

factories and other industries did exist in and just beyond the municipal boundaries, and the mobilization of World War I led to an expansion of the city's port facilities. The chamber of commerce was highly aggressive, and the major local newspaper could sense, not without some misgivings, that a new, pressing tension had invaded the lives of Charlestonians from the Battery inland. "We conduct everything at fever heat now," the *News and Courier* remarked in 1920, "where a few years ago the majority of persons worked in a quiet, sane, if in many ways unprogressive manner." Likewise, devotees of the old Charleston, like DuBose Heyward, lamented new forces which threatened local traditions:

> "The engine ripped the silence, and the jaded,
> Driven city stumbled from its sleep."[46]

Politics had long been the arena of the city's "better citizens," but in 1911 John P. Grace—a Roman Catholic and, by Charleston standards, a "liberal" Democrat—was elected mayor. Grace spoke out against corporate monopoly and privilege and called for government efficiency, street paving, expanded city services, and commercial development. He was immediately assailed by Charleston's business and civic elite, and the Commercial Club's effort to undercut his power through the creation of a city commission died with a gubernatorial veto of the measure. Grace was narrowly defeated in 1915 by Tristram P. Hyde, a conservative whose "near obsession for economy," in the words of one Charleston historian, cut city services, reduced taxes, and paved the way for Grace's reelection in 1919. His new administration faced continuing problems, however: opposition aldermen refused to attend council meetings, and Solicitor Thomas P. Stoney, a "young Bourbon," was elected mayor in 1923. Though he was "the ogre of many a Charleston businessman," according to John J. Duffy, Grace "probably did more for Charleston business than any of the businessmen mayors in the period." Despite his "florid, anti-aristocratic oratory, very little of a radical nature had resulted from his administration." Thus Charleston's government, especially after Grace's final defeat, continued in its traditional fashion.[47]

46 Charleston *News and Courier*, March 14, 1920; DuBose Heyward, "Chant for an Old Town," in *Skylines and Horizons* (New York, 1924), 71.
47 John Joseph Duffy, "Charleston Politics in the Progressive Era" (Ph.D. dissertation, University of South Carolina, 1963), 206, 208, 238–39, 275, 282–84, 342, 381, 383, 387. Also see Carl E. McCombs, "Charleston Breaks with the Past in Public Welfare Work," *National Municipal Review*, XIII (June, 1924), 341, 349.

As a seaport community, Charleston had always contained a relatively high proportion of foreign immigrants for a southern city, though their percentage of the population declined from 4.1 in 1910 to 2.6 in 1930. Blacks constituted a majority of the population until 1920, and comprised more than 45 percent of the populace in 1930. Negroes were found in all sections of the city, though many living in white neighborhoods—as in other southern urban areas—were confined to servants' quarters and back alleys. No Charleston census district contained fewer than 10 percent of blacks or whites. Negroes were most concentrated between Congress and Bee streets, and between Shepard and Calnun streets—generally toward the center of town or just off the downtown business district. They suffered from the usual deficiencies in urban services, and from a rate of infant mortality twice that of whites—to the extent that the city led the nation in this category in 1922. Charleston's older black aristocracy retained local leadership well into the 1920s and was not really displaced by rising Negro business and professional groups until the 1940s.[48]

Outsiders suspected that Charlestonians were part Chinese because they "ate rice and worshipped their ancestors," but the city was not merely a collection of extended families shut off from the outside world. According to William Watts Ball, conservative editor of the *News and Courier*, "the existence of a strange and esoteric aristocracy is the figment for the most part of outside publicity agents and penny-a-liners. The manners of Charleston's early middle-aged and younger generation have been affected by the rattlings and shakings of the last two decades, whether for good or for bad, not less than have been those of other communities, and a few old folk wring their hands and deplore in Charleston as in *partibus infidelium*." Yet the Palmetto City remained relatively unique among southern urban areas in both its lack of growth and its begrudging acceptance of the expansive vision put forth by the local business elite.[49]

A local historian recently wrote that "Knoxville in the 1920s . . . was much

48 Woofter, *Negro Problems in Cities*, 52–53; McCombs, "Charleston Breaks with the Past in Public Welfare Work," 342; Meier, *Negro Thought in America*, 152. According to Meier, "Not until the 1920s did Charleston Negroes enter into the 'co-operative' businesses dependent on the Negro market and not until after World War II did the dispersal of the better educated descendants of the old families pave the way for the rise to upper-class status of those descendants of the old house-slave class who now moved into the professional and business positions that accorded them higher social status."

49 Harriette Kershaw Leiding, *Charleston: Historic and Romantic* (Philadelphia,1931), 5; William Watts Ball, *The State That Forgot: South Carolina's Surrender to Democracy* (Indianapolis, 1932), 272.

the same sort of city it had always been—comfortable, friendly, reserved, and satisfied with a way of life that included no extremes."[50] But the city's very rapid expansion, and the urban problems and concerns appearing in the wake of that expansion, afforded considerable evidence to the contrary. The central city population grew by more than 114 percent between 1910 and 1920, the most impressive expansion of any medium-sized regional urban center outside of Texas and Florida between 1910 and 1930.

Jennie M. Bly, an itinerant book agent, commented in 1925 that she had "never found a more peculiar town" in all her travels. "The buildings, most of them, have a whacked-up look about them. Even Gay Street has a rickety appearance." Despite these small-town features, Knoxville was judged "not all bad. It is a good business town, having survived all panics wonderfully, and the people will buy, although they seem gruff and uncivil." In the short space of two or three decades, Knoxville had become a manufacturing center, with over three hundred and fifty plants primarily devoted to textiles, marble, and furniture, and the large repair shops of the Southern and Louisville and Nashville railroads. It was also the home of the University of Tennessee and a major commercial nexus for the East Tennessee region.[51]

Knoxville's population was relatively homogeneous. Largely because of its insular location and late industrial boom, it had one of the lowest proportions of foreign immigrants in the urban South. By the end of the 1920s there were eight hundred foreign immigrants in the city and only about two thousand citizens of foreign or mixed parentage. The percentage of blacks in the population was also small, though it increased slightly during the decade. Most of the city's growth stemmed from a heavy influx of native, rural whites from the mountainous areas of eastern Tennessee.[52]

Among the problems with which Knoxville's Negroes had to contend was the fact that the city was a ripe recruiting ground for the Ku Klux Klan—and one of the few places in which written records from the halcyon days of the Invisible Empire have survived. "White-collar workers accounted for about one-third of the total and included primarily salesmen, clerks, and small businessmen," Kenneth Jackson noted. "More than two-thirds of Knoxville Klansmen were laborers or blue-collar workers, most of them employed by

50 Betsey Beeler Creekmore, *Knoxville* (Knoxville, 1967), 227.
51 Jennie Margerie Bly, *Adventures of a Book Agent* (Boston, 1925), 171–72; Jackson, *Ku Klux Klan in the City*, 59.
52 Bly, *Adventures of a Book Agent*, 171–72; Woofter, *Negro Problems in Cities*, 54–55, 106.

such relatively large concerns as the Southern Railroad [and] the Foreign and Domestic Veneer Company." Of special interest is the fact that about two-thirds of Knoxville's Klan members had lived in the city for at least ten years, refuting the belief that the Klan was purely a rural phenomenon. It also suggested that the period of rapid growth and consequent social and economic dislocation in these years did create a highly favorable climate for an organization that promised to restore its members' sense of their own importance and dignity in a time of shifting values and mores.[53]

Municipal government in Knoxville mirrored similar tendencies throughout the urban South toward efficiency, economy, and the expansion of at least some city services. A city commission, assailed in the early years of the decade for corruption in the awarding of construction contracts, gave way in 1923 to a city manager government approved by a sizeable majority of the voters. The new city manager and the director of public safety were experts imported from Virginia, and in its first year the new administration reduced the costs of municipal government by $620,000, started a public improvements program, established a consolidated department of public welfare, and ordered a 10 percent tax refund totaling $280,000.[54]

Neither Knoxville nor Charleston was destined to become a commanding metropolis. The Palmetto City, even with the presence of large military installations after World War II, continued as a memento of an older civilization; and Knoxville, for all its industrialization, remained a smaller university and blue-collar city in the Appalachian foothills. Both testified to the diversity of the southern urban experience, even as Atlanta, Birmingham, and New Orleans represented the kind of "progress" to which many middle-sized regional cities aspired.

A Southern Urban Profile

In 1937 William F. Ogburn compared cities across the country according to eighteen basic population characteristics. In fourteen of these characteristics, cities of the North and South resembled each other more closely than they did

53 Jackson, *Ku Klux Klan in the City,* 59. The Klan was active in most other southern cities, of course, especially Atlanta and Birmingham. New Orleans, partly because of its significant Roman Catholic population and cultural heterogeneity, was never a place of Klan success.
54 Arthur R. Gande, "Knoxville's First Year Under City Manager Government," *National Municipal Review,* XVIII (November, 1924), 611–17; *ibid.,* XIII (December, 1924), 721.

the rural areas in their own regions. Strong resemblances in physical appearance and arrangement existed as well. The central business district of the large southern city served, as Sam Bass Warner, Jr., wrote of Philadelphia, "as an acceptable metaphor of the metropolis itself."[55] The principal commercial section—composed of department stores, business offices, restaurants, newsstands, and shops—usually centered around or bordered on a county courthouse (as in Birmingham), a state capitol (as in Atlanta and Nashville), or some other governmental structure. In this small inner core the municipal buildings, and usually a park or square, were also located.

At least one or two downtown industrial districts were found contiguous to the central business section and—in the case of the seaports and river cities—docks, warehouses, and loading areas were clustered along the waterfront. Even in an age before the widespread application of zoning laws a general spatial separation of economic activities pertained, though growth had in almost all urban centers confused patterns of land use and wedged newer stores and factories up against residential bungalows and into the older commercial and "public" sectors. And even with the rise of new buildings, the downtown districts wore a certain dingy aspect. "Sheer ugliness is still the chief mark of the business sections of the majority of southern cities," one observer noted. "A succession of flat roofed rectangular buildings down the main streets is the uninspired rule."[56]

Cutting across the increasingly complex downtown pattern were the railroad lines that tended to run along or through the business district and converge at a rail terminal or in one of the industrial sections. This disrupting of motor traffic caused by passing trains led to a rash of projects during the decade to build viaducts or tunnels. City streets were often rutted and unpaved at any distance from the main thoroughfares, and motorists were frustrated by irregular intersections and dead ends.

Skirting the central business core were the gambling dens, red-light districts, ill-kept movie houses, pool halls, and rooming houses that existed in every large regional city. Harlan W. Gilmore, in his study of Nashville during the 1920s, termed this general downtown region the "zone of deterioration." In this area, he wrote, "we find . . . 'red light' districts, 'dope dens,' and 'gang'

55 William F. Ogburn, *Social Characteristics of Cities* (Chicago, 1937), Chapter VII; Sam Bass Warner, Jr., *The Private City: Philadelphia in Three Periods of Its Growth* (Philadelphia, 1968), 187.

56 Ula Milner Gregory, "The Fine Arts," in William T. Couch (ed.), *Culture in the South* (Chapel Hill, 1934), 271–72.

lands. We also find a preponderance of old 'broken-down' people, aged widows, bachelors, old maids, widowers, and aged couples." Some lower-class white residential districts, which housed factory workers and recent poor rural migrants, were also located in this zone. "Here there were few marks of cultural or material respectability," William D. Miller observed of Memphis, "and the miserable quality of life was reflected in violence, murder, and suicide." Many blacks also lived in areas adjacent to the downtown factories and warehouses, where population density was high, housing cheerless, and sanitation poor.[57]

As one moved outward from the business district, residential areas tended to improve, with the more pleasant and desirable neighborhoods lying on the urban periphery. As a rule, some of the better white working-class and immigrant sections were located in an "intermediate" zone between the business district and the upper-class suburbs. This was, of course, the twentieth-century urban profile, drawn by sociologists as a series of concentric circles, common to almost all American cities. In the case of southern urban centers, however, blacks were not totally concentrated in a single inner-city area but scattered in one or two major clusters and in a series of smaller neighborhoods—especially in gullies, along railroad tracks and creekbeds, and in other areas which had been by-passed by whites. The industrial suburb was also a feature of large southern cities, often dwarfing in size those areas in the downtown section devoted to manufacturing. This was particularly true in Birmingham, where many of the iron and steel mills sought to escape municipal taxation and regulation. And along the urban outskirts one might find an occasional farm, caught unsuspectingly in the sprawl of the city.

This urban profile is, at best, an impressionistic portrait. Better residential areas were located both uptown and downtown in New Orleans, and the Crescent City had traditionally followed a linear rather than concentric pattern of growth. The "zone of deterioration" was also located variously in southern cities in relation to the central business section, and "vice" districts were often to be found, especially in the newer urban areas, almost solely in black neighborhoods. Cities also differed considerably in the homogeneity of their neighborhoods. But this profile, in its fundamental outlines, was quite similar to that prevailing in most other American cities.

57 Gilmore, *Racial Disorganization in a Southern City*, 50; William D. Miller, *Memphis During the Progressive Era*, 19.

The urban pattern was generally one of increasing complexity, with a proliferation of economic activities, industrial skills, neighborhoods, and populations. The working class—white and black—was hardly an undifferentiated proletariat but rather a collection of diverse elements. Likewise, large residential districts were composed of many subdistricts and neighborhoods that were distinguishable on the basis of everything from architectural style to income level and racial composition. This pattern was by no means planned in the normal sense of the term but was probably the inevitable result of population growth, technological innovations, and an increasingly specialized economy.

The emergence of these social and spatial patterns was mirrored in black areas of southern cities. A substantial black entrepreneurial class developed by the first years of the twentieth century on the basis of a "new economy" primarily dependent on a Negro market and the resources available within the black population. An older black aristocracy composed of barbers, contractors, and clergymen gave way—particularly in the more rapidly growing cities—to a newer elite of larger merchants, teachers, doctors, lawyers, and other professional and business types. As W. E. B. DuBois observed around the turn of the century, "the old leaders of Negro opinion, in the little groups where there is a Negro social consciousness, are being replaced by new; neither the black preacher nor the black teacher leads as he did two decades ago. Into their places are pushing the farmers and gardeners, the well-paid porters and artisans, the business-men—all those with property and money." At the same time, blacks were becoming more organized. Scores of black social clubs, philanthropic organizations, business associations, and women's groups proliferated on the existing base of Negro churches and mutual-benefit societies. Working-class blacks were forced out of certain occupations, like the building trades, in some cities and found new opportunities in others—such as industrial employment in Birmingham.[58]

58 DuBois, "Of the Wings of Atlanta," in *The Souls of Black Folk*, 68. The need for scholarly studies of blacks in the urban South in the late nineteenth and early twentieth centuries is especially acute. I have relied largely in my analysis on Meier, *Negro Thought in America*; Meier and Lewis, "History of the Negro Upper Class in Atlanta, Georgia, 1890–1958," 128–39; Woofter, *Negro Problems in Cities*; Zane L. Miller, "The Black Experience in the Modern American City," in Raymond A. Mohl and James F. Richardson (eds.), *The Urban Experience: Themes in American History* (Belmont, Calif., 1973), 44–60; and Zane L. Miller, "Black Communities in the Urban South, 1865–1920" (Paper presented to the Southern Historical Association, Houston, Tex., November 19, 1971); and Zane L. Miller, "Urban Blacks in the

Black neighborhoods generally lacked parks, schools, sanitation, and paved streets, and Negroes suffered severely from job discrimination, low wages, and the tightening constrictions of Jim Crow. But the evidence suggests that over the course of the half-century from 1880 to 1930 the southern urban black population grew larger, more diverse, more cosmopolitan, more self-reliant, and more prosperous. Black institutions became stronger and more varied, and an entrepreneurial elite developed which aspired to middle- and upper-class prominence while at the same time demanding equal treatment from whites and improvements in their own communities. These developments were not uniform throughout the urban South. Birmingham had no older black aristocracy to begin with; Atlanta was notable for the size and strength of its Afro-American leadership and institutions; New Orleans contained both Creole and non-Creole blacks, which maintained, to some degree, "two parallel social hierarchies"; and Charleston relied for a longer period on its older Negro aristocracy. But the general trend was toward more organized and self-conscious black urban communities whose leaders stressed self-reliance and racial solidarity—through patronage of black business, the creation of Negro civic clubs with broad membership, protests against racial discrimination, and the growth and cooperation of both old and new institutions.

This complex urban realm produced social views and environmental conceptions that were about as varied as urban conditions themselves. Probably every resident maintained a conception of the city, or at least of a particular community or neighborhood. Some views were more frequently expressed than others, of course, and some citizens were especially active in advancing their notions of the "good" or desirable city. While we know a great deal about the social and economic forces which shaped the twentieth-century metropolis, our knowledge and understanding is, however, very deficient when it comes to the role of such conceptions in the process of urbanization, or to their precise relationship with socioeconomic factors and opinions. If what men thought about their cities had anything whatever to do with how they acted in them, then this deficiency is of more than passing importance. It could, in fact, hold the key to an additional explanation of why cities developed as they did.

South, 1865–1920: The Richmond, Savannah, New Orleans, Louisville and Birmingham Experience," in Leo F. Schnore (ed.), *The New Urban History: Quantitative Explorations by American Historians* (Princeton, N.J., 1975), 184–204.

II Urban Attitudes and Advocates: The Dynamics of Community Ideology

Make loud your praise of hustling men,
Speak proudly of the busy jostling din,
Set hearts in tune with the headlong progress,
Drink deep of Builder's happiness.

—Fred Short, "Birmingham All Hail" (1926)

"EVERYONE has talked about the city except the business man," the Chicago Better Business Bureau declared in 1930. "He has been too busy making the city worth talking about, and yet he alone knows and understands the city for what it really is."[1] The same could perhaps be said of the industrial worker, the Italian immigrant, or the municipal bureaucrat—all of whom knew the city in a very special way and contributed significantly to its life. But the businessman, at least in the urban South of the 1920s, did not keep his opinions of the city to himself. As civic spokesman and urban booster he left his views—disorganized and impromptu as they might have been— strewn throughout the historical record.

What one finds in sifting through these bits and pieces of booster rhetoric and civic exhortation is, of course, a good deal of confusion and inconsistency, as one might discover in a study of folklore or popular political opinion. On closer examination, however, a pattern begins to take shape, tenuous and elusive but nevertheless much more than the product of unconnected,

1 Quote from *Chicago Through the Eyes of Business*, reprinted in Anselm L. Strauss (ed.), *The American City: A Sourcebook of Urban Imagery* (Chicago, 1968), 56–57.

39

random observations, and infinitely more tangible than the mass of individual, personal views of the city that were rarely communicated and seldom preserved.

What emerges from this mass of material, in fact, is the outline of a general conception of the city, a complex of beliefs and attitudes about the nature and role of urban life, an urban ethos that permeated the circulating media and was apparently shared in some degree by large numbers of urban dwellers—and certainly by the commercial and civic elements who dominated the channels of printed communication.

This ethos was neither a coherent policy nor a structured ideology. But it was more than a compendium of booster nonsense. In its way it was a most serious assessment of the urban condition and the urban future. Its central theme was disarmingly simple: the necessity for growth and order, change and stability, progress and preservation. It was, in all probability, both an attempt to promote economic self-interest and to resolve the conflict between the centrifugal and centripetal currents in urban society—a conflict fundamental to the life of the twentieth-century metropolis. It was also undoubtedly an effort to hold the urban community together through "acceptable" values, social norms, economic controls, and institutional restraints.

Before we can begin to fully identify this ethos, isolate the probable reasons for its existence, and trace its impact on the city—a task which comprises the major portion of this volume—we must first examine its sources, the dynamics of its formulation, and the means of its cultural diffusion. We must direct our attention for the present moment not only to urban imagery, as it is usually understood, but also to an analysis of the relationship of imagery and concepts of the city to socioeconomic factors. Who were the principal advocates of an urban ethos? Were these advocates in a position to substantially influence the course and character of urban development—in effect, did they have the power to implement their conceptions of the city in any tangible way? Finally, how was the urban ethos disseminated and articulated, to the extent that it found a measure of acceptance among a variety of groups in the urban population?

The Image of the City

When Carl Sandburg described Chicago as a "tall bold slugger" among American cities, as "Stormy, husky, brawling,/ City of the Big Shoulders," he vividly set forth an image, a personal perception, of what the city was and what its future was likely to be.[2] Urban images have ranged from the simplest visual portrayals to intricate conceptions of the environment, and have differed markedly from individual to individual and from group to group. Certainly, few were fashioned with Sandburg's literary skill. The images most commonly encountered are those centered around skylines, panoramic views, landmarks, or widespread notions about the "personality" of a specific city. They focus, in short, on one or two major attributes of a given city, whether it be the Boston landscape seen from the Charles River, the serpentine freeway system of Los Angeles, or the odor of Chicago's slaughterhouses. Cities are endlessly stereotyped in popular literature and advertising, so that New York appears as a sophisticated cultural and commercial center, Washington a haven of political intrigue, and Miami a tropical fleshpot.

As a form of mental shorthand—the basic function of most stereotypes—these images served a limited purpose. But most perceptions of the city were neither so superficial nor so easily recognizable. The image of the city maintained by most individuals, as Kevin Lynch observed, "was not a precise, miniaturized model of reality, reduced in scale and consistently abstracted. As a purposive simplification, it was made by reducing, eliminating, or adding elements to reality, by fusion and distortion, by relating and structuring the parts." In visual terms, it was not a photograph but an impressionistic portrait whose scope and form depended as much if not more on the mind of the perceiver as on reality itself. Each individual's image of the city was thus in some respects unique, created unconsciously from the assorted stuff of his own particular observations and impressions. It was rarely comprehensive in dimension but partial and fragmentary, assembled in bits and pieces to meet special needs.[3]

The urban image was often not only a spatial representation, focusing on the outward physical appearance of a city, but also social, economic, and temporal—constituting, in effect, an entire symbolic system.[4] Images of the city were inherently unstable, always changing in response to new circumstances. If a city failed to attain the expectations of a prevailing image, if its skyline was altered or its major industry collapsed, if the composition of its population suddenly shifted, then older conceptions became inadequate and

2 Carl Sandburg, "Chicago," in *Oxford Book of American Verse* (New York, 1950), 585.
3 Kevin Lynch, *The Image of the City* (Cambridge, Mass., 1960), 87, 2.
4 See Anselm L. Strauss, *Images of the American City* (New York, 1961), 32.

new ones were demanded. The image of the city was thus characteristically complex and ill-defined, continually shifting in emphasis and content. It was by its very nature imprecise and unstable, varying from individual to individual, from period to period, and from city to city. Though generally formulated in unsystematic—even unconscious—fashion, its elements were nevertheless arranged in some order of relationship to one another, so that observations, random impressions, and memories were blended together as part of the individual's attempt to comprehend the urban environment. Above all, the image was deeply personal.

The urban image was, however, as important as it was elusive and fragmentary. The extent to which it was manipulated in the mind of the individual suggests that it was not a fortuitous perception but rather a means of relating man to his world, of providing some environmental frame of orientation, some emotional and psychological relationship with physical surroundings. The more vivid and distinctive the image, the more it apparently contributed to emotional security and stability. "When the city has been symbolized in some way," according to Anselm Strauss, "personal action in the urban milieu becomes organized and relatively routinized. To be comfortable in the city—in the widest sense of these words—requires the formulation of one's relations with it, however unsystematically and crudely. Uncertainty about the environment can only engender deep psychological stress." [5]

Rooted as it was in the emotional and psychological needs of individuals and groups to establish some degree of *harmony* between themselves and their environments, the urban image necessarily operated more on the plane of symbol and myth than on the level of empirical perception. Such images were basically "nonrational" or "nonlogical" and could not be empirically verified. As one authority wrote, the truth or falsity of such nonlogical constructs "are not dependent, nor can they be, on the methods of science. They represent a different order of reality." [6]

5 *Ibid.*, 17. Also see Lynch, *Image of the City*, 2–5. Marc Fried observed in a similar vein ["Grieving for a Lost Home," in Leonard J. Duhl (ed.), *The Urban Condition: People and Policy in the Metropolis* (New York, 1963), 156] "that a *sense of spatial identity* is fundamental to human functioning." Though our discussion here relates to the city, the necessity for an "environmental image" is obviously not limited to urban areas.
6 William Lloyd Warner, *The Living and the Dead: A Study of the Symbolic Life of Americans* (New Haven, 1959), 485.

Images of the city were functional, however; since their basic purpose was to orient man to the urban environment, they always reflected a certain measure of reality. Just how closely the image mirrored reality varied greatly from individual to individual, so that this particular factor is impossible to measure with any precision. In theory, an image totally unrelated to reality would call for actions that would lead to more, rather than less, confusion and disorientation.

The realm of urban imagery is thus marked by incredible diversity and variety. As the city was divided into a number of populations, so also was it symbolically fragmented. Purely visual perceptions blended readily with social thought, historical awareness, and deeply personal hopes and fears, becoming almost a function of the individual personality. If the analysis of this multifaceted pattern of urban imagery presents a most difficult problem for the sociologist or the city planner, even with the benefit of the latest methodology, it is an impossible task for the historian. The sources he requires are among the least likely to be preserved in the historical record, certainly as far as the images of the individual city dweller were concerned, and polling the dead is as yet an undeveloped methodological art.

Attitudes toward the city must be considered not simply as assorted visual images of the physical terrain or even as general impressions of whether the city was or was not a desirable place to live; but as complex *concepts of community* that—when brought together in an articulated urban ethos— involved not only visual representations but notions about the city's history and its future, its role within the regional and national pattern, and its relationship to the individual and to various social groups.[7] We must ascertain whether significant urban groups had characteristically different ways of looking at their environment and, if so, determine which groups were the

7 Most historical approaches to the subject of urban imagery have been peripheral, a means of illuminating other areas of investigation; and visual impressions and spatial representations have been examined without adequate attention to other kinds of awareness. The failure to examine various impressions as products of specific social, economic, and cultural conditions is perhaps the most serious deficiency. Sociologists and city planners have contributed much in the way of theory—Anselm Strauss is the most notable example—but their work has generally been weakest in the attempt to apply theory to *historical* situations. Few scholars have succeeded in relating visual and social impressions of the city to a larger, more all-embracing conceptualization of the urban community. As Dwight Hoover observed, "the idea of community in American cities has yet to be done." Dwight Hoover, "The Diverging Paths of American Urban History," *American Quarterly*, XX (Summer, 1968), 314.

most effective in creating and advancing particular concepts of the city, and also in influencing the process of urban development itself.

Urban Images and Socioeconomic Status

Most distinctions drawn between various attitudes toward the city focus on whether such attitudes were favorable or unfavorable, prourban or antiurban. Of even greater significance were the differences among urban views in terms of their scope and dimension: and it is precisely here where we can establish some fairly firm relationships between concepts of the urban community and socioeconomic status.

The city meant different things to different people, and perceptions of specific areas of the city varied depending on the degree of personal familiarity with those areas. Of crucial importance, however, is the fact that conceptions of the city tended to correlate to a significant degree in their character and dimensions with the social, economic, and geographical "radius of interaction" of various urban individuals and groups, with different degrees of *participation* in the urban community. According to Scott Greer, "the lower the occupational and educational level, the smaller the scale of the individual's participation. This means, not that he is uninvolved, but that the radius of his interaction is shorter. Kinfolk and the small-scale world of the neighborhood grow relatively more important as we move through the urban landscape toward the low end of the social-rank continuum."[8]

This observation is confirmed by Mirra Komarovsky's 1946 study of 2,223 adult residents of New York City. Business and professional people—both men and women—of the middle and upper classes consistently reflected both a higher number and a broader range of institutional and group affiliations, especially membership in city-wide organizations. Fully 60 percent of the working class and 53 percent of the white-collar males "did not have a single organized group affiliation with the exception, perhaps, of a Church." Furthermore, the group affiliations of the lower classes were primarily with neighborhood churches, lodges, and fraternal orders.[9]

8 Scott Greer, *The Emerging City: Myth and Reality* (New York, 1962), 127.
9 Mirra Komarovsky, "The Voluntary Associations of Urban Dwellers," in Logan Wilson and William L. Kolb (eds.), *Sociological Analysis* (New York, 1949), 379–85.

Though income alone was not a consistent determining factor, the "radius of interaction" of the middle and upper ranking groups was obviously greater. This does *not* suggest that the lower classes were unconcerned about their communities, or that organizations like the church and the lodge were unimportant—indeed, such institutions were spawned of intense communal longings. But the pattern of institutional and group affiliations among members of the lower classes, their sphere of community interest, was considerably more circumscribed in a spatial sense than that of groups higher on the social rank scale.

Those individuals and groups in the working and lower classes therefore tended to see the city in a general way, as their social and economic radius of interaction and participation in the city dictated—in terms of their own neighborhoods, their immediate friends and family, their job, their immediate experience. Marc Fried observed, for example, that "feelings of being at home and of belonging are, in the working class, integrally tied to a *specific* place," while concepts of community in the middle class are "not as contingent on the external stability of place or as dependent on the localization of social patterns, interpersonal relationships, and daily routines."[10]

Persons with a particularly pronounced material or emotional stake in the community were among those most likely to participate in community affairs, whether at the neighborhood or the city-wide level. Merchants and home-owning residents were thus generally more involved in local activities than either a floating laboring population or a group of transient professionals in the middle or upper class. Among those least likely to develop wide-ranging group affiliations and a strong relationship with the community were, as one writer put it, "the uprooted and the isolated, the disadvantaged and the segregated, the confused and the disillusioned, and the sectarian. Those who profess a feeling of belonging are the socially secure, the active participants."[11]

It would be wrong to think that the socially and economically uprooted could not be organized, or that they made no impact on the course of urban development. What we are talking about here is an articulated conception of the city that extended beyond neighborhood lines—and the poor, the socially

10 Fried, "Grieving for a Lost Home," 157.
11 Francis C. Rosecrance, "The Community in Industrial Civilization," in Eugene Staley (ed.), *Creating an Industrial Civilization* (New York, 1952), 312.

insecure, and the transient were simply not in a position to contribute a great deal to this particular kind of conception.

A number of social scientists have attempted systematic studies of varying attitudes toward the city among urban leadership groups.[12] All the evidence strongly suggests that developed and elaborated visions of the city as a whole were largely limited to the middle and upper class groups who were more socially secure, whose radius of interaction carried them beyond the confines of a specific area or neighborhood, whose social and economic contacts led them to think of the city as a larger entity, and whose control over the urban media allowed them to articulate and disseminate their vision—their urban ethos—to other groups in the population and into the historical record. Whether their vision was accurate or misinformed, socially constructive or unconstructive, it was nevertheless sufficiently developed and articulated to permit historical analysis. Every city dweller, regardless of social position, maintained an urban image of some kind; but those in the upper reaches of the socioeconomic spectrum were virtually the only ones to attempt a reasonably systematic formulation of an urban ethos, to think such matters through and to state their thoughts consciously and publicly. Businessmen, journalists, promoters, professional men, and civic leaders all espoused at one time or another in every area of the country some form of urban vision. Such

12 Robert K. Merton's classic division of the community leadership into "local" and "cosmopolitan" influentials, "Patterns of Influence: Local and Cosmopolitan Influentials," in his *Social Theory and Social Structure* (Rev. ed.; Glencoe, Ill., 1949), 387–420, is probably the most familiar of such studies. Merton's localite was parochial and "preoccupied with local problems, to the virtual exclusion of the national and international scene." The cosmopolitan, on the other hand, regards himself as part of a larger society and does not feel "rooted in the town." Similarly, Everett Carll Ladd, Jr., *Ideology in America: Change and Response in a City, a Suburb, and a Small Town* (Ithaca, N.Y., 1969), especially 166–67, 172–77, argues that ideological and political conflict is best understood in terms of "cosmopolitanism" and "parochialism," rather than in terms of the more conventional dichotomy between "liberalism" and "conservatism." The urban historian will sense that, in many respects, this kind of distinction can easily be overdrawn. Urban boosterism—and the urban rivalry in which it was so often rooted—was an endeavor that entailed not only a pronounced loyalty to the home community but also a considerable knowledge and appreciation of regional and national developments and opportunities. A far more important distinction, at least for understanding the sources of the urban ethos, was that between the upper and middle classes and those groups lowest on the socioeconomic scale—as suggested in Zane L. Miller, *Boss Cox's Cincinnati: Urban Politics in the Progressive Era* (New York, 1968), especially Chapter 7, "Boosterism and Reform," 113–28. Other essays on the local-cosmopolitan distinction include Thomas Dye, "The Local-Cosmopolitan Dimension and the Study of Urban Politics," *Social Forces*, XLI (March, 1963), 239–46; and William Dobriner, "Local and Cosmopolitan As Contemporary Suburban Character Types," in Dobriner (ed.), *The Suburban Community* (New York, 1958), 132–43.

individuals and groups were most definitely present in the burgeoning cities of the South, especially after 1880.

The Commercial-Civic Elite in Southern Cities

An Atlanta publication complained in 1926 about the lack of any "real aristocracy" among the social and economic leaders of the city: "You can go down the list and find dozens of houses now prominent in social life, the family trees of which sprouted out of a whitewash bucket, a second-hand furniture shop, or a grist mill, and in one well-known case, out of a peddler's pack."[13] This assessment was a bit drastic; but the business-oriented middle class that asserted itself in southern cities in the late nineteenth century became dominant in virtually every regional urban area after 1900. The conflict between an older aristocracy of birth and a newer elite of entrepreneurial spirit had given way by the 1920s in most of the larger southern cities to a pattern of cooperation among the members of the upper classes, due to intermarriage and the power and influence of the rising businessmen.

The business-oriented middle class in southern cities during the 1920s cannot be defined precisely. It was composed primarily of those businessmen and civic leaders whose social and economic interests extended beyond the boundaries of a single section or neighborhood yet were focused mainly in the local urban area. Since the membership of this group included a wide range of local leadership, it is perhaps best to refer to a *commercial-civic elite*, composed of larger merchants, real estate agents, insurance brokers, bankers, contractors, and a variety of other persons who were either associated directly with commercial enterprises or agreed substantially with business middle-class goals and priorities—attorneys, journalists, physicians, educators, clergymen, and city officials. Though some of the largest businessmen were very much a part of the local elite, they were often less interested in purely local matters because they represented absentee economic interests in manufacturing firms, shipping companies, and railroads. The principal sphere of interest, activity, and concern for members of the commercial-civic elite in southern cities during the 1920s was the downtown business district.

The activities of the commercial-civic elite were evident on every hand,

13 *Atlanta Life*, November 27, 1926.

but perhaps most notable was the impressive array of voluntary civic organizations that cropped up throughout the urban South, the type of association which Oscar Handlin termed "the characteristic social unit of the modern city."[14] Men's luncheon clubs held weekly meetings in downtown hotels and restaurants, initiated philanthropic projects, raised funds for existing religious and charitable agencies, formed women's auxiliaries, proclaimed "social service" as their primary goal, and joined with similar organizations in other cities. The Rotary, Civitan, and Kiwanis clubs, among others, assembled their membership from the "outstanding citizens" of the community and firmly eschewed any narrowly commercial purpose. Though often ineffective in achieving their declared goals and rarely willing to tackle the most controversial of local issues, these organizations nevertheless functioned as forums of discussion, centers of social activity, and originators of recommendations bearing on public policy. Because many drew their members from different elements of the middle and upper classes they undoubtedly contributed to a certain unanimity of views among the local business-oriented elite, and since their members were among the most powerful and influential men in the community they naturally exercised some authority in the councils of city government.

Most important of all such organizations were the chambers of commerce that not only sought to unify urban business interests but also appropriated to themselves the task of defining and encouraging general community growth and well-being. In addition to holding regular meetings, most chambers sponsored a variety of civic activities, created dozens of committees, placed advertisements in national publications to attract tourists and new business, provided information to out-of-town visitors, and published their own magazines and periodic reports. Crucial to all of these activities, and raising the funds to support them, was the chamber secretary, a hired "professional booster" who devoted his efforts full-time to an expanding array of promotional and "service" responsibilities—the more active the secretary the more grandiose and flamboyant the promotion. Every large southern city had a chamber of commerce or a board of trade by the 1920s, noted for its diverse civic activities and for, as one observer put it, "a wild-eyed secretary whooping it up."[15]

14 Oscar Handlin, "The Social System,' in Lloyd Rodwin (ed.), *The Future Metropolis* (New York, 1961), 22.
15 William J. Robertson, *The Changing South* (New York, 1927), 281.

In Atlanta a new chamber of commerce succeeded the Board of Trade in 1871 and became especially active after the turn of the century. Its consolidation with the larger Business Mens' League made it, in the opinion of one historian, "a dominant group rivaling even the City Council for industrial and civic leadership." The chamber played a considerable role in the success of a $3,000,000 bond issue in 1910; called the Southern Hook-Worm Conference; hosted a visit by President-elect Taft in 1909; and created the Chamber of Commerce Realty Company and the Atlanta Convention Bureau in 1912–1913. By 1920 the group's membership reached 2,890, and a year later the chamber supported an $8,850,000 bond issue and formed the Junior Chamber of Commerce and the Division of Women's Affairs. Several presidents of the organization—notably Asa G. Candler and Ivan Allen—were also mayors of Atlanta. The chamber's most ambitious project was a coordinated drive among the city's 350 commercial and professional organizations in 1925 to raise $1,000,000 for a nationwide "Forward Atlanta" advertising campaign. By 1927, ninety local civic groups were represented in the Presidents' Club, originally formed in 1915 under the slogan, "United for Civic Advancement." The Atlanta Rotary Club was organized in 1913 by Evelyn Harris (son of Joel Chandler Harris), Henry W. Grady, Jr., Ivan Allen, and Howard Geldert, and similar groups appeared shortly thereafter—the Kiwanis Club (1917), the Civitan Club (1920), and the Exchange Club (1922).[16]

A Business Mens' League and a Merchants' and Manufacturers' Association were formed in Birmingham in 1909. In the same year, the Birmingham Commercial Club established its permanent headquarters in a ten-story "skyscraper," proudly changed its name to the Chamber of Commerce, and increased its already aggressive promotional activity. One of the most notable of the national civic associations, the Civitan Club, was founded in the Alabama metropolis in March, 1917 (the eighth national chapter was established in Atlanta). By the 1920s, Birmingham included a full range of commercial and civic groups.[17]

16 Thomas M. Deaton, "Atlanta During the Progressive Era" (Ph.D. dissertation, University of Georgia, 1969), 99–100, 103; Walter G. Cooper, *Official History of Fulton County* (Atlanta, 1934), 339, 350, 361–64, 367–68, 393, 802–803, 806, 808–809, 811; Ivan Allen, *Rotary in Atlanta: The First Twenty-five Years* (Atlanta, n.d.); Atlanta Forward Atlanta Commission, *Report of the . . . Commission* (Atlanta, 1930).
17 Martha C. Mitchell, "Birmingham: Biography of a City of the New South" (Ph.D. dissertation, University of Chicago, 1946), 177–78; Birmingham *Age-Herald*, June 7, 1921, January 10, 1922.

Nashville was likewise noted for a variety of voluntary associations. "All the business 'service' clubs are here," wrote Vanderbilt professor Edwin Mims, "with the usual mixture of boosting, standardized foolishness, and really good intentions and public service." Interaction among various elements of the city's elite was encouraged by a half-dozen mens' clubs composed of academics, businessmen, ministers, and other leaders which met weekly to consider questions of importance to the community. According to Mims, their discussions not only resulted in tangible public benefit but also served to break "the supposed uniformity of Southern thought." The Nashville Boosters drew representatives from different civic groups and sponsored trips throughout the region to promote the city's social and economic advantages. One member of this group, a local clergyman, characterized Nashville civic organizations as "the quickest avenue to associations with men really worth while." A "Sell Nashville to Itself" program was inaugurated in 1926 and the president of the chamber of commerce suggested that the thirty-nine-week campaign be supported through public taxation so that every citizen would be forced to do his civic duty.[18]

Memphis and New Orleans also contained well-organized and active civic bodies. The Memphis Chamber of Commerce was one of the largest in the South, with a membership of 3,821 by July, 1919. In 1920 the organization boasted thirty-four standing committees and divisions concerned with such matters as conventions, traffic and transportation, education, publicity, farm development, art, athletics, entertainment, postal services, reading, taxation, and social agencies—to name a few. The chamber maintained a full-time secretary and ten other salaried officials, including a statistician and a "market expert"; sent speakers throughout the South and delegations across the country to inspect the operations of other civic groups and projects; and put particular emphasis on the development of a highway system in the mid-South.[19]

In New Orleans, the Association of Commerce contained 4,709 members in 1920 and 5,100 by 1928 from virtually every significant commercial firm

18 Edwin Mims, *Adventurous America: A Study of Contemporary Life and Thought* (New York, 1929), 106, 108–109; Nashville *Tennessean*, June 2, 1924; *Nashville This Week*, I (January 11–18, 1926), 7 and (April 19–26, 1926), 10.
19 *Memphis Chamber of Commerce Journal*, II (July, 1919), 143, V (October, 1922), 22; Memphis Chamber of Commerce, *Annual Reports, 1919–1920* (Memphis, 1920), 6.

and professional practice in the city—organized into five departments, a dozen bureaus, and eighty-six active committees. Like similar organizations in other cities, it maintained an official lobby in the state legislature and was engaged in raising funds for an ambitious $450,000 national advertising campaign. [20]

The pronouncements and activities of chambers of commerce, civic clubs, and social service groups were dutifully recorded in the urban press. To a remarkable degree, such organizations were represented by the major newspapers—which were, after all, large business enterprises rooted in the affairs and concerns of the downtown section—as the most promising focal points for community action on virtually any significant local problem, no matter how remote it might appear from the realm of the countinghouse or the marketplace.

"The Chamber of Commerce is the clearing house for all communal endeavors," the *Nashville Review* proclaimed in 1922, and greater progress would be insured when all voluntary civic associations sat in common council and set about to "perpetuate their ideas with a will." "The Association of Commerce represents us all, in a way," the New Orleans *Times-Picayune* concluded, and the Birmingham *Age-Herald* endorsed the chamber because it "assumes a genuinely representative character; it aids in the crystallization of the best opinion in the community on issues of large public moment, and is in a position at all times to throw the whole weight of the community behind worthy business and civic enterprises." The editors of the Memphis *Commercial-Appeal* envisioned the city without a chamber of commerce. "What body would then take up propositions that daily come before the city in its business, in its efforts for better transportation, in its efforts for road improvements and a thousand and one other things that go to make up the economic and social life of a great modern city?" [21] The answer, of course, was that there were few other organizations that were prepared and willing to discuss and act on such a multiformity of subjects.

Such attitudes were not confined to white publications. The Nashville *Globe* looked to the local Negro Board of Trade "to draw the people together

20 *New Orleans Association of Commerce News Bulletin*, II (March 29, 1920), 3; New Orleans Association of Commerce, *The Achievements of Organization, New Orleans, 1928: Annual Report of the Association of Commerce* (New Orleans, 1929), 5–10.
21 *Nashville Review*, III (January, 1922), 6; New Orleans *Times-Picayune*, February 15, 1921; Birmingham *Age-Herald*, June 11, 1926; Memphis *Commercial-Appeal*, February 5, 1922.

and to unite them in every effort that is put forth for the good of the
community." Similarly, the Norfolk *Journal and Guide* proclaimed that the
city's Negro Chamber of Commerce would concern itself with general affairs,
"just as the white Chamber of Commerce takes an interest in everything that
promotes the welfare of the community."[22]

Commercial-civic spokesmen themselves ardently put forth the notion
that voluntary associations were the best vehicles for welding diverse urban
elements together in thought and action. The New Orleans Association of
Commerce reacted vigorously against any suggestion that the interests of
commercial bodies were limited to industry and trade. "Nothing is further
from the truth," the editors of the *News Bulletin* wrote. "The commercial
organization which followed so narrow a policy would have no excuse for
existing as an organization which made claims to representing a city." And
commercial organizations did, regardless of evidence to the contrary, claim to
represent the entire metropolis and the interests of all its citizens. "The people
of this city," the *Memphis Chamber of Commerce Journal* commented, "want
the Chamber of Commerce to serve as a central civic agency for the good the
service will do, irrespective of its business value."[23]

Given the reluctance of most voluntary commercial and civic bodies to
encourage discussion of issues that were genuinely controversial, and might
thus fragment their membership, a real question exists as to whether such
groups were effective in voicing or influencing public policy. Their stated
philosophy was often merely a collection of commonly accepted assumptions
concerning home, family, the benefits of hard work, and the virtues of local
boosterism, all laced together with cliches, laden with religious homilies, and
expressed through a sometimes semihysterical promotion of trade. Indeed,
their very existence depended on an ability to appeal to the common
denominators of the business-oriented middle class, and this in turn necessitated a watering down of ideology and a certain minimum of action in the
quarrels of local politics.

On the other hand, their expressed purposes and activities are significant
precisely *because* they reflect such common denominators, and thus suggest
the essential points of agreement among the middle- and upper-class segments

22 Nashville *Globe*, July 12, 1912; Norfolk *Journal and Guide*, June 4, 1921.
23 *New Orleans Association of Commerce News Bulletin*, III (July 12, 1921), 2; "Civic Activity Is
   Good Business," *Memphis Chamber of Commerce Journal*, V (January, 1923), 22.

of the southern city. Real estate salesmen, industrial magnates, bankers, downtown merchants, and attorneys could, and did, disagree on municipal tax policy and on other important urban priorities—but they expressed substantial unanimity on many goals and ideas, including a prevailing concept of the city during the 1920s. And, when they were able to reach agreement on specific public policies, they could play a significant role in the urban decision-making process.

The "power structure" in southern cities was neither monolithic nor open to all significant social, economic, and ethnic groups. The white commercial-civil elite was by far the most articulate, influential, and effective leadership group throughout the decade, and its members exercised a dominance in urban affairs that was rarely challenged—at least directly. This elite group was diverse in the sense that it was a collection of special interests, each of which responded to urban conditions and public policy with a predictable concern for the safety of its own particular endeavors. And its members were not in a position to direct municipal policy according to their every whim.[24] Also, the leading commercial-civic associations were not necessarily the vehicles through which elite influence was brought to bear on municipal affairs—though they were the principal forums where programs were justified, proposals explained, and an urban ethos articulated.

A perfect correlation between economic power and political influence rarely existed in southern cities in the early twentieth century, at least on the basis of those few studies which deal with the subject. Carl V. Harris recently demonstrated, for example, that the economic elite in Birmingham was not all of one mind with regard to various local issues, and by no means always successful in achieving its political goals. Within what I have termed the business-oriented middle class, Harris isolates the "upper ranking" and "middle ranking" economic interest groups. The upper-ranking groups (iron and steel corporations, utilities, railroads, banks, and coal mining firms) were generally most successful in influencing public policy, at least as it directly

---

24 Many political and economic decisions in southern cities in this period appear to have been made, as other scholars have suggested of American cities generally, "only within the constraints of a bargaining process among competing elites and of an underlying consensus supplied by a much larger percentage of the local population." Wallace S. Sayre and Nelson W. Polsby, "American Political Science and Urbanization," in Philip M. Hauser and Leo F. Schnore (eds.), *The Study of Urbanization* (New York, 1965), 132. For two conflicting views of urban elites and decision-making, see Floyd Hunter, *Community Power Structure* (Chapel Hill, 1953), and Robert A. Dahl, *Who Governs?* (New Haven, 1963).

affected their own activities. Members of this upper-ranking group were less interested in purely local issues than the middle-ranking groups, however, and many of their efforts were directed at protecting themselves from punitive municipal and state legislation. The middle-ranking economic interest groups, which comprised the core of the commercial-civic elite (real estate firms, contractors, larger merchants, and professional men) fully realized that their "prosperity was intimately bound up in the fortunes of the city itself" and therefore "displayed a broader and more intense interest in the entire range of local government policies than did most of the upper-ranking interest groups." [25]

Members of the middle-ranking group comprised "the vast majority of elected officials" and their influence was most evident in the allocation of public services, especially in the areas of education and police and fire protection. Harris confirmed that the "lower-ranking" economic interest groups (smaller merchants such as retail grocers, saloon owners, artisans, and wage earners) exercised very little influence on public policy. Members of this group were primarily interested in matters that affected them directly and "tended to express less concern for the general growth and upbuilding of the entire city and its governmental services than did the larger downtown businessmen." While they favored expenditures for education, they usually opposed higher taxes and most other "civic amenities." They never achieved a majority on any governmental board or agency and were clearly the least successful of all economic interest groups in molding public policy. Furthermore, the smaller merchants and businessmen in the lower-ranking category were not prominent participants in the chamber of commerce or in other city-wide civic associations. Neighborhood grocers, for example, tended to work through organizations such as the Retail Grocer's Association rather than through the chamber of commerce.

Birmingham's elite continued in the 1920s to be both heavily business-oriented and civically active. Of 296 individuals identified by a local

25 This information on Birmingham, unless otherwise indicated, is taken from Carl V. Harris, "Economic Power and Politics: A Study of Birmingham, Alabama, 1890–1920" (Ph.D. dissertation, University of Wisconsin, 1970), 16–17, 177–78, 326–27, 329–31, 465–71, 485. Most previous studies of Birmingham have portrayed the city's elite as much more monolithic and domineering in character. See Mitchell, "Birmingham," 78; and Irving Beiman, "Birmingham: Steel Giant with a Glass Jaw," in Robert S. Allen (ed.), *Our Fair City* (New York, 1947), 101.

journalist in 1920 as "important" in the city's affairs, over 200 were classified as businessmen. Of these, 66 were primarily involved in manufacturing, 22 in mining, 26 in real estate, 23 in banking and finance, and 80 in retail trades. Furthermore, over 130 of these same businessmen were involved in one or more "secondary" economic activities, including 35 who were engaged in some form of banking or finance and 23 in real estate. A large number of the city's most influential businessmen had at least one contact—usually in the form of a directorship—in banking, real estate, or insurance ventures. The great majority belonged to at least one civic association, 120 belonged to one or more fraternal groups, 100 belonged to the chamber of commerce, and 27 were recorded as having served as officers of that body. Almost a quarter (71) held appointive or elective public office at one time or another.[26]

The story was much the same in Atlanta. Between 1900 and 1916 a large majority of elected municipal officials hailed from the middle or upper class. Among the city's 174 councilmen and aldermen in this period, one historian found 39 salesmen, 31 attorneys, 30 small businessmen, 15 managerial personnel, 14 "professionals," and 19 laborers or labor representatives. Businessmen belonged to a variety of civic associations, the most important of which was the chamber of commerce. But Atlanta's social and economic elite was hardly unified on every issue or always successful in the political arena. As in Birmingham, the most controversial and hotly debated issues of the period were not economic but moral or religious in character (the issues of prohibition, Sabbath observance, and public dancing were especially important in Birmingham, for example), and they cut across economic interest-group lines and aroused the general populace as few others did in the early twentieth century.[27]

Conflict among different groups within the business-oriented middle class apparently existed in every large southern city during the 1920s. Their dominance in urban affairs resulted not so much from their complete agreement on matters of policy as from a pattern of values, aspirations, and expectations which they generally shared and from the fact that they faced no significant opposition from lower-class elements and nonbusiness institutions.

26. Sample taken from George M. Cruikshank, *A History of Birmingham and Its Environs: A Narrative Account of Their Historical Progress, Their People, and Their Principal Interests* (Chicago, 1920), II.
27 Deaton, "Atlanta During the Progressive Era," 365–87, 415–22, 424–25, 427–28; Harris, "Economic Power and Politics," 141–42.

While members of the commercial-civic elite might rail against the corruption and inefficiency of traditional political groups and seek to replace them with political forms organized according to business principles, municipal governments—even the "machines" in New Orleans and Memphis in the first several decades of the century—were largely responsive to their needs and demands.[28] Likewise, organized labor, the urban church, the black population, and even groups like the Ku Klux Klan posed no real threat at any time during the decade to commercial-civic interests, and their leaders tended, in fact, to support the ideas and activities of the leading civic associations.

The Klan, for example, was less a vehicle of lower-class protest against the urban elite than it was a reaction to the dislocation of rapid growth and the presumed decline of older moral and religious values. In many communities, the Klan apparently sought to play a dual role as a secret fraternal order and a voluntary service organization, and it was known on occasion to indulge in civic boosterism. Labor unions desired specific benefits for their members, but most of their spokesmen were willing to follow the lead of the commercial-civic elite in urban affairs. Labor organizations sought a more profitable relationship with business, not its overthrow. And their influence was, in any event, severely limited by their extremely small membership.[29]

The metropolitan church, as Robert M. Miller has noted, was not only a religious body but also an important secular institution with "a tremendous stake in the prevailing economic order." It is not surprising, then, that a number of city clergymen maintained an "uncritical attitude . . . toward the business community." Success in the ministry was conceived more and more in terms of promotion from a rural to an urban pastorate and increasingly measured by the city clergyman's ability to associate himself with the personalities, organizations, and activities of the commercial-civic elite. The

28 "This was an epoch," George M. McReynolds wrote of New Orleans, "in which the pronouncements of the business man and the Chamber of Commerce were considered the wisdom of the ages. Their declarations regarding what would help or hinder the economic, industrial and commercial development of New Orleans were not subject to any critical analysis, least of all by Choctaw politicians." George M. McReynolds, *Machine Politics in New Orleans, 1897–1926* (New York, 1936), 138.

29 See Kenneth T. Jackson, *The Ku Klux Klan in the City, 1915–1930* (New York, 1967), 247–48. As Robert S. and Helen M. Lynd observed in their studies of Muncie, Indiana, the working class usually tended to follow "the same symbols" as the business class, "trying intermittently, as work allows, to affirm them as loudly as does the business class, and to narrow the gap between symbol and reality." Robert S. and Helen M. Lynd, *Middletown in Transition: A Study in Cultural Conflicts* (New York, 1937), 447.

Nashville *Christian Advocate* reacted promptly in 1920 to a report that Chicago ministers were flocking to that city's civic assocations. "This procedure may be new for Chicago," the editors declared, "but it is certainly not new for most cities in the South. In almost all our towns and cities ministers are to be found in the commercial organizations—just men among men—working for the best interest of the community. This is as it ought to be."[30]

Religious revivals reminiscent of the country camp meeting proliferated in southern cities during the 1920s, and urban ministers of the fundamentalist sects usually led the opposition to any easing of the urban moral code. But the larger, established city churches became interested in "community service" as well as in saving individual souls, and many urban clergymen were among the most ardent exponents of commercial-civic values and aspirations. As Wilbur J. Cash observed, it became in the 1920s "almost as impossible as in the North to distinguish the minister from any other business executive bent on pleasing his board of directors and hanging up a record as a go-getter and a builder, or to distinguish the institution itself from another factory or Rotary club."[31]

Southern urban blacks shared very little in the material comforts of the white middle- and upper-class world, especially after disfranchisement and the increasingly formal and legalistic separation of the races. Yet developments in the late nineteenth and early twentieth centuries had brought to the fore a black entrepreneurial class—the equivalent of the white commercial-civic elite—that moved to take economic advantage of a more definable and separate Negro market. The new and more dynamic black communities that appeared in the urban South after 1880—with their relatively greater wealth and variety of social and economic institutions—seemed in many ways a tangible fulfillment, or at least a hopeful promise, of the prosperity predicted by the National Negro Business League and its local chapters and by a number of black commercial and civic clubs. Concerned with material success and social advancement, convinced of the value of hard work,

---

30 Robert Moats Miller, *American Protestantism and Social Issues, 1919–1939* (Chapel Hill, 1958), 26, 22; Nashville *Christian Advocate*, LXXXI (December 17, 1920), 1,604. The *Advocate*, LXXXVII (January 1, 1926), 3, also boasted "that the Churches are not behind business in the adoption of business methods."

31 Wilbur J. Cash, *The Mind of the South* (New York, 1941), 298. Also see Wayne Flynt, "Dissent in Zion: Alabama Baptists and Social Issues, 1900–1914," *Journal of Southern History*, XXXV (November, 1969), 523–42.

appreciative of social order and self-discipline, and hopeful about the future of their children, the members of this Negro commercial-civic elite shared many of the goals and attitudes of their white counterparts. And their views permeated the majority of black newspapers and periodicals published in the first decades of the twentieth century. Encountering only scattered opposition from other elements in the Negro population, this black elite set about to teach others "how to live clean, moral, and thrifty industrial lives." [32]

Black leaders nevertheless consistently protested against the barriers of racial segregation, the dismal conditions in many Negro neighborhoods, the prevalence of white violence and economic discrimination, and the inequitable allocation of municipal facilities and services. Many participated in those few interracial groups that existed at the time, in organizations like the NAACP and the Urban League, and—to the extent that they were able—in the arena of local politics. Those improvements in their situation or prospects which did come about, however, were due almost solely to their own efforts rather than to the policies or sympathies of white leaders. The white commercial-civic elite was neither very concerned about the plight of its black fellow citizens nor very constrained to do anything about it—except to the extent of maintaining order in the city and the racial status quo.

The concept of the city advanced by the commercial-civic elite was important not only because members of this group were usually the most powerful on the local scene, but also because their views were broadcast throughout the city by newspapers, magazines, and pamphlets. The role of the circulating media—especially newspapers—in formulating public opinion has been, and will doubtless continue to be, a source of endless controversy. And it is not possible at the present moment to venture anything more than a reasonable guess concerning the probable influence of such media in the urban South during the 1920s.

Most of the difficulty in assessing the role of the circulating media stems from the fact that they both shape and reflect public attitudes. And there are no accepted tests to measure the degree of the distinction. But if a number of different newspapers, in different cities, under different ownership, with different staffs, different audiences, and different relationships with the public, reflect even a general unanimity on any issue or point of view, it is reasonable to assume that this is not so much a case of the media's conscious manipulation of

32 Norfolk *Journal and Guide*, February 14, 1925.

the public mind as it is a case where newspaper and readership reciprocally act on one another to preserve and extend values and attitudes that are already widespread. It is here, in other words, that one begins to deal not with the conflicting attitudes of social and political controversy, but with "community ideology"—with cultural assumptions and attitudes that transcended individual cities, specific interest groups, and institutions, even though they may have been advocated forcefully by a relatively few people.

A major newspaper's dependence on a large number of subscribers insured to some degree its role as a mirror of many accepted attitudes, and its dependence on substantial advertising from local businessmen strongly encouraged its general allegiance to the prevailing economic order and the success of local enterprises. As noted earlier, the major newspapers in southern cities during the 1920s tended to reflect commercial-civic notions about the city, probably not so much because of the influence of advertisers (though this factor cannot be discounted) but because the papers were themselves businesses operating within the established social and economic system, and because such notions found wide acceptance among their readers.

Metropolitan newspapers did not, of course, speak for the entire urban community, even though this was often how they perceived their role. The majority of their readers were inevitably found among the middle class and the more stable and prosperous elements of the working class, and no white newspaper spoke for blacks, even though they did try to speak about them and occasionally at them. But since many of the same concepts of the urban community enunciated in the large dailies were also present in publications directed to more limited audiences—church papers, Negro weeklies, labor union periodicals etc.—there seems to have been some diffusion of the commercial-civic elite's urban ethos among various elements of the population. Some features of this ethos were possibly like the moral and social values that were, as the Lynds suggested of Middletown, "so familiar and so commonly taken for granted that they represent the intellectual and emotional shorthands of understanding and agreement among a large share of the people." [33]

Though we cannot be sure what role the circulating media played in disseminating conceptions of the urban community, or how widespread these

33 Lynd and Lynd, *Middletown in Transition*, 402.

conceptions really were, we can say with some confidence that the major newspapers in these cities in the 1920s were most responsive to the suggestions, activities, and goals of the local commercial-civic elite, and that these media were fairly faithful in reflecting, at least in a broad sense, commercial-civic views.

The general conception of the urban community—the urban ethos— which prevailed in these publications was not a monolithic, regimented body of ideology or a finely honed symbolic analogy. But it *was* expressed within the rigor of argument, ordered to some extent by conscious metaphor and symbolization, structured by the intellectual necessities of communication, and preserved in the finality of print. If it can be identified only through a painstaking process of collecting and arranging, it is at least—unlike the myriad individual images of the city forever lost to the historian—possible to collect and examine. It is also fairly easy to determine, if not its ultimate sources, then its principal advocates, the great majority of whom were members of the urban commercial-civic elite. Precisely what it was, and how it affected the city itself, are even more pressing matters.

III A Sense of Place: The Dimensions of Urban Consciousness

> Not all the praise of country-side and rustic scene by poet and romancer... can ever change the fact, that the meeting-place of men, where they do congregate to exchange ideas, relate experiences, formulate rules of conduct and band themselves in cooperative endeavor, in united effort for the general good, that this seat of social concourse—the city—is the type and standard of their civilization.
>
> —Edward A. Parsons, *The Latin City: A Plea for Its Monuments* (New Orleans, 1925)

> If a maladjustment between the city and country population exists at present in the South, would it not be better to remedy that difficulty by an intensive development of the manufacturing enterprises which make cities rather than by a wholesale northern migration of the surplus population of the farms?
>
> —Nashville *Tennessean*, January 2, 1924

FOR THE founders of Sudbury, Massachusetts, in the seventeenth century, the construction of a new community was, as Sumner Chilton Powell wrote, "their principal ideal, and their loyalty to the town even transcended their professions of religious faith."[1]

Local allegiances of this intensity rarely survived into the nineteenth and twentieth centuries. Geographical mobility and radical innovations in transportation and communication severely weakened the bonds of localism and even those of regional identity. On the other hand, rivalry between towns and cities for capital, trade, and population—and the continuing importance of place for many Americans—tended to underline the older pattern of loyalties and to produce a local form of patriotism that sometimes seemed as vociferous as the national variety. "There is a civic patriotism as old as the planting of new cities," Scott Greer noted, "a commitment to hallowed ground," a

---

1 Sumner Chilton Powell, *Puritan Village: The Formation of a New England Town* (New York, 1965), 179.

61

boosterism which "reflects a synthesis of the economic man's wish to improve his market and the civic patriot's identification with his city as home."[2]

Local loyalties had always been important in the South, though the country rather than the town was often their principal focus. In the late nineteenth century urban patriotism manifested itself in towns and cities throughout the region, and was frequently expressed in braggadocio reminiscent of the regional frontier. By the twentieth century local urban identification seems to have grown concurrently with the development of southern cities, and in similar degree. Local urban loyalties were quite compelling for many southern city dwellers, and they constituted the first rudimentary prerequisite for the development of urban consciousness.

Certainly, local loyalties were more than artificial devices of commercial promotion. For some, a distinctive and widely recognized community guaranteed a degree of personal recognition. "Birmingham is a city of such power and resources," a local journalist wrote in 1920, "as to confer distinction, something after the manner of ancient Rome, upon its individual citizens. The man who writes 'John Doe of Birmingham' is claiming not only a means of identification but also some prestige from the association of his name with that of a city known everywhere." For others, local loyalty was based quite simply on the fact that the individual's life was most intertwined in a specific place. As a Memphis writer put it, "My city is where my home is founded, where my business is situated, where my vote is cast, where my children are educated, where my neighbors dwell and where my life is largely lived." Consequently, "My city has a right to my civic loyalty. It supports me, and I must support it."[3]

If individual identity did depend to a degree on an association with a particular locality, then it was important that the local community be seen in some relief, with certain differentiating features that separated it conceptually from other environments. It was important also that a city be readily comprehended: anything that confused its image or its residents' perceptions of it was to be avoided or corrected. The lack of proper street markings, for example, and the fact that residents and visitors alike could become lost in the

---

2 Scott Greer, *Metropolitics:A Study of Political Culture* (New York, 1963), 10.
3 George M. Cruikshank, A *History of Birmingham and Its Environs: A Narrative Account of Their Historical Progress, Their People, and Their Principal Interests* (Chicago and New York, 1920), I, 2; "My City and I," *Memphis Chamber of Commerce Journal,* V (August, 1922), 71.

midst of the city, was a source of concern throughout the urban South.[4] For the city to be understood, it had to be seen with at least a minimum of clarity. The perceived relationship between the individual and his city thus led inevitably to the desire that the city be "legible," that it contain some distinctive features or characteristics to set it apart from other environments and from other cities.

One especially popular means of rendering the community more distinctive was to invest it with a "personality," a personification and simplification of urban reality that would express more vividly the city's various attributes. Of greatest importance, perhaps, was the degree of notoriety which a specific urban "personality" was able to achieve beyond local boundaries. The precise substance of this "personality" apparently mattered less than its wide acceptance by those in other communities. Atlanta leaders, for example, were disappointed to learn in 1920 that their city had been omitted from a discussion of "city personality" held in Madison, Wisconsin. "No citizen of Atlanta can doubt that Atlanta has a personality," one writer noted, "but that is of little importance if the personality is not so pleasing or striking as to make itself felt among the elect."[5]

Urban consciousness rested not only on the recognition of essential differences between a city and other communities, but upon the perception of important similarities. Thus, almost all cities were perceived as having more in common with each other than with rural areas. Indeed, this urban consciousness—the awareness of the complex, interdependent world that is the city, the cognizance of the city as identifiable by qualities that were distinctly *urban*—was both the recognition of the city *sui generis* and the distinctive features of a specific city. And urban consciousness provided an essential framework of awareness for the development of broader, more

4 The Birmingham *Age-Herald* (March 17, 1921) referred to the city's southside as a "veritable maze," and the Birmingham *Post* (December 13, 1926) spoke of the "thousands who have wandered bewildered in the labyrinth of Birmingham." Likewise, a Memphis writer in the *Memphis Chamber of Commerce Journal*, V (March, 1922), 17, considered the erection of street signs "imperative to the general welfare." See also Birmingham *Age-Herald*, January 12, 1921; Atlanta *Constitution*, February 9, 1922; Nashville *Tennessean*, January 22, 1925. In promoting the organization of a Nashville Symphony Orchestra, the *Tennessean* of May 16, 1920, pleaded, "Nashville must have something distinctive."
5 Atlanta *City Builder* (September, 1920), 12. See also Bayrd Still, "The Personality of New York City," *New York Folklore Quarterly*, XIV (Summer, 1958), 83–84.

elaborate views of the city and its ultimate significance. Before urban citizens could begin to construct a coherent, relatively wide-ranging urban ethos, they first had to arrive at some notion of how the city was similar to some environments and what set it apart—culturally, conceptually, and spatially—from others. No process was therefore more important in the development of urban consciousness than the comparison of a specific city with other communities.[6]

Southern cities found a multitude of different kinds of environments that invited such comparison: their own suburbs, the farms and small towns of the urban hinterland, other regional cities, and urban centers in the North and West. On occasion, urban spokesmen even juxtaposed a specific city with an "ideal" urban community. As the *Memphis Chamber of Commerce Journal* suggested in 1924, "The town can best test its strength by making comparison and contrast with other towns. Make out a score card for a model town. Apply the test to your town. Study it in the light of other towns of equal strength and opportunity."[7]

Through such contrasts southern urban spokesmen expressed various responses to particular features of rural and city life and shaped, to a considerable degree, the conceptualizations of their own communities. The *perceived* relationship between a specific city and other environments, the role or place which a particular urban area enjoyed relative to other communities, is perhaps best termed the city's *spatial identity*, or the *spatial dimension* of urban consciousness. And it was upon this elementary foundation of identification and local loyalty that more abstract visions of the urban community necessarily rested.

Most urban writers and spokesmen, and members of the commercial-civic elite in general, probably identified themselves first as Atlantans or Memphians rather than as Georgians or Tennesseans. They displayed greater interest in regional and national urban affairs than in rural life and activities. Through their awareness of the city's geographic location and its relationship

---

6 "It is, in fact," as Nels Anderson wrote, "the existence of other communities that give each a sense of identity. The internal consensus, the self-awareness that the population acquires, becomes the more readily articulate in relation to the proximity of other populations. These relationships with the outside not only contribute to the formation of a 'consciousness of community,' but they contribute in many ways to making a community the sort of place it is." *The Urban Community: A World Perspective* (New York, 1959), 43.

7 *Memphis Chamber of Commerce Journal*, VII (April, 1924), 44.

to rural areas, small towns, suburbs, and other cities, they fashioned an urban consciousness that emphasized both the particular features of their own city and the general characteristics of urbanism. To a remarkable degree, their attitudes toward other communities were shaped within a distinctly urban frame of reference, so that suburbs were thought to be logical extensions of the city, small towns were seen as poised uncertainly between city and country— and thus rarely posited as models of community—and rural areas were valued largely because they contributed both directly and indirectly to the urban welfare. They considered the city itself to be an inherently dynamic and expansive community—defined not by its municipal boundaries but by the extent of its economic and cultural influence—that aspired first to the dominance of its hinterland, then to regional prominence, and finally to national recognition.

Suburbs: Outposts of the New Urban Frontier

Population decentralization was evident by the 1920s in all major southern urban areas. Though the perceived dichotomy between city and country had not been fully replaced by a new polarity between city and suburb, as Anselm Strauss suggested of a later period, the implications of outlying residential and industrial settlement were of considerable interest to most observers during the decade. The Atlanta *Constitution* noted in 1920 that "the city is surrounded with thickly-settled and heavily-populated suburban residence communities," and a Birmingham paper observed six years later that "the tendency now in all large cities is to develop homes in the outlying districts."[8]

While there was some ambiguity concerning centrifugal population movement, the prevailing attitude in large southern cities toward outlying residential areas was sympathetic. The demographic trend was viewed as a welcome relief for congested inner cities and as a collective effort to improve individual living conditions.

A chief benefit of suburban residences, according to the literature of the time, was their proximity to nature, their "convenience to delightful woods and mountain retreats where men and women may 'commune with nature in

8 Anselm L. Strauss, *Images of the American City* (New York, 1961), 246; Atlanta *Constitution*, May 27, 1920; Birmingham *Age-Herald*, March 1, 1926.

her visible forms,' and may quickly speed from pavement and soft coal smoke to the clear air of highland and woodland." [9] Bubbling brooks, wooded fields, and untouched landscapes were obvious advantages that, when combined with excellent investment opportunities, rendered suburbs desirable from virtually any standpoint.

The central city often fared poorly in comparisons with its expanding suburbs. The journey out from the city was sometimes seen as one away from "the familiar serrated sky line, with its lofty buildings, its terrifying canyons of busy streets, jostling crowds and babel of noise and confusion" into a quieter and more healthful world; and the trip back was a return to the smoke and roar, the busy streets and teeming office buildings, and the confusion of the crowds." The single-family residence, ensconced on its modest plot of land, was an ideal widely shared during the period, and one best realized in outlying areas where population dispersal and lower real estate costs made such development possible. Rarely voiced were suspicions that decentralization might ultimately threaten the overall urban welfare. The Nashville *Banner* concluded in 1920, for example, that outward population movement "leads to a large suburban growth at the city's expense. . . . When limits are extended to take in thickly-settled suburbs, which Nashville's experience shows is some-times a difficult undertaking, then the new growth begins further out." [10] But this was about as far as southern urban spokesmen would go in casting doubts on a movement almost universally hailed as a sign of progress.

Negro publications also lauded the suburban phenomenon, notwith-standing the noticeable trend in most southern urban areas toward more concentrated black residential settlement near the city core. Groups of Memphis blacks began moving into the outlying districts as rural Negroes swelled the already congested inner-city population. In one such suburban community, a black organization called the "Orange Mound Boosters" was formed "to promote health, education, law and order, and the community spirit" as well as other suburban amenities. In Atlanta, the *Independent* called attention to the new black suburb of Rockdale Park and lamented the white monopoly on the better outlying areas. "We can't all live in town," the editors observed. "The white man is grabbing every suburban locality as a home for himself . . . that he may get out of the plague of a noisy and busy city. And we

9 Birmingham *Age-Herald*, November 11, March 1, 1926.
10 *Atlanta Life*, March 5, 1927; Nashville *Banner*, April 2, 1920.

would act wise if we follow his foot steps."[11] Members of the upper socioeconomic classes obviously had the requisite resources to participate most fully in outlying residential development, but population decentralization was not strictly confined to any single economic or racial group, and enthusiasm for suburban living was widespread throughout the urban population.

The general acceptance of the advantages of suburban living involved a blend of urban-rural images and reflected the desire, either explicit or implied, to "marry" the country and the city. As one writer put it, "Nashville home lovers" sought "a place where they may be a part of the city and yet partake of the comparative freedom of suburban life." Likewise, the Memphis *Commercial-Appeal* complimented Henry Ford's plan for a "model city" at Muscle Shoals, Alabama, a community which would extend over a seventy-five mile area and in which "the inconveniences of both cities and rural sections would be avoided." Most spokesmen accurately credited decentralization to both the desires of urban residents to leave the crowded cities and the bevy of new technological innovations that made such movement practicable. They viewed the automobile, the telephone, the radio, the highway building programs as principal forces in the outward movement of people and industry, and generally favored these innovations as essential to bringing cities and rural areas closer together.[12]

If the city is defined as an area of relatively congested population, without open spaces, and composed entirely of one dense core with a close juxtaposition of commercial, industrial, and residential zones, then the suburb was largely born—in the South at least—of antiurban attitudes. But such a definition is neither wholly accurate nor comprehensive, and it is only

11 Thomas J. Woofter, Jr., *Negro Problems in Cities* (Garden City, N.Y., 1928), 99–100, 163; Atlanta *Independent*, April 23, 1925.

12 *Nashville This Week*, I (August 31–September 7, 1925), 19; Memphis *Commercial-Appeal*, January 5, 1922; Nashville *Tennessean*, March 4, 1928. Scott Donaldson observes that the suburb, according to the planning theory of the time, "would represent the best of both worlds, which would preserve rural values in an urbanizing world, which would enable the individual to pursue wealth while retaining the amenities of country life." Donaldson, "City and Country: Marriage Proposals," *American Quarterly*, XX (Fall, 1968), 548. See also his *The Suburban Myth* (Ithaca, N.Y., 1969), 4. Schmitt contends that "nostalgia for an agrarian past played no part" in the thinking of assorted nature-fakers or suburbanites alike; "inevitably they rejected a mythology that exalted men who lived off the land." They perceived distinct differences between city and country and "looked upon fields and forests as inspirational resources for their urban life." Anselm Strauss notes (*Images of the American City*, 209) that the "rhetoric of decentralization" embodied a blend of urban-rural images.

one of the many ways in which cities have been conceived in American history. Southern urban spokesmen actually put forth several apparently conflicting notions of what characterized a city, and a great many were indeed critical of what we might call the "urban core." But this should not lead us to dismiss urban spokesmen as "agrarian" or "antiurban"—much less as "Jeffersonian"—or to ignore other, alternative definitions of "the city." The great majority of southern urban commentators in the 1920s viewed the suburb as an adjunct to an essentially urban existence; it was, in other words, neither agrarian nor rural in conception, but rather a means of enjoying urban life without population congestion and many other difficulties associated with the city core. If the suburb was an attempt to "marry" city and country, then the city was clearly conceived as the dominant partner.

Suburban development was especially noticed, of course, during census periods, on occasion becoming a way of explaining a lack of population growth within the municipal boundaries. Those cities with the most appealing natural surroundings, according to the Nashville *Banner*, were those with the least interior urban growth: "Only cities, in the main hemmed in by barren fields through which red gullies run, are showing big population increases." But this was more than pure rationalization. The realization was widespread that "the city" was, increasingly, the "metropolitan area." "We know . . . that Atlanta is vastly larger than the census indicates," the *Constitution*'s editors wrote, "because our suburbs to the north, east, west and south of our arbitrary boundary lines, are, in all respects except that of local government, each part of Atlanta; and the weight of Atlanta is really that of the metropolitan area." Similarly, Nashville leaders considered and discussed the merger of the city with Davidson County as early as 1920, in view of "the fact that the *legitimate city population* in these days of rapid transit and the extension of city conveniences and privileges is disposed to spread." [13]

In a very real sense, the suburbs were conceptually drawn within the immediate urban orbit, just as many were eventually joined with the city through formal annexation. The suburb was, of course, conceived in part as an improvement over the congested inner-city; but outlying residential and commercial development was largely seen during the period as an expansion of the city into more spacious and comfortable surroundings, an exploitation

13 Nashville *Banner*, April 3, 1920; Atlanta *Constitution*, June 6, 1920; Nashville *Banner*, April 2, 1920 (my italics).

of the immediate urban hinterland for basically urban purposes. Attitudes toward the suburb thus constituted a conceptual parallel of urban expansion and imperialism.

The prevailing view depicted the city as an organic entity almost constantly in the process of growth and formation, and virtually limitless in its potential extent. "The city," according to the *Tennessean*, "is no longer the self-contained unit that it was in an earlier day. About and adjacent to every city," the editors wrote, "there grows up a region where there is no distinguishable difference between the economic and social life and that of the city itself. The problems of the city and its environs are usually identical." In the final analysis, then, city and suburb were separated only by "an imaginary line." [14]

Indeed, much of the fascination which accompanied suburban development in the 1920s centered on the dramatic boldness with which such projects brought outlying territory within the urban domain. Even those publications most critical of the central city and its problems portrayed suburban developments as "representing the vision and courage of some real estate man or group, backed by a faith in the city and its future. New streets are being laid out, leaving scars in the green flanks of the hills, valleys are being filled up, mains are being placed, while all the natural beauty of the surroundings is, so far as possible, being retained—and all to make way for more new homes." Even though such ventures were mainly prompted by business considerations, "The American city is deeply indebted to these men with the pluck to assume the risk, to express their faith in the future in terms of brick and wood and stone, taking barren hillsides and brambled hollows and by the magic of their genius, converting them into places of entrancing beauty—places fit for the habitation of man." [15]

For members of the commercial-civic elite, especially, the suburb was not one pole of a newly emerging dichotomy but a logical, inevitable, "legitimate" extension of the city—an essential outpost of a new urban frontier. Thus, they considered the urban core the "business district" and the suburbs the "residential districts," each specialized in function and reflecting distinct features but neither self-sufficient and both parts of the more all-embracing force that was the modern city.

14 Nashville *Tennessean*, September 5, 1927.
15 *Atlanta Life*, March 5, 1927.

Small Towns: In Between City and Country

The small town, aside from its significant role in American tradition and folklore, was a most important part of the overall southern urban scheme in the 1920s. Technology permitted and encouraged the location of industry in villages scattered throughout the region, especially in the Piedmont, and communities of fewer than ten thousand people proliferated more rapidly than larger towns and cities. Southern urban spokesmen were hardly of one mind in their attitudes toward the small towns, but throughout the period they contemplated its horrors and virtues in the city press. Curiously, they approached the village with somewhat less certainty than they demonstrated with respect to either the suburb or the farm—perhaps because the small town stood precariously between the clearly urban and rural. And this urban-rural quality of the town's existence made it many things to many people.

Aspersions were sometimes cast against the provinciality and rusticity of the smaller towns, with the large city emerging from the comparison an infinitely more exciting and desirable place of residence. Those southern urban novelists who devoted some attention to the small town, rather than limiting themselves solely to the popular antebellum tales, appeared to follow the pattern of the "Main Street" criticism so noteworthy in national literary circles. Hamilton Basso's Macedon, South Carolina, for example, was not only small, but isolated and provincial: "What a stinking hole to be buried in. You might as well try to live your life in a tomb." Compared with a city like New Orleans, the town was intolerably undisturbed, insufferably complacent. "There seemed to be a dead area around it, a kind of doldrums, through which the ideas and intellectual currents that blew across the rest of the country did not penetrate." Ward Greene of Atlanta portrayed the small southern town as composed of "either a lot of busted old Joes pretending they're aristocrats when they haven't a dime's worth of culture left, or a lot of howling godhoppers running the town for purity and pep." His fictional Corinth "was snobbish as only a city can be that has outgrown the friendly country town stage and has not yet attained the variegation of the cosmopolis. It was like a naughty little girl in a new coat who snubs other little girls in yesterday's shabby dresses, including the younger sisters in her own house." [16]

16 Hamilton Basso, *Courthouse Square* (New York, 1936), 72, 198; Ward Green, *Ride the Nightmare* (New York, 1930), 10, 62.

For Greene, it was not the diminutive, placid, comfortable country town that was the object of disgust, but the growing village that clung ridiculously to pretensions of greatness.

Urban writers offered many reasons to account for the small town's lack of appeal and "progress." For one thing, the village was notoriously lacking in the amusements and recreational activities that clearly set the city apart; and those primitive amusements that did exist were limited by a traditional mentality. As the *Tennessean* commented in 1925, "It isn't a hick town unless there's no place to go where you shouldn't be." Smaller towns also lacked the rush of commercial activity and business incentive that dominated larger urban communities, one result of which was an increasing flow of talented and ambitious men and women to the metropolises. According to one labor publication, "One of the reasons why young men leave their native towns for the larger centers—and perhaps the principal reason—is that the smaller towns and villages lack enterprise. Its citizens are apt to wait on some northern capitalist or outsiders to come in and discover its advantages."[17]

Indiscriminate rural migration to the city was not encouraged by most urban observers, but it was attributed as much to the failures of small towns as to the greater attractiveness of the big cities. The bitterest denunciations were usually reserved for the occasion when a small town competed in some way with a larger center, or presumed to offer advantages supposedly limited to the larger urban areas. Nashville, for example, was outraged to discover that Meridian, Mississippi, had been successful in assembling a local symphony orchestra while efforts in the Tennessee metropolis toward this goal were just beginning. "IS NASHVILLE TO BE OUTDONE," the *Tennessean* queried, "BY A LITTLE JERK-WATER TOWN IN THE BACKWOODS OF THE COTTON BELT?"[18]

For urban Negroes, the small town was notable not only for its rusticity and lack of business incentive, but also for deeply entrenched racial conservatism. Black spokesmen were naturally quite concerned with those threats to life and liberty which Negroes encountered in the smaller centers. "Thousands of black men and women are leaving the country," the Atlanta *Independent* observed in 1920, "and coming to the cities for protection; for they have absolutely no protection for their lives and property in the small

17 *Nashville Tennessean*, March 13, 1925; Birmingham *Southern Labor Review*, VII (September 1, 1926), 8.
18 Nashville *Tennessean*, May 24, 1970.

towns and rural districts." [19] Lynchings were much more frequent in small
towns and rural areas, and the caste system which took on a certain flexibility
in the larger cities, if only because of the greater difficulty of white control of
the black population, remained highly restrictive in smaller communities.

Favorable views of the small town were expressed as well. Religious
spokesmen, especially, looked to the village for its greater commitment to the
church and traditional moral verities. "Here the throbbing social questions do
not disturb the work as in the larger cities," the *Alabama Baptist* claimed,
"and at the same time they are able to support a virile ministry." Other writers
pointed to the small town for maintenance of solid habits and values in an age
of swirling social and cultural change. "The culture of the old south," which
the Memphis *Commercial-Appeal* saw in particular abundance in the smaller
regional centers, "leavens the materialism of this region and creates in our
people a love for the beautiful and for those things that make life interesting."
Some observers yearned longingly for the primary, face-to-face, personal
relationships that made the village more humane and less confusing: "The
metropolis works for the suppression of the individual," the *Tennessean*
concluded, whereas "the little city where everyone knows the other encour-
ages his development." [20]

Even more frequent than criticism of village arrogance was praise of small
towns when they demonstrated tendencies defined as "progressive" by larger
urban standards. Some commercial-civic leaders believed that the smaller
towns and cities of the region offered greater opportunities for the solution of
pressing urban ills, and that their growth would in fact improve the health and
well-being of the metropolises. Of particular interest to southern urbanites,
apparently, was the idea that smaller communities, because of their "retarded"
growth rates, were in a position to benefit from the lessons learned in the
larger centers, especially of the necessity for intelligent planning. "Small
towns may be made as beautiful as big cities," the Age-Herald generously
conceded; "as a [matter of] fact, many of the smaller urban centers of the
country can outstrip the larger centers in work of this kind for the simple
reason that many natural lines of beauty have not been marred or broken by
over-growth." Significantly, praise for small southern towns was often based

19 Atlanta *Independent*, January 17, 1920.
20 Birmingham *Alabama Baptist*, LIII (April 20, 1922), 3; Memphis *Commercial-Appeal*,
   March 9, 1922; Nashville *Tennessean*, September 10, 1923.

on their adoption of big city values and attitudes, on whether or not they demonstrated an awareness of the big city's superiority. The *Age-Herald* took exception to Sinclair Lewis' attack on "Main Street," not so much because he was maligning those with a closer contact with nature and the "good life," but because "Main Street has its skyscrapers, its motion picture palaces, its chain stores and practically all the elements of metropolitan existence, but on a smaller scale."[21]

The small town, like the suburb, was subjected to a largely urban standard of assessment; but for most southern urban spokesmen in the 1920s it was the relatively distant small town rather than the near-by suburb that was genuinely poised between country and city. The image of the clean, quiet, simple village carried pleasant connotations for many urban dwellers, but it was most frequently employed as an abstraction to illustrate specific deficiencies in the urban environment, not as a model to be followed. The expanding town which adopted urban amenities and aspired to larger size and greater prominence was taken much more seriously—condemned on the one hand for its pretension and praised, on the other, for its craving of big city ways. But whether the small town was regarded with defensiveness or paternalism, the larger urban centers were usually considered superior in most respects, and a clearer sense of the city's spatial identity often resulted from the comparison.

City and Country: Peaceful Coexistence

An agrarian bias survived in large southern cities in the 1920s, as reflected in myriad pronouncements on the virtues of rural life and the problems of the city. On the surface, this appeared as a full-blown renunciation of urbanism in favor of time-worn agrarian virtues and traditions, an attitude that seemed particularly appropriate in the nation's most agricultural region. On the other hand, Wilbur J. Cash reminded his readers of the widespread "supercilious contempt for all countrymen, including the yeoman himself" that eventually "infected practically the whole urban population down to mere market villages."[22]

Neither view, however, is wholly accurate. Respect for agriculture—both

21 Birmingham *Age-Herald*, June 14, January 31, 1926.
22 Wilbur J. Cash, *The Mind of the South* (Vintage Books ed.; New York, 1941), 289.

as a vocation and a way of life—existed in the urban circulating media, but alongside an obviously patronizing view of the countryside. As in the case of attitudes toward small towns, southern city dwellers looked upon the country from a distinctly urban perspective, with the purpose of understanding their cities as much as promoting or disparaging the farm.

Some urban spokesmen were clearly in the tradition of the Nashville Agrarians. William Watts Ball, editor of the Charleston *News and Courier* in the last half of the decade, wrote of "ignorant" city masses and portrayed "yokels" as republican soldiers manning essential lines of defense against the malignant spread of socialism. Ball was convinced that most people caught in the swell of urban wretchedness would gladly return to agrarian pursuits if freed from the chains of industrial slavery. "Release 552,000 factory workers pent up in New York and hundreds of thousands of men, women and children would flee to the open country with them." Yet even Ball admitted that though the farmer had wrested control of his own destiny "the eyes of most city workers are so scaled that they cannot envy him." [23]

Agrarianism of this sort was often motivated more by cultural than economic sentiments, of course—the rural way of life symbolizing traditional values that seemed doomed by industrial civilization. Ellen Glasgow, hardly to be considered a practitioner of agrarianism, wrote Allen Tate in 1933 from her beloved Richmond: "I find myself definitely turning toward your point of view and away from the raucous voice of the modern industrial South. The most disheartening thing in life to me just now is to be obliged to live and work in an age that seems to have lost not only all standards but even all respect for what we used to think of as artistic integrity." [24] Such writers recommended the farm not as a practical alternative, but as a conceptual one; and they feared the city because it so aptly represented the currents of a new and troubling time.

The migration of country boys to the city was lamented on a number of grounds, including the concern that older traditions would be eroded and the quality of national life damaged. "What should be done right now, without waiting for further census revelations," the *Constitution* recommended in

23 These comments are taken from two of William Watts Ball's essays, "More Intent to Save the City Than to Save the Country" in 1931, and "The Vertical Frontier" in 1933. See Anthony Harrigan (ed.), *The Editor and the Republic: Papers and Addresses of William Watts Ball* (Chapel Hill, 1954), 143, 140, 150.
24 Blair Rouse (ed.), *Letters of Ellen Glasgow* (New York, 1958), 127.

1920, "is for the whole country to concentrate on a general, nation-wide, aggressive and effective movement to turn the trend of population growth away from the cities and toward the country." The *Southern Labor Review* employed an even more compelling analogy to make the same point: "We are today treading the road of Rome. . . . The same social and economic cancers that destroyed the vitals of that great empire are rapidly developing in the United States." Foremost among those social and economic cancers were urban financial imperialism and the movement of rural dwellers to the city. Most major newspapers called attention to the "realities" of city life: the dearth of jobs, the additional training required for success, and the back-breaking drudgery of city pursuits. "The boy who goes into a store, a bank or any other commercial institution and makes good works as hard, if not harder, than does the boy on the farm," a Memphis writer noted. "If there is any difference, it is in favor of country life." [25]

Religious spokesmen tended to see the city as tempestuous and confusing, with temptations in abundance and congregations in disarray. "Do not let the young people in the country districts be deceived by the big crowds and show windows and white lights of the cities," the *Alabama Baptist* advised. "These are but the vanity of vanities, as many thousands who live in the cities attest to their sorrow." A related fear was that lessened church activity in the rural areas would lead eventually to the collapse of the one Protestant stronghold that remained secure. The young clergyman who sought after great things in the city was most likely to "be either engulfed by or deserted by the multitudes." [26]

Even though they complained of racial injustice in the country districts, most Negro newspapers encouraged southern blacks to remain on the farm, not as tenants but as yeomen. The South, rather than the North, was the true home for the black man because, as one writer put it, "of the agricultural bent of his mind." The country encouraged "independence of thought and industry," better health, and lower mortality. Perhaps most important, the farm seemed a more viable alternative for the urban black because of the problems he encountered in cities. "The poor white man has open to him the factories, the mills, the stores and the many other occupations necessary to

25 Atlanta *Constitution*, June 4, 1920; Birmingham *Southern Labor Review*, VIII (June 8, 1927), 2; Memphis *Commercial-Appeal*, May 12, 1922.
26 Birmingham *Alabama Baptist*, LVI (May 15, 1924), 4; LIX (March 24, 1927), 4.

city life," the Nashville *Globe* observed in 1909, "whereas the black man is discriminated against in everything that the white man wants. . . . Under these conditions would it not be a strategical move for the young Negroes to answer the call and trace their steps back to mother earth?" Blacks had lived for generations in the rural South, but by the early twentieth century a flourishing black yeomanry seemed more remote a possibility than ever. The hope continued, however, that blacks could cease to be renters and consumers in the city and become producers and property-owners in the country.[27] But this was a dream prompted more by urban troubles than by rural realities; most blacks came to accept the inevitability of urban migration, and the hopes, however frustrated, that lay behind it.

Rural life was hardly judged superior by all observers. Dorinda Oakley, the leading character in Ellen Glasgow's *Barren Ground*, had found in New York "how easy it was to pursue her individual life, to retain her secret identity, in the midst of the city." Her return to rural Virginia was a disturbing and lonely homecoming. The railway station was small, "and how desolate, stranded like a wrecked ship in the broomsedge. What isolation! What barrenness!" Though Dorinda eventually adjusted to her new circumstances, she was at first "swept by a longing for the sights and sounds of the city." Birmingham's Jack Bethea surveyed the south Alabama Black Belt with a critical eye. "Farmhouses were as untidy as the fields and with as little evidence of care. . . . Mostly the farm buildings were unpainted, bleak, and unadorned, surrounded by outbuildings with sagging roofs and gaping windows." One Nashville writer concentrated on the unhealthy conditions in rural areas. "Solitude—even the solitude of open fields and healthful skies—is an enemy to health; on the other hand, there are in the densely populated ghettos of New York, of London and Paris, surrounded by conditions that would seem to make health impossible, persons so old that time appears to have passed by them." The *Tennessean* commented in 1923 that rural youngsters suffered more from poor diets and inadequate exercise "than the children of the clean city pavements and parks."[28]

27 Atlanta *Independent*, April 2, 1925; Nashville *Globe*, September 3, 1909; Norfolk *Journal and Guide*, July 9, 1927.
28 Ellen Glasgow, *Barren Ground* (New York, 1925), 200, 250, 306; Jack Bethea, *Cotton: A Novel* (Boston, 1928), 3; *Nashville This Week*, V (May 20, 1929), 1; Nashville *Tennessean*, July 22, 1923.

Many writers recognized the farm-to-city migration as the product of profound social and economic forces and attributed it primarily to the greater opportunities in the city. "As long as the reward for labor in the towns and cities is greater than it is in the country," the *Tennessean* suggested, "we need not expect this movement to be checked. Nor for business reasons should we be anxious to check it." The migration would improve the working conditions and economic opportunities of those who remained in the country, while at the same time expanding the urban market for farm produce. The movement of rural blacks to the cities was, according to the Atlanta *Independent*, an "index of the prostrate and unprofitable condition of the farming industry," and served notice "that the colored race is undergoing some industrial evolution, that it is making progress in the skilled trades, and that it is no longer merely a reservoir of unskilled labor." [29]

The agrarian bias that remained in the urban South was frequently couched in terms of the city's self-interest, suggesting that historians have perhaps read the Agrarian Myth a bit too literally. The Birmingham *Age-Herald*, for example, lamented the migration from farms to cities, not because the movement would destroy the foundations of the Republic or sap the nation's vitality, but because it would inevitably lead to housing problems, increased congestion, and rising food prices within the city. Other papers expressed similar fears. Increasing city populations at the expense of producing farms would only fuel an escalating cost of urban living. The prospect of thousands of farm migrants, unskilled and uneducated, pouring into a city labor market which could not absorb them, and into residential areas that were already crowded, was not a welcome one. Some labor spokesmen complained that rural immigrants were frequently used as strikebreakers, which imperiled the labor movement and depressed prevailing wage scales. Black publications observed the overabundance of unskilled Negro workers in cities, and recommended that potential migrants remain in the country and buy their own farms, thus contributing to the prosperity of the race without adding to the already considerable burdens of their urban brethren. The *Tennessean* noted that a major disadvantage of the migration was that it served "to aggravate the troubles of the city dweller and the industrial worker." The

29 Nashville *Tennessean*, April 25, December 7, 1927, December 26, 1922, April 26, 1923; Atlanta *Independent*, November 2, 1922.

principal fear was that migration of rural blacks and whites would only serve to worsen existing urban conditions, a fear that "there is not room enough for all in the cities."[30]

Fervent pleas on behalf of the family farm were most frequent in the first years of the decade, during the postwar agricultural depression and the slow and fitful urban economic resurgence in the temporary setback of 1920–1922. When urban economic conditions improved toward mid-decade, lip service was still paid to the humble farmer and his needs, but it was much less emphatic and far more abstract. This suggests the role that urban spokesmen may have played in every period of economic difficulty in advocating movements "back-to-the-farm" and should lead historians to a reconsideration of what this role portends for their conceptions both of the Agrarian Ideal and the city itself.

Urban attitudes toward farm-to-city migration thus correlated to some degree with urban social and economic circumstances but bore little relation to rural conditions. Indeed, the postwar agricultural depression continued throughout the decade. There was therefore no inherent contradiction between the desire for continued urban population growth and discouragement of the extensive rural migration which augmented that growth. In periods of economic prosperity, the migration was generally accepted as inevitable, and urban expansion was advanced as a principal goal. And, in any event, most urban writers looked unfavorably only on those rural migrants who were untrained and unlettered and thus more likely to become burdens on the city rather than contributors to its prosperity.[31]

The view that the integrity of rural districts should be preserved to protect

---

30 Birmingham *Age-Herald*, January 14, 1921; Knoxville *Journal and Tribune*, February 22, May 8, August 13, 1920; Nashville *Tennessean*, February 4, 1920; Birmingham *Labor Advocate*, October 21, 1922; Norfolk *Journal and Guide*, August 8, 1925; Nashville *Tennessean*, January 2, 1923; Birmingham *Age-Herald*, November 16, 1921.

31 As Clayton R. Robinson observed, "As long as the city was prosperous, the migration of rural people into it was encouraged; local boosters pointed with pride to the growing population." In times of economic difficulty, however, "these same local leaders would begin to talk about the advantages of living in rural self-sufficiency. They began encouraging rural people to return to the farms they had abandoned, or had been forced to abandon." See Robinson, "The Impact of the City on Rural Immigrants to Memphis, 1880–1940" (Ph.D. dissertation, University of Minnesota, 1967), 92–3. To my knowledge, Robinson is the only other scholar to note this emphasis on urban rather than rural interests in the urban advocacy of agricultural pursuits. But, as with so much else in this disappointing dissertation, the observation is neither taken to its obvious conclusion nor subjected to adequate analysis.

urban residents from rising unemployment, lower wages, and deteriorating housing and working conditions was often expressed through the belief that city and country should ideally exist in a state of mutual dependence and peaceful coexistence, each fulfilling its unique social and economic role in the larger society. The editors of the Atlanta *Constitution* considered prosperous farms essential for a prosperous city, "for without a strong, thriving rural population to sustain it and back it up, a great city might as well be a city of card-houses." By contributing resources and talent to the growth of urban areas, the "farms are the city-builders." Indiscriminate population movement from farm to city was therefore discouraged, though migrants with special skills and incentive were always welcomed.[32]

"The city cannot live on the country unless the country is full of people," the Memphis *Commercial-Appeal* declared, "and the countryman who moves to the city is, in a business way, cutting his own throat." On the other hand, urban development, as the Norfolk *Journal and Guide* pointed out in 1926, created jobs and opportunities in the country by providing an expanding market for farm products. Since city and country each had important roles to perform, and neither was entirely self-sufficient, mutual dependence was beneficial to all concerned and was best attained through cooperation. As the *Alabama Baptist* put it in 1924, "The produce of the world on which men must live does not grow on concrete pavement. Conversely, those powers which create ideas and mould thought—newspapers, magazines, books, colleges—do not grow in corn fields." Interaction between city and country was thus inevitable. "And the man who for selfish interests seeks to arraign one district against the other," the editors continued, "as many politicians have done, is unfit for office in either place."[33]

As with urban attitudes toward suburbs and small towns, views of the rural districts were shaped by an urban perspective and oriented to essentially urban interests. Many proposals to improve farm life, for instance, consisted largely of bringing urban amenities to the country. "The solitude of the country must be done away with," declared the *Commercial-Appeal*. "Our country people may finally meet this by living in small villages and going out from them every morning to their farms." That the city was more appealing than the farm to

32 Atlanta *Constitution*, June 9, March 5, 1920.
33 Memphis *Commercial-Appeal*, April 13, 1920; Norfolk *Journal and Guide*, June 19, 1926; Birmingham *Alabama Baptist*, LVI (July 31, 1924), 3.

young people was a virtually unchallenged proposition during the decade. The *Age-Herald* frankly remarked in 1926 that "Young people, once given a taste of life in urban centers, will not be content on the farm unless something is provided to take the place of city attractions. Nor can they be blamed for this attitude." [34] Many urban spokesmen obviously believed that the only hope for rural areas was the adoption of city conventions and standards of "progress," the replacement of isolation and outmoded habits of life with community-oriented institutions and recreation.

Another important theme in the circulating media directly reflected urban expansionism. The Nashville *Banner* called for "as close and convenient a connection" as possible between the city and its surrounding territory, while the New Orleans Association of Commerce declared: "To-day we aspire to link our destiny along with our great and prosperous hinterland"—a hinterland which included large portions of the central South. Cities tended to stand jealously astride their surrounding territory, and to resist all outside commercial intrusions. "There is no reason," the *Age-Herald* stated, "why either Memphis or Atlanta should be allowed to ship goods into the Birmingham jobbing zone. There is a certain territory that belongs to this city quite legitimately, just as there is a certain territory that belongs to these other cities." [35] Urban interests struck deep into the rural hinterland, as commercial "spheres" were carved out in the continuing process of urban imperialism; and the awareness of these spheres was an important part of the southern urban spatial identity in the 1920s.

The Agrarian Ideal, as enunciated by rural spokesmen and by literary figures like the Nashville Agrarians, included economic as well as cultural elements, of course; but a principal emphasis was placed on agriculture as a way of life which encouraged independence, hard work, pure thoughts, and simple pleasures. The agrarian bias of commercial-civic spokesmen in the urban South, however, rarely concentrated on this aspect but emphasized the importance of a prosperous countryside to the survival and health of the city. Without the food and new citizens provided by the farms, the metropolis could hardly aspire to greater growth and prosperity. Conversely, a dying countryside not only imperiled the urban supply of foodstuffs and raw

34 Memphis *Commercial-Appeal*, April 17, 1920; Birmingham *Age-Herald*, January 3, 1926.
35 Nashville *Banner*, December 8, 1921; *New Orleans Association of Commerce News Bulletin*, II (January 19, 1920), 3; Birmingham *Age-Herald*, March 14, February 16, 1920.

materials but also inundated the city with unskilled labor and posed immense demands for urban institutions. Preservation of the country was, like the attraction of industry and the construction of new transportation routes, considered necessary for unhampered urban development.

Other Cities: Identity Through Rivalry

Urban spokesmen manifested their concern for conditions in suburbs, small towns, and rural areas in a variety of ways throughout the decade, but this was substantially eclipsed by their attention to the events, activities, and attitudes in other large cities, especially in the South. Interest in other regional centers was to some extent, of course, a natural outgrowth of the urban struggle for capital, markets, and population—or, as a Memphis writer put it, "for mastery of empire, trade and things cultural." [36]

The meteoric rise or notable resurgence of a nearby urban area was thought, in fact, to present repercussions and possibilities to the home-city far beyond those of even an agricultural depression. Urban competition in the region took place on every conceivable level, and comparisons between cities were constantly drawn on the basis of everything from bank clearings and construction permits to crime rates, civic improvements, and cultural attractions. Southern cities competed also, of course, with urban areas in the North and West; but cities within the region were usually the principal reference points in southern urban rivalry.

The most important criterion of comparison was the census enumeration which took place at the beginning of each decade and constituted for many southern urban leaders not only a population count but an interurban struggle of almost heroic proportions. The competition for population between Atlanta and Birmingham was particularly vigorous during the 1920s. Eugene R. Black, president of the Atlanta Chamber of Commerce, warned his fellow citizens in 1920, "Unless the people here wake up to the fact that a census is being taken to see that each Atlantan is enrolled, Atlanta is going to fall behind Birmingham." The Birmingham *Age-Herald* advanced the belief, only slightly in jest, that Atlanta surreptitiously watered its census report: "The Georgia metropolis has a way, it is said, of counting week-end visitors, and in

36 Memphis *Tatler*, I (June 15, 1929), 12.

a pinch hotel registers and morgue records." The census not only recorded population but ranked cities in what seemed an inviolable order of size and growth—to stamp them, at least for a decade, with a clear and portending judgment. Thus, the census was regarded as a vehicle in the struggle for regional and national urban recognition. "Obviously," the *Age-Herald* explained in 1920, "it is to the advantage of Birmingham to make the best showing possible, for we are in a spirited race with other southern cities. To fall below the population we have been claiming for several years will be humiliating and a blow to our prestige." The competition was thus not only for jobs, capital, and population but also for recognition in a larger urban community: "It will not be pleasant to endure the jibes and jeers of rival cities if Birmingham fails to make a showing proportionate to her claims."[37]

Some comparisons with other regional cities were occasions for relatively serious self-appraisal. The *Banner*, for instance, explained Nashville's failure to equal Atlanta's growth rate as the result of the Tennessee capital's comparatively untouched hinterland. Sometimes comparisons were frivolous, even playful. According to the *Tennessean*, nothing of consequence ever happened in Atlanta "except the daily arrival of the 3:53 from Nashville; the annual benefit ball of the soda jerkers' society, and the occasional singing of Geraldine Farrar." A degree of bitterness was also noticeable from time to time, often because the recognition accorded a competing urban center implied a loss of prestige to the home-city. Though most regional cities favored an aggressive local patriotism and regarded Atlanta as the prototype of such sentiments, there was occasional resentment over the reckless bravado of the "Atlanta spirit." The Memphis *Commercial-Appeal*, with little generosity and less good taste, described the Atlanta booster as a publicity-mad fanatic: "The average Atlanta man is like a negro at a hanging, he is willing to be hanged if he can be the center of a large crowd."[38]

Perhaps because of the awareness invariably sharpened by interurban competition—and the emphasis on urban excellence primarily by regional standards—southern cities also relied on one another for ideas and examples concerning local improvement. Most often, admirable events in other cities were cited to arouse local pride, to spur civic action along similar lines.

37 Atlanta *Constitution*, January 16, 1920; Birmingham *Age-Herald*, March 14, February 16, 1920.
38 Nashville *Banner*, October 23, 1921; Nashville *Tennessean*, March 23, 1920; Memphis *Commercial-Appeal*, October 16, 1920.

Nashville's efforts to promote a one-and-a-half-million-dollar bond issue included references to the success of a similar proposal in Memphis. "The progress and prosperity of Memphis," the *Tennessean*'s editors wrote, "is told in its growth in population and increase in property values and by its faith in itself and its courage to issue bonds necessary to build a city." The Charleston *News and Courier* was forever pointing out the development of Savannah to counteract the lethargy it detected in the Palmetto City. While Savannah prospered, the paper commented, "Charleston makes no progress at all but, instead, goes backward." Similarly, the *Commercial-Appeal* reprimanded its readers that "The Atlanta citizen does more for Atlanta than we do for Memphis. . . . The people of Georgia and Atlanta get publicity throughout the nation as the people of Memphis and this territory should get."[39] In most instances, the emulation of one southern city by another involved some specific program or characteristic—governmental organization, property values, promotional campaigns, or streets and other public facilities.

Intense civic loyalty usually precluded the unadulterated praise of a competing city, since local superiority was a prime ingredient of urban patriotism. Suggestions to maintain or exploit such assumed superiority, however, were not regarded as "unpatriotic," and the rhetoric employed was usually a curious mixture of civic pride and envy. "If advertising can quicken the industrial and commerical pulse of Atlanta and other Southern cities," thought Nashville businessmen, "it can do the same thing for Nashville. As a matter of fact," they added, "Nashville has advantages not enjoyed by several other cities that are successfully using publicity." Birmingham admired the new construction underway in Atlanta, but the *Age-Herald* cautioned, "We should not envy Atlanta. We should look about and see if we cannot somehow catch the Atlanta building stride."[40]

Southern city fathers normally rose to the defense of their own in the face of criticism, real or implied, from outside the region. The *Banner* reacted vigorously to President Warren G. Harding's "scolding" of the South on the racial question when he spoke at Birmingham's semicentennial celebration in 1921. "The people of the South," the editors protested, "would have liked something from the President that congratulated Birmingham on its rapid

---

39 Nashville *Tennessean*, December 16, 1925; Charleston *News and Courier*, March 3, 1921; selection from the Memphis *Commercial-Appeal* reprinted in the Atlanta *Constitution*, July 4, 1920.
40 *Nashville This Week*, I (May 31–June 7, 1926), 3; Birmingham *Age-Herald*, July 21, 1920.

growth and remarkable industrial development that produced such a splendid city." In fact, praise or criticism of one regional city by a nonsoutherner was often regarded as applicable to all southern cities, an attitude which both reflected and strengthened the bonds that existed between urban areas in the section. The awareness of a regional urban community grew throughout the decade, underlined by the notion that development of one city contributed directly or indirectly to the development of others. An Atlanta religious and civic leader suggested in 1922, for example, "that the wider the influence of other cities extends, the greater Atlanta's growth will be, and that no other city can grow or expand its influence at the expense of another city."[41] Many city leaders tended to blur essential differences between southern cities just as they tended to overlook those between the city and its suburbs. A meeting of southern urban businessmen in Atlanta in 1925 occasioned this advice to southern city dwellers from a popular local poet: "Atlanta's ours, we clothe its every need—/ But better yours and mine when this we heed:/ 'One great Southeast in perfect union blent!' " Through regional urban rivalry, the remaining strength of southern sectionalism, and the focusing of attention of most southern cities on one another, a stronger cognizance of mutual southern urban interests emerged in the early twentieth century. Regardless of the differences between southern cities, the *Age-Herald* reminded its readers, "We are part and parcel of the same destiny."[42]

It is something of an American tradition for urban citizens to criticize the cities of other regions while lauding those closer to home. Southerners had a habit in antebellum times of denouncing northeastern cities as corrupt while finding their own urban areas to be centers of republican virtue, good taste, and refined culture. This phenomenon was by no means confined to the South; cities in the West in the same period considered themselves the hearts of a vibrant new civilization, whereas those of the East were merely outposts of a decrepit Europe.[43] While not as fervent during the 1920s, such a tendency was still discernible in southern urban thinking. Attention to cities

---

41 Nashville *Banner*, October 27, 1921; Frederic J. Paxon, "A City of Friendships," Atlanta *Christian Index*, CII (December 7, 1922), 12.

42 Platt Young, "Welcome—Southeastern Cities," Atlanta *City Builder* (November, 1925), 3; Birmingham *Age-Herald*, May 23, 1920.

43 Charles N. Glaab and A. Theodore Brown, *A History of Urban America* (New York, 1967), 54; Charles N. Glaab, "The Historian and the American Urban Tradition," *Wisconsin Magazine of History*, XLVII (Autumn, 1963), 22.

outside the region focused primarily on New York and Chicago, not only because of their obvious metropolitan significance but also because they were symbols of both the best and the worst features of the urban environment. Attitudes toward the North and northern urban centers were often shared, of course, by the great majority of white southerners—regardless of where they resided. Nevertheless, the views of northern and midwestern cities expressed in the southern urban media generally heightened not only the sense of a particular urban identity but deeply colored the awareness of a regional urban community.

Attitudes toward the largest cities in the "North" (which included the Midwest) often centered on features widely believed to be distinct from urban conditions in the South—substantial alien populations, rampant crime and disrespect for law and tradition, and deep-seated economic and political corruption. The threat of large foreign populations in nonregional cities seemed ominous indeed, especially in the early years of the decade. The *Tennessean*, reflecting the nationwide hysteria over "reds" and foreign radicals, fired a critical barrage at its favorite target—Chicago: "We take pleasure in informing the North—and Chicago in particular—that it must clean its doorstep of these men who would plot against the safety of this country." Hardly any southern metropolitan newspaper avoided the opportunity to comment on the dangerous concentrations of foreigners in the urban North, or to boast that the Palmer "Red Raids" in January, 1920, had left southern cities virtually untouched. Seventy-two cities in the country were scenes of the crack-down on "radicals" and dissenters, with arrests in the South confined to Louisville, Kentucky, and Jacksonville, Florida. Most editorial writers in the region claimed, as did the Atlanta *Constitution*, that this record was "a splendid tribute to the broad Americanism of the south, which has remained untarnished and untouched by the insidious monster that is gnawing at the vitals of our national government."[44]

Though the Red Scare eventually faded, deep suspicions of foreigners and their impact on American life lingered. "The foreign populations are becoming a menace," the *Tennessean* warned in 1921. "They are jeopardizing American ideals." The gravest fear was that these irresponsible, even

44 Nashville *Tennessean*, January 4, 1920. (The paper persistently referred to Chicago as "Little Germany." See, for example, the issue of March 2, 1920.) New Orleans *Times-Picayune*, January 5, 1920; Atlanta *Constitution*, January 10, 1920.

disloyal, groups would gain political ascendancy over other areas of the country. Echoing a familiar refrain, the Knoxville *Journal and Tribune* predicted that New York City alone might well account for more representatives in Congress, after reapportionment, than the total number of representatives from Kentucky, West Virginia, and Virginia, and that Chicago would wield more national inflence in the lower house than Alabama and Mississippi combined: "It can be seen that the country in the future is likely to be ruled by the cities. And along with that comes the thought that a very large proportion of the population is not American, but decidedly un-American."[45]

There were few calls for a more equitable distribution of foreigners throughout the country; southern urban leaders generally delighted in the fact that "The South is free from the scum of Europe." Alfred E. Smith was a symbol of northern big city ways even before his national confrontation with Herbert Hoover in 1928; and it was not his urban origins, but his association with "foreign" and "corrupt" elements in the city that most disturbed southern urbanites. "'Al' Smith," the *Age-Herald* declared in 1926, "does not appeal to South and West, where traditions and habits of mind have little in common with those reared on New York's East Side." In contrast, most southern urban commentators depicted their own cities as largely homogeneous communities, ignoring in the process, of course, many significant local ethnic, racial, religious, and class divisions. As the *Tennessean* expressed it in 1920, "There is only one class here, really, and its membership is based on service to country."[46]

The southern urban press often associated large "alien" or "mixed" populations with lawlessness, moral depravity, and political corruption. "The criminal classes from Europe have flocked to America," the *Christian Index* claimed, turning large American cities into "centers of sedition and lawlessness." Bloody vendettas among gang bosses and the rising influence of organized crime were only parts, however, of a larger sweep of depravity and corruption that many southern writers detected in the urban North. Northern cities were known for race riots, "black and tan" social affairs, dope dens, and

45 Nashville *Tennessean*, May 18, 1921; Knoxville *Journal and Tribune*, February 28, 1920.
46 A. T. Robertson, "American Cities and the Criminal Classes," Atlanta *Christian Index*, CV (October 29, 1925), 5; Birmingham *Age-Herald*, August 22, 1926; Nashville *Tennessean*, February 10, 1920.

underground subversive activity. "Without its great mass of wickedness," the Norfolk *Journal and Guide* declared, "Chicago would not be Chicago at all, any more than Monte Carlo would be any such thing if its gaming tables were all smashed and fed to the flames." As far as the *Tennessean* was concerned, the midwestern metropolis was "a cesspool of immorality."[47]

Southern city newspapers followed the ups and downs of Chicago bosses with particular interest, and most editorial writers attributed the city's crime, labor violence, and general disorganization to dishonest government and inefficient public service as well as to substantial alien populations. The overthrow of Chicago's "Big Tim" Murphy in 1923 was proudly applauded throughout the urban South, and Mayor William Hale Thompson was frequently made the epitome of all that was wrong, or could go wrong, with American cities. The Memphis *Commercial-Appeal* described Boston as a city "of crooked streets and politicians none too straight," while the *Southern Labor Review* persisted in its attacks on the violence and "merciless intrigues" of "the great, corrupt political parties and their murderous machines."[48]

Southern urban spokesmen were quite aware that crime, public dishonesty, and changing moral patterns existed in their own cities, of course, but such problems were perceived as being infinitely less serious and disquieting. It is especially important to note that, for the most part, criticism of northern cities was not directed at cities per se, but at certain undesirable urban characteristics thought to be particularly abundant in nonregional metropolises. Many southern urban novelists, for example, portrayed northern cities as much more stifling and congested than southern centers. One of Ward Greene's characters, sounding a note of Dreiserian determinism, saw New Yorkers "struggling, like insects, for a crumb of happiness, until a big foot squashed them with the quest still blind." And Albert Bein of Nashville wrote of Chicagoans living in a "forest of buildings like boxed mice." Antipathy to the urban North centered around the issue of those foreign populations and influences that were judged to render crime, corruption, and moral laxity especially ominous. This attitude was undoubtedly born to some extent of the

47 Robertson, "Amercian Cities and the Criminal Classes," 5; Nashville *Banner*, August 31, 1921; Norfolk *Journal and Guide*, April 10, 1926; Nashville *Tennessean*, March 2, 1920.
48 Nashville *Banner*, March 1, 1923; Nashville *Tennessean*, February 24, 1927; Memphis *Commercial-Appeal*, March 4, 1920; Birmingham *Southern Labor Review*, VIII (April 13, 1927), 2.

regional fear of ethnic and racial heterogeneity, but it was also a product of southern defensiveness. As Will Alexander, director of Atlanta's Commission on Interracial Cooperation, noted in 1925, the southerner, often accused of mindless violence, was quick to cover his own sins with a blanket of accusations hurled back at his tormentors: "When a lynching occurs in his own community, such a man begins to point to the murder record of New York and Chicago."[49]

The migration of southern blacks to the urban North precipitated considerable discussion in the circulating media during the decade, and the issue was in many respects a perfect vehicle for comparisons of cities in the two sections. Most southern white writers traced the sources of the migration to rural poverty and a misguided desire for greater economic opportunity, rather than to repressive social conditions; but they largely decried the movement, whatever its causes, on the grounds that it threatened to deplete the South's supply of cheap labor—a major regional advantage in the competition for industry. In addition, many whites—and some blacks— believed that Afro-Americans "belonged" in the South. "The negro," according to the *Age-Herald*, "has no friends as reliable and sympathetic as the best type of southern white people. There is no need for him to seek friends in strange climes." Consequently, strict measures were instituted in some of the smaller towns and cities to discourage the migration. Though drastic action was generally not initiated in the larger southern urban centers, the view that blacks were essential, or at least highly important, to regional economic development was widespread. "The South needs the negro," observed the *Tennessean*. "He is part of it. Without him there must be a readjustment of our economic life."[50]

Southern urban blacks expressed a variety of opinions on the migration,

49 Greene, *Ride the Nightmare*, 279–80; Charles Walt [Albert Bein], *Love in Chicago* (New York, 1929), 67. Will W. Alexander, "Encouraging Mob Violence," Atlanta *Christian Index*, CV (January 5, 1925), 7.
50 Nashville *Christian Advocate*, LXXXIV (June 22, 1923), 779; Birmingham *Age-Herald*, October 10, 1920, October 18, 1922, November 23, 1922; Nashville *Tennessean*, May 20, 1923. Also see St. Clair Drake and Horace R. Clayton, *Black Metropolis: A Study of Negro Life in a Northern City* (Torchbook ed.; New York, 1962), I, 58–59. It is unnecessary, and in any event impossible, to attempt a comprehensive discussion of attitudes toward black northward migration here. A perceptive and balanced commentary on this phenomenon during the period, however, came from the pen of Will Alexander. See his "Going North," Nashville *Christian Advocate*, LXXXIV (June 22, 1923), 778, and "The Recent Negro Migration and the South," *ibid.*, LXXXV (February 29, 1924), 264.

but they were usually quite emphatic in attributing the movement directly to social injustice as well as rural poverty. It seems fairly certain that a large majority of southern blacks believed that economic opportunities were more abundant and social repression and racial harassment less severe in northern cities than in the South, even after the violent racial conflagrations in 1917–1919. And the Negro press paid great attention to the economic and social activities of black communities in New York, Chicago, Boston, Philadelphia, Detroit, Baltimore, Washington, D.C., and other nonregional urban areas.

Since most black papers were, however, in one way or another committed to the improvement of local urban conditions, they rarely encouraged their readers to move North en masse. Southern black businessmen were naturally concerned lest the migration northward reduce their own markets. James C. Napier, for example, called for measures to reduce the movement in his presidential address to the National Negro Business League in 1917: "One thing to be considered by this League and all local leagues, is what can we do to stop the migration of our people to other parts of the country. It hurts us. It hurts our business." [51]

White urban spokesmen were deeply suspicious of activities in northern black communities which reflected, in their view, not only inherent Negro weaknesses but the enervating and dangerous influences of the urban North. Editorial writers reacted predictably to rumors of interracial fraternization in New York and Chicago, especially when such contacts carried sexual overtones. Particularly irritating were black publications that occasionally reached the editorial rooms of southern urban dailies: "One of these publications is a newspaper, several copies of which have been received by the *Age-Herald*. This newspaper and others like it would not be tolerated in the South." The very existence of vast "black belts" in northern cities appeared to threaten the southern racial pattern. Negroes were not only concentrated, and thus better able to communicate with one another, but they exercised their relatively unrestricted right of free speech to the discomfort of white southerners satisfied with the status quo. Blacks were also in a position to flex their political muscle, and many white writers drew a direct connection between the northern

51 See Atlanta *Independent*, November 1, November 15, 1923; and the survey of Negro high school students in W. D. Weatherford, *A Survey of the Negro Boy in Nashville, Tennessee* (New York, 1932), 116–18.

political machine and the foreign and Negro population that was believed to support it.[52]

Most typical, and most revealing, of southern urban reactions to black migration was the assertion that Negroes were in reality dissatisfied in northern cities. "They have learned," stated the *Alabama Baptist*, "that the paradise of the North is a Utopian dream." Black urban communities in the North were depicted in the white media as crowded; ravaged by tuberculosis, pneumonia, and infant mortality; threatened by crime and violence; characterized by broken and deteriorating family structures; and haunted by joblessness, poor working conditions, and race prejudice. The Memphis *Commercial-Appeal* claimed in 1922 that more blacks had been killed in race riots in East St. Louis and Chicago than were lynched in the South in the preceding twenty years. Chicago blacks were "more dissatisfied than in any other city," according to the *Banner*, and many writers held that a massive black return to the South was precluded only because northern Negroes were caught in industrial slavery or simply lacked sufficient funds to make the trip home.[53]

Southern cities, however, were thought to offer a much more congenial environment for the Negro. "If he has gone to a city in the South," the *Christian Advocate* remarked, "he likely has near some negro friends from the old neighborhood with whom he can still associate and from whom he can still receive some comfort. His old-time church is easily reached, and the happy songs of the congregation are a consolation to him." The *Age-Herald* boasted that "Birmingham has retained its negro population and added to it because remunerative employment for the race is found here and because the negro is treated with consistent fairness." Conditions in Chicago, in contrast, were "not adapted to the southern negro's needs."[54] The majority opinion, then, at least among white spokesmen, was that if blacks insisted on moving to the cities, the wisest choice would be a regional urban center where

---

52 Charleston *News and Courier*, December 6, 1922; Birmingham *Age-Herald*, June 23, 1920. A cartoon illustrating an article attacking Al Smith in *Atlanta Life* (September 15, 1928), for example, portrayed a black New York City official dictating a letter to a young, attractive white secretary.

53 Birmingham *Alabama Baptist*, LII (January 19, 1922), 4; Nashville *Christian Advocate*, LXXXIX (March 9, 1928), 291–92; Nashville *Banner*, June 22, 1920; Birmingham *Alabama Baptist*, LVI (April 2, 1925), 4.

54 Nashville *Christian Advocate*, LXXXIX (March 9, 1928), 292; Birmingham *Age-Herald*, December 19, 1920, March 30 1927.

conditions and social attitudes were more conducive to their health and progress.

Increasing urban rivalry in the North and South also encouraged comparisons between cities in the two sections, and southern commercial-civic spokesmen often employed nonregional cities as examples to be either emulated or avoided. Significantly, the largest and one of the oldest southern cities—New Orleans—devoted relatively more attention to national rather than regional urban developments. After the census results of 1920 were announced, Crescent City leaders did not appear concerned with the rapid growth of Atlanta and Birmingham; rather, they were most attentive to the expansion of Detroit, Cleveland, and Los Angeles and deeply interested in the close competition between New Orleans and Washington, Minneapolis, and Seattle in the national census reports. As one of the major ports in the country, New Orleans regarded even New York as a direct trade rival, and in 1920 the *Times-Picayune* announced proudly that the city had surpassed San Francisco for the first time in the comparative shipping statistics. Charleston, while not in a position to compete significantly with larger cities, apparently felt a closer bond with established East Coast centers such as Boston and Philadelphia than with newer urban areas. According to William Watts Ball, Philadelphia and Boston were thought of as "lifelong acquaintances and companions," while upstarts like Cleveland, Dayton, or, for that matter, even Birmingham, were not Charleston's concern.[55]

Attention to the national urban scene was not limited to the oldest or the largest among southern cities. Most urban writers noted at one time or another the more auspicious aspects of city development outside the region. Atlanta and Birmingham both looked to Los Angeles as something of a kindred spirit in the race for urban growth. The *Constitution* recommended that local boosters could do with a dose of the "Los Angeles spirit," though the editors added that Atlanta had "immeasurably greater opportunities to do greater things" than the California metropolis possessed. The *Age-Herald* specifically mentioned Los Angeles' successful efforts toward developing port facilities and a highway system as befitting emulation by local officials and businessmen. Birmingham and other southern cities increasingly employed

55 New Orleans *Times-Picayune*, January 12, January 10, January 5, 1920; William Watts Ball, *The State That Forgot: South Carolina's Surrender to Democracy* (Indianapolis, Ind., 1932), 271.

national comparative standards in measuring their own success, though they usually chose to emphasize those aspects in which the home community could compete—even if this involved the stretching of a point. The *Age-Herald* asserted confidently that the Steel City's amusements were comparable to those of New York and Chicago, and the *Tennessean* devoted an editorial to the fact that funeral costs in Nashville were $260 less, on the average, than those in New York, Cleveland, Detroit, Chicago, or St. Louis![56]

Southern writers recognized that many problems afflicted cities regardless of regional location. The traffic difficulties of Atlanta were seen as virtually identical to those in New York, Chicago, Boston, St. Louis, "and other great cities in her class." Housing shortages and health problems were also identified as genuinely urban and national in scope, and some southern dailies reported developments along these lines in considerable depth. Judicial reform in New York City prompted the *Banner* to observe, "The whole country could well afford to take a leaf out of New York's book." City planning was another aspect of urbanism in other regions that especially interested southern city leaders: the *Constitution* suggested that "Atlanta's new city planning commission can profitably emulate the policy under which New York is operating," and the *Commercial-Appeal* likewise considered this program "the finest sort of object lesson for all other cities in the country." Birmingham was interested for a time in the city-county merger programs that appeared so successful in Denver, Los Angeles, and Baltimore; and community advertising campaigns, which were highly popular in southern centers during the decade, were an additional point of interest. Charleston admired the civic spirit prevalent in Philadelphia, Atlanta sought to duplicate the large-scale promotional campaign in St. Louis, and Birmingham lauded the cooperation between cities on the West Coast in advertising and mutual publicity. Southern city officials also traveled to other cities throughout the country to examine at firsthand various innovations in administration, education, law enforcement, and traffic control, and these journeys underlined a growing sense of national urban identity.[57] The list could be extended

56 Atlanta *Constitution*, Feburary 6, 1921; Birmingham *Age-Herald*, June 19, February 10, 1920; Nashville *Tennessean*, February 18, 1928.
57 Atlanta *Constitution*, October 2, December 25, 1920; Atlanta *Independent*, January 27, 1924; Nashville *Banner*, April 28, 1922; Atlanta *Constitution*, October 20, 1920; Memphis

almost indefinitely. As was the case throughout most of American history, cities engaged in economic and political rivalry while at the same time drawing extensively from one another in specific areas of urban policy.

Cities of other regions provided numerous examples of undesirable conditions and characteristics that southern urban leaders consciously set about to avoid. The *Tennessean* found Boston too "pedantic" and Detroit too purely industrial and admonished local officials to encourage urban diversity and to make full use of the city's "natural advantages." The *Age-Herald's* editors employed a contrast between Detroit and Pittsburgh to reveal the best future course, as they saw it, for Birmingham. Pittsburgh, a steel town with which the Alabama metropolis was often identified, was seen as boss-ridden and politically medieval, afflicted with serious labor problems. Detroit, on the other hand, was politically "free" and the home of the businessman's hero, Henry Ford. Birmingham leaders were also alert to the problems of Cincinnati, because the midwestern city was growing rapidly and yet was somewhat eclipsed by Cleveland—a situation with which Birmingham could readily identify because of its frustrating comparison with Atlanta.[58]

There was general sympathy with the problems of urban areas outside the region, and a realization, expressed or implied, that similar conditions would produce comparable problems everywhere. "Nashville and every other city in the land," the *Tennessean* recommended, "should profit from the awful experience of Chicago. There is no reason to believe that similar conditions if permitted to exist in Nashville would make us any less immune to their consequences than has been the case in Chicago." Suggestions appeared in southern newspapers and business publications advocating closer cooperation between cities in the eradication of common problems. "We shall be making a mistake," a business spokesman in Memphis observed, "if we do not learn the lesson of the value of cooperation taught by the experience of cities like Cleveland, Pittsburgh, and Detroit." Competition between cities was seen as inevitable and, to some extent, desirable, but a consistent argument began to develop for increased cooperation between cities across the country. "With all

---

Commercial-Appeal, May 19, 1922; Birmingham *Age-Herald*, January 22, 1923; Charleston *News and Courier*, June 4, 1921; Atlanta *Constitution*, January 15, 1921; Birmingham *Age-Herald*, January 5, 1926.

58 Nashville *Tennessean*, May 1, 1920; Birmingham *Age-Herald*, October 21, 1926, February 24, 1920.

the cities working on the matter," the *Tennessean* wrote, "and exchanging ideas, each city has the advantage of the best thought and experience of the others."[59]

While few southerners expressed any affinity or sympathy for large "alien" populations or highly organized political machines, and most were quick to attack the urban North for its perceived mistakes and transgressions, many commercial-civic leaders also expressed the aspirations of their cities to be ranked among the nation's urban elite, their readiness to be identified with the country's largest and most prestigious metropolises. Atlanta, of course, referred to itself as the "New York of the South" and attempted, through the encouragement of local literary talent, to become the "Boston of the South" as well. A Birmingham spokesman observed that if the Alabama city continued its pace of urban expansion it could well become the Gotham of the southern region in the not-too-distant future, and the aspiration was not thought unworthy. A general fascination with the sophistication and excitement of the nation's largest city was reflected in O. O. McIntyre's regular feature column, "Bits of New York Life," carried in many southern dailies (including the Atlanta *Constitution*, the Birmingham *Age-Herald*, and the Knoxville *Journal and Tribune*).[60] A related theme was the widespread imitation of metropolitan conventions and amenities by both small towns and large cities in the region—a tendency that, in the opinion of many writers, could be taken too far. One character in a Katherine B. Ripley novel spoke disparagingly of such efforts in a small southern city: "If a man were to swallow an alligator on the corner of Forty-second and Broadway tonight, by morning somebody'd have swallowed a lizard on the corner of Arch and Merchants here." Similarly, the *Tennessean* complained that southern cities were far too imitative of northern urban architectural styles, even when they were inappropriate in the local setting: "If New York has a skyscraper, so must we; if Manhattan boasts of something which is necessary to her economic life, we immediately pounce upon it, though there is no justification for it." Even

59 Nashville *Tennessean*, March 31, 1928; "Our Opportunity," *Memphis Chamber of Commerce Journal*, II (July, 1919), 143; Nashville *Tennessean*, June 15, 1924.
60 Atlanta *Constitution*, January 26, 1920; Birmingham *Age-Herald*, January 11, 1927. Though Atlanta welcomed the title "New York of the South," one writer eagerly noted that "The average New Yorker is well satisfied with his city—and ignorant of what it contains. The average Atlantan," on the other hand, "is merely gratified with his city and will not be satisfied until it becomes one of the world's greatest centers of population." See John R. Hornady, *Atlanta: Yesterday, Today and Tomorrow* (New York, 1922), 4.

business boosters in the South's most culturally distinctive metropolis were known for their efforts to bring New Orleans into the national urban mainstream. As one promoter told a visitor to the city, "Modern New Orleans patterns herself after New York and Chicago. She is *chic.*"[61]

If urban rivalry underlined the tendencies of local patriotism to assert the city's distinctiveness and superiority, it also contributed to the view that the problems and conditions of nonregional cities differed from those of southern urban areas more in degree than in kind. Indeed, southern urban spokesmen increasingly expressed the notion of a national urban community with problems and possibilities not regionally defined or limited. Business writers in Nashville noted, for instance, that due to "fundamental far-reaching forces" the nation was growing into "*one* community," with growth and its consequent opportunities and challenges in cities everywhere, with the same retail goods to be found on the shelves in New York, Chicago, or Nashville.[62]

Thus, the frequent comparisons between southern cities and those both within and without the region led to a growing sense of urban identity which rested on two types of awareness: that the city in question was distinctive and worthy of comparison with the best cities in the land, and that the city was irrevocably a part of a larger regional and national urban community. These types of awareness were not mutually exclusive but rather mutually dependent—a sense of urban identity developing out of the recognition of similarities as well as differences. In like fashion, southern cities considered other regional centers their principal rivals for trade and prestige, while at the same time emphasizing their role within a national urban pattern. Urban loyalties were therefore in many ways both terribly provincial and quite cosmopolitan.

Spatial Identity and Urban Consciousness

Part of the "psychology of American urban expansion," as Anselm Strauss perceptively observed, was the shifting relationship between urban reality and the image of the city as perceived by urban residents: "When a city grows larger," for example, "it tends to change its rivals; for it is likely then to change

---

61 Katherine Ball Ripley, *Sand Dollars* (New York, 1933), 44–45; Nashville *Tennessean*, March 24, 1920; Mildred Cram, *Old Seaport Towns of the South* (New York, 1917), 275.
62 *Nashville This Week*, IV (October 29–November 5, 1928), 3.

from a local into a regional center, or from a regional into a national metropolis. Imagery is only keeping pace with changed economic functions and added size."[63]

In illustration of this point, all major southern cities in this study had reached beyond a purely local identity by the 1920s, and all in one way or another aspired to regional prominence and judged their development by regional urban standards. And some, especially New Orleans, sought to play a significant role on the national scene. In all cases there was a realization that the city was inherently *expansive*, that its influence and its energy touched areas far beyond its own boundaries. The city was not an isolated pinpoint on a map, but a dynamic entity affecting, and in many respects determining, economic and cultural currents that extended outward from its center. Most urban spokesmen also understood that the city was, in turn, dependent on other areas for its very survival.

A business writer in New Orleans expressed it well: "For every center there is a circumference. For every city, center of distribution, there is trade territory. The greater the territory, the greater the center." And, he might have added, the greater the city the more extensive the area of its impact. Conceptions of this "circumference" varied, of course, from city to city— reflecting the prevailing "spatial identity" and the perceived relationship between the city and the "outside" world. For Knoxville, it largely referred to the "rapidly developing section" of eastern Tennessee; for New Orleans it included "that great community" of the Mississippi Valley and the Gulf states, and even some Latin American regions that could legitimately be considered part of the city's "trade territory." Whereas Charleston conceived of itself as the "Metropolis of the Carolinas," Atlanta, Birmingham, and even Nashville classified themselves, variously, as "the artistic center of the South," "the greatest industrial center of the South," or "the greatest city in the South." And regional dominance naturally led, it was assumed, to national prominence. The editors of the Nashville *Globe*, for example, liked to think of their city as "the one point in the South on which the eyes of the nation are centered." Definitions of the city's "circumference" were sometimes based purely on economic and commercial considerations. Thus, the Memphis Chamber of Commerce declared that the city "has a vital interest in every influence that affects transportation on the Mississippi River." At times, that definition rested more generally on the desire for regional or national

63 Strauss, *Images of the American City*, 204.

recognition: chambers of commerce sought to "sell" their cities "to the world," and one writer simply wished that Birmingham "take its rightful place among the really big cities."[64]

The prevailing conception of the city which appeared in the public prints was rarely consistent or precise. But the overwhelming majority of southern urban spokesmen recognized the city as a relatively larger entity on a regional or national map that dominated a less populous surrounding territory, that its influence spread throughout a growing "sphere of influence," that it resembled other cities across the country in general form and in its reliance on the arteries of commerce and communication which linked urban areas together. Even seventh graders in the Atlanta public schools were taught to think in just these terms: "Place your hand palm downward, stretch out your fingers, imagine Atlanta on your palm, and you have a concrete illustration of the city as a distributing center," one school book recommended. "Each finger represents the railroads which stretch themselves to the sea or connect with the Gulf or link with the great trans-continental trunk lines."[65]

This view of the city, though composed of an immense variety of attitudes from different perspectives, consistently portrayed the city as expanding both in terms of population and territory. This was to some extent, of course, a means of adjusting the urban image to urban reality; cities were, after all, increasing in size and urban influences were spreading over larger and larger areas. But it was also an expression of an apparently widespread, almost visceral, belief that cities were inherently dynamic—that it was the urban destiny either to expand or deteriorate. The trouble with growth, however, was that it pulled and tugged—and even threatened to rend—the existing fabric of urban life. It presented a variety of challenges to social and economic order that members of the commercial-civic elite found almost as disquieting as the presumed consequences of urban stagnation. And these challenges were vividly, tangibly manifested in myriad "urban problems" with which municipal and civic leaders wrestled throughout the decade.

64 "The Stuff Cities Are Made Of," *New Orleans Association of Commerce News Bulletin*, VI (July 29, 1924), 2; Knoxville *Journal and Tribune*, January 5, 1920; *New Orleans Association of Commerce News Bulletin*, VII (August 11, 1925), 2; Charleston *News and Courier*, February 11, 1923; Marjorie Mathis, "Atlanta's Writers Gain Wide Audience," Atlanta *City Builder* (April, 1925), 10; Birmingham *Southern Labor Review*, IV (March 29, 1922), 3; Nashville *Globe*, July 21, 1911, January 10, 1913; *Memphis Chamber of Commerce Journal*, V (August, 1922), 50; *Birmingham*, I (May, 1925), 6.
65 Atlanta Public Schools, *City of Atlanta by Seventh Grade Pupils of the Atlanta Public Schools* (Atlanta, 1921), 101.

IV   A Plethora of Problems

New Orleans has a bigger and more important role to play in the future among the citizens of the world. But it is imperative that she put her own house in order before she can fulfill this destiny in the fullest possible measure.

—*New Orleans Association of Commerce News Bulletin*, July 12, 1921

URBAN BOOSTERS have been the perennial optimists in American history. No destiny was too grand, no challenge too great for the city of their aspirations. But even boosters had their sober moments, when the city's opportunities were measured against its problems and future prospects set beside present realities. Southern urban spokesmen frequently approached urban problems piecemeal, one at a time; on other occasions, they grouped them together in lengthy lists and catalogs. In either case, a discernible current of concern for the future of the urban community ran just below the surface of their thinking, if not in plain view.

The most common worry expressed by commercial-civic leaders during the 1920s was that the city had somehow "outgrown almost all of its public facilities." The addition of new populations and territories in the twenty or thirty years before 1920 introduced a continuing strain on the capacity of municipal facilities and services—especially in Atlanta, Birmingham, and Memphis. "At present Birmingham's problems are critical," a local college professor wrote in 1925. "For a municipality of a quarter of a million, she is

99

remiss in the matters of paving, sewerage, lighting, and police protection. Her park system is very inadequate." In other regional centers the same note was sounded in a consistent refrain. The *Constitution* observed at the beginning of the decade that "Atlanta is suffering, every day of its existence under present conditions, by reason of the inadequacy of its public municipal facilities." One writer found conditions in Nashville sufficiently disturbing to "raise the inquiry as to whether there is any civic spirit, or anybody cares."[1]

Urban writers offered official intransigence, inadequate tax revenues, and citizen indifference as explanations for the failure of urban services to meet public needs. But the most frequently cited cause was the rapid, unprecedented expansion of those needs, to the point where the city seemed hard put to keep up with the dynamism of its own growth. Whatever else one might say about the successes or failures of urban leadership in this period, spokesmen for the commercial-civic elite can hardly be accused of complete ignorance of urban ills. In fact, the causes, manifestations, and possible remedies of city problems tended to underlie, if not dominate, most discussions of the nature and destiny of the urban community which appeared in the public prints.

An awareness of the full panoply of problems that were identified as peculiarly urban in character or extent—from garbage collection to street lighting, from crime to traffic congestion—served to set the city apart from rural areas and small towns and complement the spatial identity of urban consciousness. More important, the concern for urban ills mirrored a larger apprehension on the part of commercial-civic leaders that the process of urbanization was becoming less susceptible to control and direction—that uncontrolled, rapid development might actually undermine the city's opportunity for continued growth and "progress." Certainly, the promotion of growth at virtually any cost—characteristic of earlier "boom" periods—seems to have partly given way by the 1920s to a desire to deal with the consequences of that growth.

Business middle-class responses to these urban problems were often only halfhearted and partial, to be sure, and purely rhetorical complaints cannot be

1 Birmingham *Age-Herald*, January 8, 1926; Harrison A. Trexler, "Birmingham's Struggle with Commission Government," *National Municipal Review*, XIV (November, 1925), 662; Atlanta *Constitution*, July 4, 1920; Edwin Mims, *Adventurous America: A Study of Contemporary Life and Thought* (New York, 1929), 104. See also New Orleans *Times-Picayune*, January 8, 1920; Birmingham *Labor Advocate*, July 10, 1920.

accepted at face value. Furthermore, the emphasis on the severity of specific difficulties was not uniform throughout the city; various members of the commercial-civic elite were more concerned about some problems than others, depending on how these problems affected their particular economic interests. And very few white writers were terribly offended by the plight of urban blacks. But municipal policy, conceptions of the city, and urban boosterism were all fashioned within a general context of *perceived reality* which prevailed among most business middle-class spokesmen during the period. Urban boosterism was rooted firmly in a particular framework of awareness, and its vision of the city's destiny invariably rested to some degree on a cognizance of those urban ills which were thought to threaten that destiny.

Most of the problems in the urban South during this period were familiar; indeed, they had been endemic to cities almost from the beginning— transportation, water supply, health, safety, housing, and trade. The decade was somewhat distinctive in the level of working-class unemployment that prevailed in the years from 1920–1922 and persisted in some measure down to the Great Depression. And the problems with transportation technology were virtually unprecedented. The motor vehicle, specifically, registered its first major urban impact during the decade and symbolized for many observers both the possibilities and the dangers of technological innovation. In general, however, it was not the nature but the degree of these difficulties (at least as *perceived* by urban spokesmen) that heightened their importance during the decade. This was hardly the first period in which urban southerners complained about local conditions; yet one can detect in the largest cities a comparatively higher level of expectations among the members of the commercial-civic elite. As their cities aspired to regional and national prominence, as they sought to play a larger role in a larger urban community, the nagging problems attendant to growth may have appeared less acceptable than before.

The public discussion of urban ills shifted in emphasis from one specific problem to another, from general lamentations to precise analyses, from thoughtful considerations to emotional outbursts. On one level, problems were examined pragmatically as challenges requiring solution; on another level, they were implicitly or explicitly regarded as symbols of change which suggested crucial implications for the metropolis. The principal common denominator in this diverse body of observations and concerns was, however, a general apprehension—even a fear—that the urban environment was deteriorating; that the city population—increasingly bereft of deep roots in any particular community—was growing less responsible, stable, and orderly; and that the problems of urban expansion threatened the future growth and stability of the metropolis and the leadership of the commercial-civic elite.

A Deteriorating Urban Environment

When commercial-civic spokesmen complained about the inadequate municipal facilities—garbage collection, sewers, law enforcement, public health, fire prevention, streets and street lighting, public utilities, and transportation—they were disturbed by more than the fact that urban living conditions could be better. Poor services and facilities, in their view, rendered the city less attractive to new citizens and industry and hindered the city's capacity to absorb larger populations and territory. Among those problems identified as relatively serious in the circulating media of the period were atmospheric pollution, housing, and inadequate recreational facilities.

Though not a major industrial area, Nashville suffered some of the most severe spells of atmospheric pollution that afflicted larger southern cities during the decade. The *Tennessean* reported in 1921 that the downtown section "hides under a pall of smoke. All day long the office and factory worker breathes in air and soot in equal quantities." Two years later, the *Banner* noted that the simple act of respiration "involves taking into the lungs quantities of foul and ill-smelling smoke." And in 1925 the dark skies seemed the product of a lunar eclipse: the sun was visible only as "a big molten ball in the eastern sky that struggled to penetrate the black pall that Nashville's chimneys sent skyward." [2]

Aside from a pervasive sense of gloom, atmospheric pollution resulted in obvious damage to persons and property. "Damage in a thousand ways—" a Memphis business writer commented, "soiled clothing, sooty offices, ruined merchandise, interior decorations made dingy, domestic cleaning, to say

2 Nashville *Tennessean*, January 26, 1921; Nashville *Banner*, January 10, 1923; Nashville *Tennessean*, January 23, 1925. These periods of intense air pollution usually occurred in the depths of winter, suggesting that residential and commercial coal furnaces, rather than industrial effluents, were primarily responsible for the problem.

nothing of the effect on health, is the daily effect of the unregulated boiler and furnace." The Birmingham *Post* even made a connection, rare for the 1920s, between atmospheric pollution and the carbon monoxide produced by motor vehicles: "a serious menace to health to tens of thousands of people in our downtown buildings," the editors wrote.[3]

The broad ecological implications of atmospheric pollution went unnoticed during the 1920s; but many urban commentators did regard it as a potential threat to health and property and a very real unpleasantness of significant proportions. On the other hand, most tended to accept a degree of pollution—dirt, noise, smoke—as an inevitable partner of urban growth and progress. Though the problem never assumed in the 1920s the ominous overtones of forty years later, its direct association in the public mind with urban development strongly implied a disquieting realization that it would grow worse with industrialization and population expansion. And some spokesmen were worried that it might, in time, become intolerable. "While a smudge may be honestly acquired and be in itself a mark of progress," a Birmingham writer cautioned, "it should not be permitted to remain on the tip of one's nose indefinitely."[4]

Much more serious for the immediate quality of urban life was the shortage of new dwellings, especially in the first half of the decade, and the rent profiteering that exacerbated the housing problem. The paucity of adequate housing in Nashville was termed "acute" in 1921, and the *Tennessean* recommended that banks and insurance companies establish a special fund for home mortgage capital. The *Journal and Tribune* reported in 1920 that "Never before in the history of real estate business in Knoxville has the shortage of housing facilities . . . been so short as now." Virtually everyone realized that the problem was shared in some degree by all cities in the country, but newspaper editors were also quick to note the local severity of the housing shortage. The *Commercial-Appeal* called for the construction of thousands of new homes to meet the rising demand. "Whatever can secure this building, whether it be municipal loans, reduction in material costs or a combination of both should be adopted." The dwelling shortage was

---

3 *Memphis Chamber of Commerce Journal*, V (January, 1922), 7; Birmingham *Post*, June 20, 1923. The editors, however, could think of no immediate solution other than requiring that automobile exhaust pipes be pointed downward rather than upward!
4 Birmingham *Age-Herald*, May 4, 1920.

compounded by a considerable increase in rents in the immediate postwar years. A committee of the Birmingham Civic Association charged in 1920 that rents in the city had risen as much as 1,000 percent over the preceding few years and demanded action by the state legislature and the establishment of a "conciliation board" by the City Commission to negotiate reasonable rents with landlords.[5]

Increasing movement to the suburbs vacated older houses near the central city that were often converted to multiple-family dwellings. Large numbers of recent rural migrants were confined to company towns, as in Birmingham, or to rooming houses and squatty tenements near downtown industries, warehouses, and railroad shops. The detached bungalow or single-family dwelling still predominated in most southern cities during the period and was certainly considered the desirable norm, and the multistory tenement was not a prominent feature of the urban landscape. Regardless of the type of dwelling involved, Wilbur J. Cash noted that by 1930 "a large part of Southern labor . . . was living in slum or semi-slum conditions."[6]

To some extent, of course, the housing crisis affected the business middle class directly and certainly revealed some difficulties in the private economy. But the housing shortage and high rents struck most sharply at lower-income groups, and concern for the problem among commercial-civic spokesmen was neither completely an expression of direct economic self-interest nor of disinterested benevolence. Most commentators saw inadequate rents as threats to urban order, just as home ownership was thought to be, both socially and economically, a major stabilizing factor in American life. The *Tennessean* even equated the tendency toward apartment-dwelling and home-renting with the state of insecurity characteristic of farm tenancy. And such conditions might produce a propertyless, dissatisfied, and restive working class. The failure to provide sufficient dwellings for a rapidly increasing population obviously offered little comfort to those who contemplated even

5 Nashville *Tennessean*, May 22, August 14, 1921; Knoxville *Journal and Tribune*, March 3, 1920, February 4, 1922; Memphis *Commercial-Appeal*, October 1, 1920; Birmingham *Labor Advocate*, June 5, 1920.
6 Wilbur J. Cash, *The Mind of the South* (Vintage Books ed.; New York, 1941), 278–79. According to one of the leading home mortgage companies in Atlanta, the "typical" new dwelling in that city during the 1920s was a five-room wood frame bungalow, ranging in cost from $2,500 to $3,000. See First Federal Savings and Loan Association of Atlanta, *Atlanta: Forty Years of Progress, 1924–1964* (Atlanta, 1964), 2.

greater future growth and suggested that a deterioration of city housing relative to rising demands would make future expansion less stable and discourage community spirit among the mass of urban citizens. "Conditions in the cities are already well nigh intolerable," a Birmingham clergyman remarked in 1920, "and bid fair to grow worse. . . . The fact is that rentals are already doing a large part in maintaining the restless spirit of the country."[7]

Urban parks and recreational facilities were, like city housing, considered much more significant in the scheme of urban life than mere amenities. And, like the shortage of adequate dwellings, those areas set aside in earlier years for recreational purposes seemed woefully inadequate after the vast population expansion which most southern cities experienced since the turn of the century. The *Constitution* complained in 1923, for example, that only two hundred of the thousand acres of potential park property in Atlanta were "actually developed." On the surface, this concern appears as little more than a penchant for naturalism and perhaps a nostalgia for the joys of a simpler, rural existence. "It is for the very reason that his life is intense that the city man feels the actual need of the open air and the simple things which the open air brings," a Birmingham writer concluded. And a group of Atlanta businessmen referred to a proposed series of downtown parks as "the lungs" of the city.[8]

Commercial-civic spokesmen, however, regarded parks not so much as the repositories of a romanticized Nature as safety valves for the release of urban tensions. In the intense and disorganized pattern of metropolitan life, recreational areas supposedly acted to relieve urban anxieties, minimize conflict, and divert children and young adults from criminal or socially undesirable pursuits. Many writers expressed an interest in directing and organizing the leisure hours of the city population, to insure that free time was put to "constructive purpose." Disorder, crime, and conflict were just as much the products of poor housing and inadequate recreational opportunities, many spokesmen reasoned, as of unemployment, poverty, and immorality. "There is a direct connection," the *Tennessean* noted, "between

7 Nashville *Tennessean*, June 11, 1921, September 19, 1927; Birmingham *Alabama Baptist*, LI (May 20, 1920), 4.
8 Atlanta *Constitution*, May 29, 1923; Richard A. Johnston, "For Good of the Community," Birmingham *Age-Herald*, May 26, 1922; "The Lungs of a City," Atlanta *City Builder* (August, 1923), 3, 5.

the lack of urban recreational facilities and the prevalence of crime." In Nashville the Rotary Club and the City Park Commission cooperated in a program to encourage the planned use of individual leisure time: "They want," the *Tennessean* reported, "to help the city catch the waste hours and turn them to a healthy accounting." [9]

This was not a complete acceptance of an environmentalist explanation for crime and disorder: many still attributed these social ills to immorality and deficiencies of character. Yet commercial-civic spokesmen gave every indication of concern lest a deteriorating urban environment serve to exacerbate these deficiencies and encourage a further fragmentation and disorganization of the urban population.

What begins to emerge from an examination of these discussions of urban problems, in other words, is a connection in the business middle-class mind between specific urban ills and broader currents of instability and disorder— and a correlative emphasis by commercial-civic spokesmen on the necessity for social control. Inadequate housing and parks, poor municipal services, and even air pollution were thought capable—certainly when joined with crime and economic dislocation—of altering the existing social structure and undermining the stable and progressive character of the city. This was not a desire to avoid or retard growth, but to maintain a particular pace and character of expansion most beneficial to commercial-civic interests and goals.

A Wayward Population

The southern metropolis was, like other large American cities, a collection of different populations, clustered according to residence, work, race, and income. The disparity between wealth and poverty, between the successful and the jobless, could hardly be completely ignored by even the most dedicated city booster. The commercial-civic elite in southern cities during the 1920s, concerned as they were with their own urban interests and role, found the complexities and divisions of the urban population extremely troubling—not because they believed in social or economic equality, but because a fragmented population constantly subjected to new demands and

9 Nashville *Tennessean*, January 24, 1928, November 29, 1922.

crises was, in their view, an inherently unstable compound. Unemployment and vagrancy signaled deeper problems among the lower classes. Crime, lawlessness, and corruption seemed ominous manifestations of moral degeneration and social irresponsibility. The deterioration of the tightly knit family threatened what was believed to be a basic unit of social stability. And an apparent falling away from older habits and values suggested a reevaluation of tradition that seemed both "progressive" and potentially disruptive.

The Birmingham Civic Association declared urban unemployment to be exceptionally serious in 1921 and initiated efforts to feed and clothe the families of destitute workingmen. The Atlanta Junior Chamber of Commerce reported in 1922 that more "beggars", lined the streets "than at any previous time in the history of the city." Large layoffs from wartime industry and the temporarily nationalized railroad system, coupled with postwar strikes and other economic readjustments, threw considerable numbers of men and women out of work and either into the streets or on the road in search of jobs. According to the *Constitution*, it was not a question of the scarcity of laborers, "for there are plenty of idle men, strong and husky and amply able to work. It is simply a question of the unwillingness of such men to do work that is fairly begging for them." The "loafer" should "be run out of town," the editors recommended, "out of the state, and out of the country as an undesirable citizen and an impediment to progress." Such irresponsible behavior was not only an affront to the accepted American work ethic but was abhorred because, as the *Age-Herald* wrote, "Idleness breeds crime." [10]

Some writers suggested charitable assistance and public works to aid local vagrants. But most commercial-civic spokesmen recommended police harassment as the best means of dealing with "outsiders." The greatest danger, in their view, lay in the accumulation of a mass of irresponsible and potentially dangerous persons in the city. The secretary of the Knoxville Associated Charities declared "that every community should take care of its own helpless and for this reason we cannot let Knoxville become the dump-heap for other cities." Likewise, the *Tennessean* observed in 1921 that while "Nashville can provide for its own . . . this is not the year when hospitality can be extended to those who drop in without credentials." The solution was for the police "to keep this floating population on the move."

10 Birmingham *Labor Advocate*, June 25, 1921; Atlanta *Constitution*, July 21, 1922, March 28, 1920; Birmingham *Age-Herald*, May 27, 1920.

The slogan advocated by the *Age-Herald* as an appropriate guide to public policy was "Work or Move On." [11]

The enforcement of vagrancy statutes has long been a means of regulating the labor force in a capitalist economy and was perhaps especially important in a region which competed for national industry by promising a cheap, docile working population. "While the method of controlling Southern labor is radically different from the method of controlling the foreigners in Northern mills," Ivan Allen of Atlanta explained, "Southern workers are amenable to control and . . . are apt to understand the situation as it exists." But idle men and women clearly represented more for the business middle class than just unproductive workers. The position of the unemployed in a complex urban society was highly undefined and without institutional "responsibility," and their presence was considered not only a burden on the community but a possible threat to its stability. In addition, such fears carried racial overtones in southern cities. "The time is ripe in Birmingham for a real war on vagrancy," the *Age-Herald* concluded in 1927. "There are too many idle negroes in this city, and idleness is at the bottom of many of the recent crimes of violence which have shocked the city and brought about a situation which has grown in seriousness from day to day." [12]

Crime, lawlessness, and corruption were (for the business-oriented middle class) the most tangible manifestations of urban irresponsibility and disorder. Atlanta's police chief reported at the beginning of the decade that he could not "remember when we had so many crimes in such a short period as Atlanta has shown in the past few weeks." According to the urban press, the pace of crime continued unabated throughout the 1920s, though concern was especially pronounced in the first years of the decade as the nation readjusted to a peacetime economy. "Have conditions reached such a pass in Atlanta," the *Constitution* asked in 1922, "that neither life nor property is safe from molestation by day or by night?" Robberies had become so frequent, the *Independent* observed, "that people leave their homes with great apprehen-

11 Atlanta *Constitution*, May 23, 1921; Knoxville *Journal and Tribune*, May 1, 1920; Nashville *Tennessean*, August 19, 1921; Birmingham *Age-Herald*, November 30, 1922.
12 Ivan Allen, *Atlanta from the Ashes* (Atlanta, 1928), 79. (Allen indicated that his intention was "to present his city to the executives of American business.") Birmingham *Age-Herald*, February 23, 1927. For a provocative discussion of vagrancy laws and relief policies as means of regulating the labor force, see Frances Fox Piven and Richard A. Cloward, *Regulating the Poor: The Functions of Public Welfare* (New York, 1971).

sion, for they do not know when they may be robbed or killed." A Birmingham paper wrote in 1920 that "Hold-ups and other crimes... have become so prevalent that people may well ask themselves if it is safe to leave their homes after dark." Similar complaints were voiced in every major southern city. "Murders of a shocking nature have become so frequent in Nashville," the *Banner* noted, "that they have almost ceased to cause excited comment." As far as many commercial-civic spokesmen were concerned, "Crime, crime, crime, seems to be the order of the day." [13]

Corruption in various agencies of municipal government was singled out from time to time as one reason for the apparent ineffectiveness of law enforcement. In Atlanta, for example, special grand-jury investigations in 1921 charged widespread collusion between the police department and an organized coterie of gamblers, thieves, and confidence men which Solicitor General John A. Boykin described for the Chamber of Commerce Forum as a "HORRIFYING CONDITION"; the *Constitution* concluded, "Society has reached a point at which human life, to say nothing of property, is not even reasonably safe and secure." Attention centered not so much on the ethics and conduct of police officers and city officials, however, as on the dangers of what would later be termed "street crime"—the robberies, beatings, and murders which most obviously threatened life and property and suggested deeper currents of disorder in urban society. At times, public concern reached the point where groups of citizens held "law and order" meetings, as in Birmingham, and volunteered to actively assist law enforcement authorities in apprehending suspects and intimidating potential criminals. [14]

Many writers pointed to the prevalence of concealed firearms as a major reason for violent crime. "The pistol," the Charleston *News and Courier* declared, "is a curse to this country." The availability of handguns was directly connected by most spokesmen with the murder rate and was especially lamented since the least trustworthy elements of the population were, in the business middle-class view, most likely to possess deadly weapons. The *Journal and Tribune* exclaimed that the "rough element of the population" went "armed as if it were in war or living in a jungle," and the

13 Atlanta *Constitution*, December 23, 1920, November 22, 1922; Atlanta *Independent*, January 5, 1922; Birmingham *Age-Herald*, October 26, 1920; Nashville *Banner*, September 26, 1921; Atlanta *Constitution*, November 28, 1920.
14 Atlanta *Constitution*, March 17, January 18, 1921; Birmingham *Labor Advocate*, December 16, 1922.

Tennessean called for restrictions on the sale of such weapons "as to minimize the likelihood of their falling into the hands of irresponsible and criminally inclined people." [15] The commercial-civic elite associated violence with lower-class groups, whether it be the "flogging" perpetrated by the Ku Klux Klan (though these were occasionally defended as supportive of "law and order") or attacks by blacks against whites. The urban press was continually concerned that substantial numbers of lower-class citizens were prepared, at any moment, to engage in wholesale violence.

Southern cities have been notorious in the twentieth century for higher rates of homicide and physical assault—and relatively lower rates of suicide— than nonregional urban areas. This suggests a greater tendency toward interpersonal aggression in the South than elsewhere, as Sheldon Hackney and others have pointed out. To this extent, business middle-class spokesmen had good cause to lament the frequent occurrence of southern urban violence, though the statistics do not bear out the consistent, substantial rise in the incidence of violent crime so often described in the contemporary press.

In Atlanta, Nashville, and New Orleans, the number of homicides per 100,000 population increased between 1920 and 1930 from 39.8 to 52.6, 13.5 to 38.3, and 16.1 to 23.2 respectively. But Birmingham (46.5 to 48.5) and Knoxville (21.5 to 22.5) showed little change, and in Memphis—still popularly designated the "murder capital of the world"—the homicide rate actually declined from a peak of 89 in 1916 to 62.8 in 1920 and 58.7 in 1930. Much of the rise in the overall crime rate was, in fact, attributable to motor vehicle and liquor law violations, both relatively new forms of legal transgression. Among the largest increases in arrests during the decade were for drunkenness, disorderly conduct under the influence of alcohol, and vagrancy—and these were, apparently, less for the purpose of disinterested law enforcement than for the control of largely lower-class, and especially black, populations. As the *Times-Picayune* expressed it from the commercial-civic standpoint in 1921: "Because of the large numbers of persons out of employment and the many undesirables at large, it is necessary to enforce rigidly the police ordinances against dangerous and suspicious characters. Any

15 Charleston *News and Courier*, December 31, 1923; Birmingham *Age-Herald*, January 29, 1922; Knoxville *Journal and Tribune*, August 15, 1922; Nashville *Tennessean*, April 5, 1924. Also see Birmingham *Age-Herald*, May 30, 1922.

police weakness will lead, as it has done in London, Montreal and other foreign cities, to disorders and rioting." [16]

An often unwritten assumption in the southern urban press was that most criminals and vagrants were black. Many commentators, in fact, explained the high incidence of violence in regional cities by pointing to their large Negro populations. Certainly, black homicide *victims* considerably outnumbered whites proportionate to population, though crimes of violence perpetrated by blacks were in the great majority of cases committed against other blacks. The white commercial-civic elite was most disturbed, however, by those cases of violence committed by blacks against whites, for it was here that they perceived the greatest threat to the existing social system. A series of ax murders in Birmingham in the early years of the decade, for example, led to a state of public semihysteria. On the basis of scattered evidence that the culprit was dark-skinned, the Ku Klux Klan organized, with the full approval and praise of white city authorities, a motorcade through black neighborhoods to intimidate the "criminal element." And cartoons appeared in the urban press portraying a large Negro hacking his way through a number of helpless white victims. [17]

Another source of disorder according to commercial-civic spokesmen was the degeneration of the home, the disintegration of the stable family unit. Many religious leaders predictably lamented the passing of the "family altar" as a constant source of spiritual inspiration. "The picture show and the automobile call the people, young and old, from their houses and every year adds to the problem of conserving the family life," one Nashville minister wrote. But such concepts were not confined to the clergy. "In cities the family circle has become almost obsolete," the *Age-Herald* commented. Because of

16 See Sheldon Hackney, "Southern Violence," *American Historical Review*, LXXIV (February, 1969). 906–25; Austin L. Porterfield, "A Decade of Serious Crimes in the United States," *American Sociological Review*, XIII (February, 1948), 44–54; William D. Miller, *Memphis During the Progressive Era, 1900–1917* (Memphis, 1957), 168; William D. Miller, "Myth and New South City Murder Rates," *Mississippi Quarterly*, XXVI (Spring, 1973), 143–53; U.S. Bureau of the Census, *Mortality Statistics: 1930* (Washington, 1934), 50; New Orleans *Times-Picayune*, February 21, 1921. Sociologist Raymond D. Gastil recently argued in "Homicide and a Regional Culture of Violence," *American Sociological Review*, XXXVI (June, 1971), 412–27, that "high homicide rates in the United States today are related primarily to the persistence of Southern cultural traditions developed before the Civil War and subsequently spreading over much of the country."
17 U.S. Bureau of the Census, *Mortality Statistics: 1930*, 50; Birmingham *Age-Herald*, January 27, 1922. Also see *Atlanta Life*, August 3, 1929.

improved roads and communications, the motor vehicle and public amuse-ments, "the average family spends less time together and under the parental roof than it did when our population was largely rural and not largely urban as it is today." Though these forces were "evidences of progress" they were nevertheless responsible for taking "people more and more away from the home," and lessening the discipline and order of the family environment. The fragmentation of the tightly-knit family was undesirable because it contributed to problems of juvenile crime, divorce, and immorality, and because it cast thousands of young women into the world of commerce and industry, thus—in business middle-class opinion—undermining public mor-als and standards of decent conduct.[18]

A falling away from older moral standards, especially among young people, was in the opinion of many writers a possible threat to the prevailing social system. A number of editorials appeared in the urban dailies on the dangers of "extravagance" and the benefits of thrift, with emphasis on their social as well as economic implications. "Extravagance is contrary to the traditions of a people who became great through frugality and plain living," the *Age-Herald* remarked. "Those maxims of thrift and hard work which are now being laughed at will sound in the ears of the improvident like a funeral knell." The irony for many commentators was that such problems often accompanied progress, and might in fact be inevitable results of general social improvement. "Unquestionably every advancement mankind makes is ac-companied by new and grave problems," the *Tennessean* observed. "It is seemingly a rule of nature, a law of life, that every step of progress requires payment of a price." On most occasions, however, commercial-civic spokes-men responded to the apparent decline of the family and public morality by promising a renewed effort to preserve viable urban institutions: "We will bend every effort," the *Tennessean* declared in 1925, "to the reclaiming of our discontented and restless young men and insure the perpetuation of our institutions and the safety of society from that disintegration which lawless-ness, disregard for the rights of the individual and a very evident weakening of the moral fabric of the nation threatens."[19]

18 The Rev. Richard L. Ownbey, "The Church and Leisure," Nashville *Christian Advocate*, LXXXVIII (January 14, 1927), 42; Birmingham *Age-Herald*, June 27, 1920; Nashville *Tenessean*, May 1, 1926; Charleston *News and Courier*, March 16, 1920.
19 Birmingham *Age-Herald*, May 15, 1920; Nashville *Tennessean*, January 5, 1967, March 26, 1925. For other representative statements on thrift and extravagance, see Memphis

Most commercial-civic spokesmen opposed restrictive legislation, however, because it gave the city an unfavorable national reputation and deprived the urban masses of "constructive" and socially acceptable amusements and recreational facilities. Moral issues cut across class and economic lines during the period, and stirred the political waters in the urban South as no other controversies did. The business middle class was divided on questions of public dancing, film censorship, and Sunday amusements, and it debated the virtues and dangers of alcohol before the passage of the Eighteenth Amendment. But the commercial-civic viewpoint, as it was expressed in the urban prints, did not favor "blue laws" and prohibitions against dancing and motion pictures, even though it publicly supported the provisions of the Volstead Act.

The joining of such issues in Birmingham is particularly revealing. A proposal to open a public dancing pavilion was defeated in the City Commission in 1922, and the *Age-Herald* lashed out immediately against what it considered an unwarranted interference with individual prerogatives and policy that would make the Magic City seem less than sophisticated. "The attempt to regulate public morals in Birmingham is being carried too far," the editors charged. The Reverend Middleton S. Barnwell, a frequent contributor to the paper and a participant in many civic activities, pointed to the 150,000 citizens who were not regular churchgoers and who desperately needed supervised amusements, especially on Sundays. The churches, he thought, should be "less interested in laws and more interested in life." [20] The proposal was finally defeated in a city-wide referendum, 10,877 to 7,220.

Motion pictures on the Sabbath, banned in a municipal election in 1918, became the most hotly contested issue in Birmingham during the 1920s. Scores of clergymen united to support the continuation of the ban, while spokesmen for both organized labor and the major newspapers adovcated its repeal. Labor unions and major manufacturing firms clearly favored Sunday amusements after church hours, as did many commercial-civic leaders. But the ban was upheld in a public referendum which recorded the largest vote ever polled in a municipal election up to that time. [21]

Commercial-Appeal, December 26, 1920; Nashville *Tennessean*, January 20, 1924; Knoxville *Journal and Tribune*, February 8, 1920.

20 Birmingham *Age-Herald*, January 4, 10, 1922.

¯1 Birmingham *Age-Herald*, April 25, 1928. For an analysis of earlier moral controversies in Birmingham, see Carl V. Harris, "Economic Power and Politics: A Study of Birmingham, Alabama, 1890–1920" (Ph.D. dissertation, University of Wisconsin, 1970), 429–32, 437–41.

Similar debates occurred in most other southern cities, though they were considerably more muted in New Orleans than in Birmingham, Atlanta, or Nashville. The major urban dailies maintained a stance of calculated moderation, expressing support of church attendance and the retention of moral and religious values while lamenting excessive restrictions. What they most desired, apparently, was an end to the controversy. "Let us, by all means," the *Tennessean* wrote, "preserve our cherished ideals of the Sabbath as a day of rest and of religious devotion: but let us not lapse into fanaticism." Most civic bodies followed suit by rarely participating directly in discussions of divisive moral questions or announcing formal positions on moral issues. [22]

The unemployment, crime, and inadequate municipal facilities, recreational areas, and housing of which whites complained were infinitely more severe in black sections and were compounded by police harassment, racial discrimination, and economic exploitation. With some understatement, James C. Napier of Nashville declared in his presidential address to the National Negro Business League in 1917 that "Mob law, the 'Jim Crow' system, poor housing, poor and short-term schools, inadequate educational advantages, disfranchisement and a general abbreviation of citizenship, are the things with which none of us are satisfied in this Southland." [23]

Spokesmen for the black business-oriented middle class were, like their white counterparts, fearful of disorder and interested in stabilizing the black community under their leadership and preserving the foundations of the prevailing economic system. But the racial and caste patterns that whites employed as means of social control only served—as far as the black commercial-civic elite was concerned—to undermine order, frustrate worthy ambitions, and minimize the power of Negro leadership. Municipal governments continually failed to treat black neighborhoods equally in the allocation of services, and Negro spokesmen consistently protested this failure. For blacks, civic loyalty was deeply rooted in their own communities and in the imperatives of self-help and racial solidarity.

In Atlanta, the *Independent* expressed a recurrent complaint that Negro neighborhoods suffered from the lack of even minimal public facilities. "Negroes pay taxes on more than five million dollars worth of property, yet their streets are unwashed, unswept and unmended." At the very least, whites

22 Nashville *Tennessean*, February 9, 1926. Also see Atlanta *Constitution*, November 14, 1920.
23 James Carroll Napier Papers, Special Collections, Fisk University.

should have recognized that such conditions posed dangers for the entire city. "Haven't our neighbors sense enough," the editors asked "to know that filth, lack of lights and police protection in a black settlement is a menace to the health and protection of the white settlement? It seems that our neighbors would rather die and go to hell with the Negro than to live in heaven with him. These conditions constitute a civic shame to Atlanta." Inequities in the distribution of public services made the paucity and fragmentation of black political power even more difficult to bear. "When we notice the improvements being made in every section of the city," the Richmond *Planet* observed, "except that portion occupied by our people . . . we are forced to ask when will these little groups of colored folks come together and under one sane leadership endeavor to accomplish something in this city and State worthy of the name?" The Norfolk *Journal and Guide* took some comfort from the fact that "Progressive cities no longer 'skimp' and discriminate between groups in the matter of street and other municipal improvement," but few services ever found their way into black neighborhoods without a concerted effort by blacks themselves. [24]

Members of the Negro business middle class lamented widespread unemployment, the unavailability of industrial and semiindustrial jobs, and the crunch of urban poverty. For "those who are poor and can barely make a living," the *Independent* advised, "the city is the last place they should go." The migration of rural blacks to southern cities only increased the difficulties of overcrowding, since Negro sections were constricted by increasing tendencies toward residential segregation. Many spokesmen for the black commercial-civic elite were also concerned with the disorganization and instability they perceived in the urban black population, and they usually supported strict enforcement of the vagrancy statutes to encourage proper work habits, promote community discipline, and prevent crime. Yet they also deeply resented police harassment, the maintenance of illegal curfews in Negro areas, and the unfortunate readiness of white patrolmen and streetcar conductors to fire on blacks with the least provocation. "It is evident," the *Planet* observed, "that colored people are the objects of particular care and observation on the part of the officers of the law." [25]

24 Atlanta *Independent*, May 29, 1920; Richmond *Planet*, October 2, 1920; Norfolk *Journal and Guide*, September 24, 1927.
25 Atlanta *Independent*, October 27, 1921, May 17, October 11, 1923, March 17, 1921, November 13, 1924, May 18, 1922; Richmond *Planet*, April 17, 1920.

Each periodic crackdown on local crime brought scores of arrests throughout the black community, while city authorities usually condoned the white ownership of pool halls, gambling dens, and bordellos in Negro sections. Unrestrained urban boosterism under such conditions was understandably difficult. "It is realized that picking out conspicuous defects in one's home city is not good advertising," the *Journal and Guide* admitted, "but neither is a high death rate, poor health standards and low morality. And if the latter can be minimized by a concentration upon the former, no public spirited citizen can escape the moral obligation to shout upon the housetops." [26]

Urban Transportation: Crisis and Opportunity

If there was a "unique" problem for the urban South of the 1920s, it was the automobile. And the subject of urban transportation elicited more comment and stirred more concern from commercial-civic spokesmen than any other during the period. The significance of transportation in shaping the pattern of American economic growth was not lost on those urban southerners who staked their personal and business fortunes on trade and expansion. Indeed, the interurban competition for good roads and automotive facilities had by the 1920s replaced the railroad as a perceived determinant of city development. But in the same measure that urban transportation was a promise of economic salvation and social improvement, its problems and failures were seen as potentially harmful to the city and its capacity to expand. "Water, air and light are vital to the life of a community," the *Commercial-Appeal* remarked, "but when a large country has scattered over it large cities, transportation approaches a vital part of the machinery of its existence." [27]

Commercial interests and the major newspapers generally welcomed the automobile as a sign of "progress" and material prosperity, and sales figures during the decade attest to the motor vehicle's wide popularity. An era marked by motor-car travel was envisioned as one both modern and affluent. The editors of the Nashville *Tennessean* concluded in 1920 that "The operation of automobiles, even purely for pleasure or relaxation, entails no vices. . . . It is one of the great blessings that has come to us who live in this age, and its

26 Norfolk *Journal and Guide*, May 10, 1924.
27 Memphis *Commercial-Appeal*, February 25, 1920.

influence on our national life is so good and so powerful and far-reaching as to challenge our imagination as to what its final results will be." [28]

Businessmen lauded the automobile because it promised to open up new channels of commerce, expand the pool of customers for downtown merchants, and make available large expanses of outlying territory for urban growth and economic development. As the *News and Courier* predicted in 1920: "It is likely that as highway development proceeds we shall have fewer small villages in South Carolina. People will go in future to the larger towns where they can buy to better advantage." Communication between cities would be improved markedly by motor vehicle transportation, and this development was thought to be, at least in theory, to the commercial advantage of all concerned. In addition, some spokesmen saw in the growing automotive tourist industry a direct and highly promising economic opportunity. Business leaders in Nashville complained that while their city was "ideally located for an automobile camping site" the interruptions in the highway linking Nashville with Chattanooga and Atlanta meant that "this city and the cities to the south and east of us are losing thousands of dollars because of the road embargo." Local promoters in Charleston envisioned that as soon as the related problems of adequate hotels and roads had been solved, the city would become "before a great while, one of the principal tourist centers of America." [29]

The major issue concerning businessmen in major southern cities during the 1920s was not whether the automobile was desirable, but whether roads, highways, and related facilities could be provided rapidly enough to insure the maximum degree of economic advantage. The Good Roads Movement in the South, and throughout the country, had always received the support of prominent business groups, and in the 1920s most chambers of commerce in the larger cities established committees especially charged with the task of promoting highway construction and the repair of existing roads. This was a policy largely shared by city officials. David E. McLendon, president of the Birmingham City Commission, declared in 1922 that "the greatest project and the one that, when completed, will mean the most to the people of our city" was the connection of city roads with county highways, which would

---

28 Nashville *Tennessean*, August 9, 1920. Also see Atlanta *Constitution*, April 4, 1922.
29 Charleston *News and Courier*, April 28, 1920, March 5, 1921; Nashville *Tennessean*, June 20, 1921; Charleston *News and Courier*, June 24, 1924, June 26, 1923.

make the city more accessible to outside trade, commerce, and communication. The cry for good roads by the business middle class became so shrill by 1926 that the editors of one labor publication complained that it threatened to drown out more important issues, such as education.[30]

Growing problems in traffic congestion, motor vehicle accidents, and inadequate parking space, however, led members of the business middle class to voice considerable concern if not second thoughts about the ability of the automobile to answer the city's principal transportation needs. In the course of the decade, motor vehicle registrations rose from approximately 12,000 to 40,300 in Nashville; from 20,000 to 58,000 in Memphis; from 20,000 to 64,200 in Atlanta; from 16,000 to 70,000 in Birmingham; and from 20,000 to 70,000 in New Orleans.[31] While traffic congestion was hardly new to southern cities, these dramatic increases in the numbers of motor vehicles were tangibly manifested in a glut of automobiles and trucks in the downtown sections. At the beginning of the decade the *Constitution* claimed that Atlanta was "confronted with perhaps as serious a traffic situation as has existed in any city in the United States," and the chamber of commerce magazine gave substantial emphasis to a statement by the chairman of the City Planning Committee that Atlanta's traffic congestion was "well-nigh unbearable." Toward the end of the decade many observers shared the opinion of the *Age-Herald* "that the automobile which was formerly such a source of

30 Quote from David E. McLendon in an unidentified magazine article (c. December 25, 1922) in "The Administration of Commission President D. E. McLendon, Nov. 7, 1921–Nov. 2, 1925: A Scrapbook of Newspaper and Other Clippings Compiled in the Office of the Commission," I, 285 (Birmingham Public Library); Birmingham *Labor Advocate*, June 5, 1926. Southern cities competed vigorously for air transportation during the 1920s as well, and chambers of commerce played a prominent role in the development of municipal air terminals. But these efforts were largely peripheral to the more central problem of dealing with motor vehicle traffic in the central city.

31 These figures are compiled from a variety of sources, including the statistics contained in *Facts and Figures of the Automobile Industry*, published annually in New York by the National Automobile Chamber of Commerce, and the following: *Annual Report of the Chief of Police of the City of Atlanta* (1930), 39; Ross W. Harris, "Traffic Survey on the Vehicular and Street Railway Traffic Situation of Birmingham" (Bound typescript in City Clerk's Office, Birmingham, Ala., 1927), 61, 57; State of Tennessee, Department of Revenue, Motor Vehicle Division, "Registration by Counties for 1930" (Typescript in Motor Vehicle Division, Department of Revenue, Nashville, Tenn.), 1–2; Nashville City Planning and Zoning Commission, *A Traffic Survey of the City of Nashville, Tennessee* (Nashville, 1934), 3; Miller McClintock, "The Street Traffic Control Problem of the City of New Orleans" (Typescript report in the City Archives, New Orleans Public Library, 1928), 75. Figures given are for the counties containing the five principal cities under consideration, with the exception of New Orleans where the municipal limits coincided with the boundaries of Orleans Parish.

convenience and means of swift transportation is rapidly becoming a serious handicap in downtown business centers." [32]

Both a cause and a consequence of traffic congestion in the downtown business district was the lack of adequate parking space provided either privately or by the city. The number of garages or vacant lots was apparently never sufficient to meet the rising demand during the 1920s, and most public parking space was located on city streets, which further hindered the flow of traffic. The problem did not go unnoticed. "About one-fifth of the automobile drivers are lucky enough to find parking space downtown," a Memphis writer complained, "and the other four-fifths burn up gasoline and lose time looking for it. Finding an unoccupied space large enough to park a car in the business district is like sighting an oasis in the desert." [33]

The automobile presumably brought additional customers into the central trading district, but vehicular congestion also made movement in the downtown sections increasingly difficult. In such circumstances, the vision of an expanding market often gave way to fears of economic isolation. "It is a fair conclusion," the New Orleans commissioner of public safety announced in 1927, "that millions of dollars have been lost in the business area because of inadequate provisions for traffic regulation and control." Yet some spokesmen were as apprehensive of the cure as they were of the disease. The elimination of on-street parking and the replacement of diagonal with parallel parking areas were measures of improving the traffic flow initiated in every major southern city. But this posed a painful dilemma for many downtown merchants: while such restrictions made vehicular movement easier—and thus supposedly encouraged customers to frequent the business district—it also eliminated many parking spaces. If there were dangers to business in traffic congestion, it remained vital that customers have some place to temporarily store their vehicles while they shopped. "Lack of parking space causes purchasers to patronize suburban rather than downtown stores," a Nashville business publication noted in 1926. "The necessity for measures to control street traffic is admitted by all. However, it is unfortunate that this should work a hardship on those who are among [the] city's largest taxpayers." While industrial firms and outlying businesses were not overly concerned

32 Atlanta *Constitution*, February 5, 1920; W. J. Sayward, "City Planning Committee Urges Survey," Atlanta *City Builder* (January, 1920), 13; Birmingham *Age-Herald*, January 13, 1927.
33 Memphis *Tatler*, I (May 25, 1929), 5.

with the problem, many downtown merchants, large and small, concluded that "To isolate the downtown section creates a situation much worse than traffic congestion."[34]

There were no major controversies between various elements of the business middle class on matters of motor vehicle regulation, but there were differences of emphasis on the basis of varying economic interests. Virtually all spokesmen decried traffic congestion and inadequate parking facilities, and the great majority proposed to solve these difficulties by constructing new roads, widening and improving existing streets, and expanding the central business district. But the problem certainly weighed most heavily on downtown businessmen, especially the smaller merchants. In 1926 Thomas H. Pitts reluctantly closed his well-known cigar store and soft-drink bar located at Five Points, a major intersection in downtown Atlanta. "I think the real thing that did it was automobiles, and more automobiles," he lamented. "Traffic got so congested that the only hope was to keep it going. Hundreds used to stop; now thousands pass. Five Points has become a thoroughfare, instead of a center." And even the larger department stores began to regret the problems consequent to rising numbers of motor cars. "It was formerly said that the growth of skyscrapers and the attendant congestion in small areas was the greatest problem faced by growing cities," the *Age-Herald* remarked in 1927, "but it is now found that this is unimportant as compared with the vehicular congestion which is making movement so difficult."[35]

As the numbers of automobiles rose, the patronage of municipal street railways declined. Streetcars not only had to contend with private passenger cars but with commercial motor bus lines and, in Atlanta and Birmingham especially, five- to seven-passenger "jitney" automobiles which competed directly with street railways along the most heavily traveled routes. No matter how much the automobile might constitute the wave of the future, commercial-civic spokesmen invariably supported at least the maintenance of existing mass transportation facilities.

To some extent, perhaps, this was because streetcar companies were large businesses with influence in the chamber of commerce as well as at city hall.

34 *Official Proceedings of the Commission Council of the City of New Orleans*, October 4, 1927, 1 (City Archives, New Orleans Public Library); *Nashville This Week*, I (May 10–17, 1926), 3.
35 Quoted in Franklin Garrett, *Atlanta and Environs: A Chronicle of Its People and Events* (2 vols.; New York, 1954), II, 822; Birmingham *Age-Herald*, January 13, 1927.

But it was surely more than that: even with the increasingly widespread ownership of motor vehicles, the majority of those citizens who came into the downtown business district—to work and to shop—traveled by means of the streetcar. The *Tennessean* reported in 1921 that some 100,000 persons were dependent on the street railway system for transportation: "Nashville has reached the stage," the editors concluded, "where rerouting and the removal of automobiles from certain streets appear essential if reasonable service is to be provided."[36]

Rarely were such drastic measures seriously considered, much less effected. But the survival of urban mass transit was for many writers, as the Birmingham *News* contended, "the most vital question in an urban community in relation to its growth." The street railway was "everywhere the backbone of development." The Memphis Chamber of Commerce also ranked convenient urban transportation as "at the base of progress in the modern city" and predicted dire consequences if the street railways were removed: "Business would slow down, industries would not operate fully, amusement places would note a lack of patronage, real estate values would drop, and the fabric of the whole commercial life of the city would be weakened. Madame could not do her shopping, and the servant girl would not be on time for work." In addition, streetcars were essential for urban expansion and considerably less expensive to operate than private cars.[37]

Commercial-civic representatives joined with the local streetcar companies in Atlanta and Birmingham to severely restrict or eliminate the operation of "jitneys." The Atlanta *Independent* was a leader of this opposition, charging that jitneys were irresponsible and inadequate means of mass transit. In Birmingham, the Chamber of Commerce, most of the civic associations, the major urban dailies, some leading labor spokesmen, and the City Commission all came out publicly in support of the Birmingham Railway, Light, and Power Company and its campaign against jitneys, though

36 Nashville *Tennessean*, June 28, 1921. A survey of Birmingham in 1926 revealed that the street railway was responsible for 64 percent of the passengers carried in and out of the downtown area, the private automobile accounting for only about 28 percent of the total passenger traffic. See Ross W. Harris, "Traffic Survey on the Vehicular and Street Railway Traffic Situation of Birmingham," 28.

37 Birmingham *News*, March 19, 1923; "City's Progress Depends on Street Car Service," *Memphis Chamber of Commerce Journal*, V (July, 1922), 11–12.

several labor publications attacked the utility and defended the jitney as the vehicle of the workingman.[38]

Given the general business middle-class fascination for the automobile—and, indeed, for all technological innovations that promised a greater degree of prosperity and urban growth—the elimination of private motor cars was hardly seen as a practical, or possible, answer. "We need both the automobile and the street cars," the Memphis *Tatler* commented in an editorial with which most commercial-civic spokesmen would have agreed. "It is possible to promote the use of one by a more liberal patronage of the other. We would benefit individually and collectively if we made proper use of both."[39]

The most pressing consequence of increased automobile registrations was traffic control. Speeders endangered lives, streets were glutted with illegally parked vehicles, and the number of automobile mishaps rose alarmingly over the course of the decade. Civic groups, business leaders, and even governmental agencies loudly complained that the traffic laws were not being enforced. The Atlanta City Council passed a resolution in October, 1922, requesting the chief of police "to enforce the present traffic ordinances," especially parking restrictions in the downtown area during peak traffic hours. The Jefferson County grand jury protested in December, 1923, that traffic-safety regulations were widely violated in Birmingham and demanded "rigid enforcement" by municipal authorities, and a similar resolution was adopted by the local Kiwanis Club in June, 1927. The Civic Bureau of the New Orleans Association of Commerce conducted a traffic study in 1926 and concluded that lax enforcement, inadequate penalties for violations, and lenient courts were the major causes of motor vehicle accidents in the city. Police spokesmen responded by pointing to their understaffed, underfunded departments and, like Charleston's chief, asked that municipal governments "enact ordinances that will be sufficiently effective."[40]

Even with the aid of new traffic signal devices, there were simply not

38 See, for example, Atlanta *Independent*, January 17, 1924. For a detailed account of this controversy in Birmingham, see Blaine A. Brownell, "The Notorious Jitney and the Urban Transportation Crisis in Birmingham in the 1920s," *Alabama Reveiw*, XXV (April, 1972), 105–18.
39 Memphis *Tatler*, I (May 25, 1929), 5.
40 City of Atlanta, Council Minutes, XXVII, 724; Birmingham *Age-Herald*, December 10, 1925; Birmingham *News*, June 23, 1927; *New Orleans Association of Commerce News Bulletin*, VIII (October 26, 1926), 1; *Year Book, City of Charleston: 1919* (Charleston, 1919), 290.

enough traffic officers available in most cities to contend with the mass of motor vehicles. "There are only two Birmingham traffic cops," the *Post* complained in 1923, "who devote their full time to looking after speeders, drunken drivers and the like." The problem seemed so immense even at the beginning of the decade that the city's public safety commissioner asked private citizens to report traffic violations to the police, who would in turn send "polite" warnings to the offending motorists. On the other hand, the new traffic-control demands imposed on law enforcement agencies threatened the maintenance of order in other areas. "The increased traffic on our streets has made it necessary to take a large number of officers off of patrol duty," Atlanta's police chief reported in 1928, "and put them to regulating traffic, thus leaving a large portion of the city without police protection."[41]

Police difficulties were compounded by the fact that many traffic violators, not to mention dangerous criminals, were better equipped to avoid capture than authorities were to apprehend them. Southern police forces moved slowly to acquire modern motor vehicles and new equipment, but the many officers still on foot or mounted on horses or bicycles during the 1920s were quite ineffective against lawbreakers with the latest technology.

By the 1920s southern cities faced a mounting transportation crisis. Increasing numbers of motor vehicles choked existing streets and severely tested unimproved dirt and gravel roads. Overextended and financially troubled streetcar lines lost patrons to jitneys, motor-bus lines, and private automobiles. Motor-vehicle accidents took their toll in lives and property while city police forces turned part of their attention away from serious crime and the control of "undesirables" and vagrants and concentrated on the regulation of traffic. The motor car was seen as a dangerous tool in the hands of criminals and reckless drivers, an obvious temptation to youth, and a threat to the tightly knit family. As in the case of handguns, business middle-class writers recommended that strict licensing procedures be employed to insure, as the *Tennessean* put it, "the responsible character of every man who is permitted to own and operate a car."[42]

Perhaps most frustrating for members of the commercial-civic elite was

41 Birmingham *Post*, July 4, 1923; Birmingham *News*, December 16, 1921; *Annual Report of the Chief of Police of the City of Atlanta* (Atlanta, 1928), 8, 3.
42 Nashville *Tennessean*, January 31, 1928.

that such a crisis occurred at precisely the moment when technological innovations promised a degree of transportation and communications efficiency and urban expansion unprecedented in American history. The automobile became for them a genuine symbol of modernity—representing the disruptive potential as well as the beneficent promise of new technological opportunities.[43]

Members of the commercial-civic elite were anxious, in short, to take advantage of new opportunities for growth and development while preserving their own status and controlling position in the city. Thus, while they often either exaggerated or underestimated the seriousness of urban ills, the urban boosterism and concept of the urban community which they fashioned must be understood primarily from within this framework of perception. "All men who think agree that this is perhaps the most restless period in the history of this generation," a Birmingham clergyman observed. "It is certainly so since reconstruction in the Southern States. Nothing is settled; business, economics, the whole of the social order with its ramifications is in a state of ceaseless effervescence." Such instability was more than an inconvenience. Members of the commercial-civic elite were confronted with what they interpreted as a basic dilemma: the very growth and expansion that they promoted and welcomed was accompanied by troubling and unpredictable consequences which threatened to undermine their interests and the type of city which they believed essential for progress and continued growth. If the difficulties attendant to growth could not be solved or meliorated, as Atlanta's mayor put it in 1920, "we have grown big enough, and do not deserve to expand any more."[44]

43 See Blaine A. Brownell, "A Symbol of Modernity: Attitudes Toward the Automobile in Southern Cities in the 1920s," *American Quarterly*, XXIV (March, 1972), 20–44.
44 Birmingham *Alabama Baptist*, L (February 12, 1920), 4; quoted in Atlanta *Constitution*, July 6, 1920.

V The Corporate-Expansive City: Concepts of Urban Growth and Community

Can you visualize Knoxville with neighborly houses following one another closely until they press upon the ridges to the north and east, can you see an expansion far into the country on the west; can you see that beautiful country south of the Tennessee river built up into a closely knit community?

—Knoxville *Journal and Tribune*, March 1, 1920

THE CITY should become bigger and better—but in many essential respects it should not change. This belief, this delicate balance between transformation and continuity with all its possible contradictions, was firmly rooted in southern urban commercial-civic opinion during the 1920s. Economies and cities had to grow in order to survive, the familiar explanation ran, while fundamental alterations in social structure, economic organization, and patterns of civic leadership were inimical to the urban welfare.

In one of his most perceptive observations, W. J. Cash noted that members of the rising southern urban middle class which appeared before 1900 were basically quite conservative, "precisely because of the gathering knowledge within themselves that the Southern *status quo* presented a nearly perfect stage for the working out of their personal ambitions." "Their will to maintain the *status quo*, as it was represented, would be simply and exactly their will to see the South go along the road to Progress."[1] But these

1 Wilbur J. Cash, *The Mind of the South* (Vintage ed.; New York, 1941), 228, 237.

skyscraper builders, civic leaders, and business types were not just responding to the call of the "southern mind" or regional patriotism—at least by the time of the 1920s—as Cash contended. They were primarily anxious to reconcile growth with order, diversity with unity, and change with stability—to guide their cities into a metropolitan world while retaining control of that world—through notions of *local* patriotism, civic consensus, and a corporate urban community.

When commercial-civic leaders spoke of "community" they did not pause to define the term with any precision. But what they almost always meant was the entire city, conceived in broad geographical terms—interdependent, sharing basically the same interests, and united behind business middle-class goals by a sense of civic responsibility and loyalty. Some may have derived notions of "genuine community" from their small-town backgrounds. But for most the village had very little to offer the city in terms of concrete examples for the improvement of urban life. While many commentators called for greater unity of purpose and for strengthened local loyalties, few expected that face-to-face relationships would ever prevail among all people in the metropolis. The search for order and community in the city was, in fact, due in large part to the realization that the metropolis was fundamentally different from the small town. This search was, in other words, not so much an effort to model the city after the village, as an attempt to maintain the viability of urban life.

Members of the commercial-civic elite were aware that special interests, occupational groups, and even classes seemed to proliferate at the same time that social and economic interdependence increased. Social solidarity and urban consensus (which had existed previously only in relative terms) appeared to diminish just as society was being drawn together by innumerable threads of commerce and communication. This social fragmentation, which held the seeds of urban discontent, put the commercial-civic elite more and more at the mercies of new complexities, problems, and social divisions that they might not be able to control. And they proposed to meliorate such fragmentation not by fundamental social and economic reorganization but by economic growth (which would create a greater store of wealth to benefit all citizens) and by civic loyalty (which would fix the attention of all city residents on common aims). The efforts of commercial-civic spokesmen to disseminate a call for urban unity reflected their belief—or at least their hope—that if citizens were informed of their mutual dependence, and of the dangers of fragmentation and disorder, a sense of cooperation and community spirit *within the existing social and economic system* would inevitably emerge.

Urban boosterism was thus not merely an extension of economic competition and a form of interurban salesmanship. It was also a message to the city population and a means of expressing a concept of the urban community held by members of the business middle class. This concept of community—this urban ethos—was built on basic commercial-civic assumptions concerning growth, citizenship, and the nature of urban society. And it was both a conceptual effort to deal with an increasingly complex urban reality and one vehicle of achieving a greater degree of social control in the emerging metropolis.

Growth and Progress: The Values of Urban Expansion

Growth and increasing size were, for commercial-civic leaders, fundamental reflections on the health and character of a city. "Speed of growth, and surpassing size" might not be the "highest ambitions for a municipality," the New Orleans *Times-Picayune* admitted; but they were most definitely "indices of success, of efficient management, of contented workers, of an enthusiastic citizenry," a "direct refllection, usually, of the homely virtues of good municipal housekeeping." Of all the various measurements employed to assess the character of urban development, none was so compelling as the quantity of the city's population. Through most of American history, a city had to become bigger to be "better"; a rising population did not simply parallel "progress" but was one of its principal determinants. As Edd Parks wrote in 1934, "Bigness for its own sake had become a megalomania" in the 1920s, with southern cities struggling vigorously for higher and higher standings in the census statistics. To be a great city was, in this sense, to become the very opposite of the small town. The Birmingham *Labor Advocate* was proud to have "witnessed the evolution of a giant among industrial centers from a small village sitting in ignorance upon the millions of untold wealth buried under the soil of her farms and gardens, to a commanding figure among the industrial giants of latter day commerce and manufacturing cities." The

Constitution reminded its readers that Atlanta was, fortunately, "no longer a village nor a town, but a big, prosperous and growing city."[2] The very words themselves in such passages conveyed the power of size and hinted at the advantages of power.

The worship of growth was by no means limited to middle-class businessmen, nor for that matter to any racial or economic group. Atlanta's major black newspaper joined wholeheartedly in the campaign to increase the city's population by 100 percent during the 1920s, an effort, the editors declared, which "deserves the united cooperation of every citizen in the city without regard to race, color, creed or politics. It is an undertaking for the city, for the benefit of all the people in the city." And the Memphis Ku Klux Klan joined the booster chorus by adopting the slogan "A Bigger and Better Memphis" in their 1923 municipal political campaign. The consequences of growth were often troubling and in some cases nearly disastrous. But growth was rarely questioned as essential to progress, and progress was thought to be "the soul of our civilization." The principal goal of all major southern urban centers was quite simply, according to the *Constitution*: "Expansion! Expansion! EXPANSION!"[3]

Population was the major measurement of urban growth and progress, but it was not the only one. Other criteria included everything from financial transactions to wages, and even agricultural prices. Downtown construction was an especially notable sign of urban expansion—the taller and more numerous the buildings, the more impressive the skyline, the more imposing the city. Even the city's chaos was, on occasion, justified as an indication of its vitality. "Observant strangers who come to this city," a Birmingham writer

2 New Orleans *Times-Picayune*, August 15, 1920; Edd W. Parks, "Southern Towns and Cities," in William T. Couch (ed.), *Culture in the South* (Chapel Hill, 1934), 505; Birmingham *Labor Advocate*, May 22, 1920; Atlanta *Constitution*, January 6, 1920.

3 Atlanta *Independent*, March 6, 1920; Kenneth T. Jackson, *The Ku Klux Klan in the City, 1915–1930* (New York, 1967), 51; Memphis *Commercial-Appeal*, January 1, 1920; Atlanta *Constitution*, January 7, 1920. It is not coincidental that most of these comments were made in 1920, when southern cities were deeply concerned with the decennial census returns. The emphasis on growth and expansion in American cities has been noted by most urban historians, and Robert S. and Helen M. Lynd encountered the same mutual dependence of growth and progress in their study of Muncie, Indiana in the 1930s, *Middletown in Transition: A Study in Cultural Conflicts* (New York, 1937), 405. Scott Greer has referred to the promotion of urban growth as a "fertility drama" which rested "upon an anxiety suspiciously similar to that of the real estate broker when business is slow." See Scott Greer, *Metropolitics: A Study of Political Culture* (New York, 1963), 13.

commented in 1926, "cannot fail to be impressed by certain things indicative of quick growth, undirected expansion, a certain rugged irregularity in the lines of a great urban plant, in the placement of industries, business houses, great buildings, looming large among squatty structures reminiscent of another and earlier life in the time of the community." Though not artistically appealing, this irregularity was nevertheless "suggestive of a growth that has refused to wait upon plans."[4]

The juxtaposition of newer, more modern edifices with older buildings offered an opportunity to measure "progress" in a very tangible way, the new skyscrapers standing as solid proof of the city's success and potential. The whole process was lyrically described by a Birmingham poet:

> A brand new building's going up today
> The workmen are toiling away
> Shaping the brick the mortar and stone
> Into a figure, whose head is thrown
> High up into the tinted sky
> Seeming a titan to passer-by
> While other houses clustered about
> Are faded, old and near worn out
> Progress has touched this spot again
> Bringing its beauty and glory and gain
> It is good to see their efforts anew
> God may our souls bloom sweeter too
> Climb high into the clearer air
> Cast out the drab, enthrone the fair.[5]

Growth seemed to have an almost inexorable quality about it. "A great city cannot be halted in its growth by any minor impediment," the *Age-Herald* remarked in 1923, "and, like a mighty stream, is likely to carry with it all objects upon its surface or within its volume." If a city aspired to regional or national prominence, if it desired to become "better," expansion was essential. "A city cannot thrive unless it has large payrolls," a black Norfolk writer concluded. "It cannot have large payrolls unless there are big factories, big railroad and shipping terminals and shops, big grain elevators and other industries." The most crucial prerequisite for growth, according to the logic of the time, was growth itself. "It is growth and prosperity that serves

4 Birmingham *Age-Herald*, March 31, 1926.
5 Ray Short, "Building," in *Hilltops* (Birmingham, 1926), pages not numbered.

[*sic*] as magnetism," a Knoxville editor observed; "it is an irresistible power in the attraction of the elements that are the essentials of growth." The city which failed to expand was almost certainly destined to decay—"it must go forward or it will go backward." Commercial-civic spokesmen did not consider growth to be a particularly difficult achievement during the 1920s; it was most commonly regarded as the "natural" and expected path for any healthy urban community. As the president of the Knoxville Board of Commerce put it, "There is nothing now that can stop our growth except our own unwillingness to grow." [6]

As long as urban expansion and a rising city population reinforced social and economic "progress," or at least posed no apparent threats to it, virtually any kind of quantitative expansion of the city was welcome, whether in population, territory, buildings, or business enterprises. But the changes attendant to growth increasingly presented a wide range of problems that could neither be ignored nor easily explained, and rampant, haphazard expansion led more often to chaos than to order. The increasing recognition of serious urban ills—especially the problems associated with population density and overburdened city institutions—threatened to lead ultimately to the conclusion that cities could only get "better" by not becoming bigger. This, of course, would have weakened or destroyed the connection between growth and progress and was far too severe a revision of older attitudes to be readily tolerated or accepted.

Most commercial-civic spokesmen therefore resorted to other means to reconcile growth and progress, quality and quantity—to continue, in a sense, their faith in the future and viability of the city. To some extent, the problems of rising population could be meliorated by expanding municipal territory, by insuring low population density while at the same time enlarging the city. Another, equally popular, means of dealing with the problem was to further define and qualify the process of growth itself, maintaining expansion as a

6 Birmingham *Age-Herald*, March 1, 1923; Norfolk *Journal and Guide*, April 25, 1923; Knoxville *Journal and Tribune*, June 29, 1922, March 14, 1920. The belief that decay was an inevitable consequence of the absence of growth was endemic to American social thought and doubtless rooted in the reality of an expansive capitalist economy. It was, in an economic sense (the necessity for ever-larger markets and increased production), a basically accurate perception, based as much on experience as on entrepreneurial enthusiasm. But the full social consequences of this idea were only beginning to be suspected in southern cities during the 1920s.

principal urban priority by distinguishing between constructive and destructive, desirable and undesirable, patterns of growth.

The great city, the healthy city, was one capable of experiencing growth without devastating consequences, a city in which growth actually contributed to stability and permanence. Optimum growth was thus almost universally regarded as "steady" and "natural" rather than excessively rapid. "Birmingham is better off for not having grown more rapidly than it has if urban growth was to have been at the expense of symmetry," the *Age-Herald* declared. The Alabama metropolis had gone beyond its reputation as the "Magic City" to become an urban center "whose foundation has been solidly laid and whose development has attained an impetus that of itself points to more." The "days of experiment" had happily passed, and the city now marched with "a steady pace of certainty."[7] The concept of "symmetrical" growth was rarely defined, but the term clearly implied that optimum expansion took place evenly, across a broad front. The basic idea was to assert the city's claim to permanence and stability, to reconcile vitality with order in such fashion that each would reinforce the other. And behind this interpretation of urban development was the thinly veiled hope that the mature city could contend with its problems and cope with the conquences of the necessity to expand.

Ironically, several southern cities categorized by many Americans as among the most notable "boom" towns of the land were eager to be bereft of the reputation. "While Atlanta's growth has been steady, though rapid, in every instance we find it has been entirely natural and healthy," a local architect boasted. "There is no taint of boom about it. It offers all the elements of endurance and stability." The mayor of Memphis proudly greeted the 1920 census because the city's expansion was not "the result of any boom or undue war activities." And the *Banner* wrote: "Nashville has had no sensational growth, but one that means much. Its growth has been based on its worth, which is not emphemeral, but of a most lasting character." The overwhelming southern urban attitude was definitely that "boom" development was to be avoided, that haphazard growth would deform the urban structure, perhaps beyond remedy. "Nashville is comparable to a man's figure," the *Tennessean* commented, "well proportioned and symmetrical,

7 Birmingham *Age-Herald*, September 12, 1922, October 18, 1920.

while some of the other cities resemble misshapen cripples, with dwarfed legs and hurculean arms." Even Knoxville, one of the most notable "boom" towns in the region between 1910 and 1920, attempted to avoid the unfavorable implications of excessively rapid expansion. "There has been nothing of inflation," the *Journal and Tribune* asserted, "nothing of the mushroom variety to mark this growth." Great cities did not grow through the "unnatural expansion of land booms and speculative realty furores [*sic*]" or from "some unhealthful stimulus." [8]

The "great" city, according to commercial-civic writers, had successfully weathered the "boom" of its earliest years and entered into the "soberer grooves of thought and habit" which marked the stage of urban maturity and stability. It was at this point that civic loyalty and self-awareness were most welcome and constructive. As the *Age-Herald* put it, "It is only after a new place has found itself, and attained a measured and steady stride and feels the confidence of attainment that it begins to look around about itself." [9]

Southern urban spokesmen employed a variety of metaphors and analogies in their endless attempts to comprehend and explain urban development. The most popular of these was organic in form, which lent itself most readily to the portrayal of city development as vital, yet disciplined by rational and "natural" patterns. A Nashville business publication likened city growth to that of a massive oak: "The progress is gradual, natural and irresistible. . . . Thus the oak tree grows into the land out of the land. This is the process of growth, the process of natural, gradual increase of which the enlarged dimensions are the result rather than the cause." On occasion, this line of argument was a rationalization of a poor showing in the census returns, or a lower than anticipated rate of expansion—if the city's growth was not exceptional, it was at least stable, secure, and predictable. Or it could be employed to explain the realities of the urban condition. The *Tennessean* compared the "sooty, ill-kept, and ugly business center" of the city with a grub. "A homely and careless worm this is, not yet come even to the dignity of a cocoon state, but a rather wonderful worm, for all this, keeping at his grubby

8 Quote from G. Lloyd Preacher, architect and engineer, in "Why Is Atlanta?" Atlanta *City Builder* (December, 1923), 7; quote from Mayor Rowlett Paine, Memphis *Commercial-Appeal*, April 9, 1920; Nashville *Banner*, July 15, 1923; Nashville *Tennessean*, May 1, 1920; Knoxville *Journal and Tribune*, August 4, 1922; *Nashville This Week*, I (March 8–15, 1926), 3.
9 Birmingham *Age-Herald*, August 2, 1926, August 27, 1922.

work in the midst of grime and disorder, yet evolving at the same time a winged self whose dreams of serenity and beauty trail through our city suburbs." Few metaphors approached the dimensions of this ambitious attempt, but the *Age-Herald* did exceed it in terms of complexity. The newspaper's editors contrived an elaborate analogy on the basis of organic tissue formation that must stand as the most remarkable device of its genre. "Accretion," they wrote, "is the addition of new cells to the outside of those already existing. Intussesception is the deposition of new particles of formative material among those already embodied in the tissue." The city, like the organic body, "is undergoing both kinds of growth. Accretions on the outside are constant while intussusception is likewise continually underway in the interior vacant spaces." [10]

Also quite popular were variants on the organic theme, personifications of the city and analogies based on the stages of the human life cycle. Carmelite Janvier, for example, described New Orleans as "a grown up child," proud and petulant. "New Orleans," she wrote, "is not only a city with so much population, so great an area, so many imports, so many exports, all to be written neatly in columns and looked upon with pride. Besides all that, she is a woman, and a Creole woman, which is more." Cities suffered through the pangs of adolescence, maturity, and old age, and were often described as "a full-grown man making shift with a boy's waistcoat" or a growing youth who finds his clothes too restricting with the passage of time. Urban writers commented through such analogies on the inadequacy of municipal budgets and facilities as well as on the nature of city expansion. [11]

10 *Nashville This Week*, I (March 8–15, 1926), 3; Nashville *Tennessean*, June 9, 1923; Birmingham *Age-Herald*, March 24, 1926. As Charles N. Glaab and A. Theodore Brown wrote in *A History of Urban America* (New York, 1967), 251, "Notions of the urban community as organic (at least from some points of view) and of the desirability of consciously shaping the urban environment have always been present in American thought." "Organicism" had become especially popular for describing the process of city development by the 1890s, and it persisted in the city planning movement and in the social thought of the first decades of the twentieth century. See Dana Francis White, "The Self-Conscious City: A Survey and Bibliographical Summary of Periodical Literature on American Urban Themes, 1865–1900" (Ph.D. dissertation, George Washington University, 1969), 98–99; and Roy Lubove, *The Progressives and the Slums: Tenement House Reform in New York City, 1890–1917* (Pittsburgh, 1962), 218, 242. Nor has organicism ceased to be useful in modern urban theory. See Leo F. Schnore, "The City as Social Organism," *Urban Affairs Quarterly*, I (March, 1966), 58–69.
11 Carmelite Janvier, *Whimsical Madam New Orleans* (New Orleans, 1928), 16, 5; Atlanta *Constitution*, January 6, 1920; Memphis *Commercial-Appeal*, January 17, 1920; *Atlanta Life*,

The majority of southern commercial-civic writers chose to promote a solidarity of thought and action in the metropolis, an expansion of community spirit that would be sufficient to resolve the most serious social and economic difficulties. "The greatness of a city," the *Tennessean* commented, "is not in its commercial temples of sculptured and beaten brass. Those are merely the outward show of an inward spirit of the citizenry. It is the civic spirit which determines a city's real size." [12] And it was this very spirit, this mysterious quality, that would redeem the city from its apparent shortcomings and preserve the stability of urban life in the midst of expansion and change. That the notions of the commercial-civic elite about the realities or potential of urban community were often unrealistic or impracticable, that they were usually based on goals or priorities dear to the members of the business-oriented middle class who espoused them, detracted not at all from their urgency or significance in the efforts to deal conceptually with the challenges and realities of the modern city. Southern commercial-civic spokesmen proposed to meliorate the consequences of expansion—and insure the constructive and symmetrical character of urban growth—by intensifying and broadening a metropolitan sense of community and citizenship.

The Ideal of Urban Community

Southern urban spokesmen emphasized the relationship between the city's destiny and the dedication of its citizens in numerous ways throughout the decade, but the basic idea was the same: "the spirit of a city is the collective will of its citizens"; "a community is merely a reflection of the lives of those composing it"; "a city is but the expression of its citizens, and becomes just

---

August 6, 1927. Though organicism predominated, other types of analogies were employed for various purposes. The Atlanta *City Builder*, for example, drew a comparison between the city and a mighty ship. The "old fashioned hulk," adorned with "barnacles of indecision" and having run aground, was in desperate need of repair. The editors recommended that the windworn sails be replaced with "twentiety-century engines—powerful and reliable." An analogy was made by Nashville writers between urban growth and a campfire, both beginning fitfully and then blazing bright and hot when interested citizens "got right down into the choking smoke and began blowing the flame." See Atlanta *City Builder* (January, 1920), 16; and *Nashville This Week*, I (October 19–26, 1925), 3. The majority of such literary devices were patently overdrawn and inept, but they were important aspects of the popular urban literature of the period and were apparently motivated by a desire to explain concepts of urban expansion to the general populace in terms that everyone could understand.

12 Nashville *Tennessean*, May 26, 1920.

what its citizens purpose in their hearts it shall become, no less and no more."
The character of the city was determined, in this view, by the character and
initiative of its population, and the life of each resident was, in turn,
dependent on the urban community: "Only so far as the community is
healthy and prosperous, are its individuals healthy and prosperous." [13]

Cities were presumably judged by outsiders on the basis of their civic
commitment. "The hidden truth that men seek in a city," according to a
Nashville writer, "is the spirit of its people." Charleston would be assessed by
others, the *News and Courier* remarked in 1920, "by our spirit of faith in
Charleston and loyalty to Charleston." Similarly, an Atlanta bard observed
that, in praising the city's accomplishments, "We think not of her sky line,
but/ The spirit of her men." [14] Like a form of secular religion, civic patriotism
had its own ritual, its own liturgy, and faith in the gospel was crucial to its
practice.

This attitude placed a tremendous burden on social solidarity, on the
ability of each citizen—at least in theory—to rally unselfishly to the city's
cause. Citizens were ceaselessly warned, "What you are, your city will be,"
and the success or failure of the city to grow and prosper was considered a
direct reflection of the state of local "civic consciousness." Social and
economic prosperity were not, the New Orleans Association of Commerce
concluded, "the soil out of which grows civic advance." Rather, "all property
values, all business values and all professional values that exist in any city are
made by the spirit of its citizens." [15]

"Civic consciousness," "community spirit," "civic pride," or "community
mind" were hailed as the essential ingredients of the successful urban
formula, the keys to explain past growth and assess future prospects. These
terms were wielded more with rhetorical flourish than with precision. A
business writer in New Orleans admitted the difficulty of defining "civic
consciousness" because it was, after all, "an attitude of mind" not subject to

13 Nashville *Tennessean*, May 21, 1920; Memphis *Tatler*, I (May 4, 1929), 4; Atlanta *City
Builder* (October, 1924), 10; Atlanta *Independent*, December 13, 1923.
14 Atlanta *City Builder* (February, 1921), 14; *Nashville This Week*, I (November 9–16, 1925), 3;
Charleston *News and Courier*, April 9, 1926; Dudley Glass (ed.), *Men of Atlanta* (Atlanta,
1924), 1.
15 "1924, New Orleans and You," *New Orleans Association of Commerce News Bulletin*, VI
(January 1, 1924), 2; Birmingham *Age-Herald*, March 3, 1922; Lucius E. Wilson, "Community Spirit," *New Orleans Association of Commerce News Bulletin*, II (December 7, 1920), 2.

exact measurement. But the man who held such an attitude, he concluded, "could say with sincerity: 'I am conscious of the duties which devolve upon me as a citizen.'" According to the Norfolk *Journal and Guide,* which came as close as any to a definition, community spirit "means that everybody in the community decides that 'we'll all go forward together.'... It means that everybody shall 'pull' for everything that will add to the growth and prosperity of the community." A pronounced unity in the pursuit of common urban goals reinforced the practical value of local loyalty and envisioned the individual as so dependent on the community that "civic pride" became simply "self respect on a large scale." [16]

One would almost think from reading such passages that commercial-civic leaders were attempting to revive the Greek notion of *civitas,* the individual commitment to the city-state. They made no explicit avowal of such an intention, but their rhetoric clearly called for a degree of civic spirit that can only be described as a sort of local patriotism. Their notion of "citizenship" was built according to their conception of the urban community and required a dedication to business middle-class goals and priorities. The "good citizen" was one who functioned within the parameters of the system, followed the leadership of the commercial-civic elite, and actively pursued urban growth and progress with booster zeal. Those who could not be so described were cast beyond the pale of citizenship.

Loyalty was "the first requisite for the ideal citizen," the major attribute of the individual who dismissed the notion of self-interest and "does all in his power to make the city a better place in which to live." The "booster" was the hero and the "knocker" the villain in the drama of urban patriotism. The full requirements of the booster role were demanding. "No matter how successful you may be or how high your character," a chamber of commerce writer in Birmingham declared, "you are not a good citizen unless you are doing something unselfishly for the good of the city you are privileged to call your home." The trouble with many "good citizens," the *Tennessean* complained in 1926, was that while they lived "exemplary lives," violated no laws, and resisted all forces of corruption, "they are not positive forces for good." The booster was, almost by definition, a community activist, the epitome of the

16 *New Orleans Association of Commerce News Bulletin,* IV (August 1, 1922), 2; Norfolk *Journal and Guide,* February 10, 1923; *Memphis Chamber of Commerce Journal,* V (January, 1923), 22. See also *Birmingham,* IV (November, 1928), 11.

good citizen, and "live and let live" became a strange slogan dreamed up by small-town folk.[17]

The "knocker," who "incessantly finds fault with social or economic conditions," who "is forever objecting to something," was the scourge of the community, an individual voluntarily cast adrift from the mainstream of urban progress, "and nothing better than an excrescence." This type of vivid characterization is most remarkable in that it rarely referred to any specific individual or group. It occasionally appeared in the context of a particular political or economic debate, with opponents of a municipal bond issue or other urban project being branded as "knockers" or perpetual malcontents. In most instances, however, the "knocker" was an abstract representation of those who might, in their cynicism or passivity, threaten the principal tenets of the commercial-civic conception of the city. Basically, knockers existed as a negative reference group for that true booster spirit of "optimism, friendliness, and a militant civic loyalty."[18]

Of all the forms of southern urban boosterism, the "Atlanta spirit" reigned supreme, "inextinguishable and all-pervading," the envy of smaller towns and cities throughout the region, the prototype of intense civic patriotism. Atlantans themselves conceded that it was a mysterious force, like electricity or the weather, which was somehow transmitted to virtually every resident, young and old, city father and newcomer. "Whether inherited, or absorbed through the environment, they all possess it," the president of the chamber of commerce declared in 1922. "Children and grandchildren of the early settlers cannot be distinguished from other children and grandchildren of those who moved to Atlanta last week." Cultivated like precious fruit, protected as a municipal treasure, "Atlanta's faith in Atlanta" was even included in the local school curriculum and made a part of daily recitation.[19]

17 Norfolk *Journal and Guide*, April 9, 1927; *Birmingham*, I (July, 1925), 1; Nashville *Tennessean*, September 11, 1926. The general concept of *civitas* was, of course, not unique to southern cities of the 1920s. As Jack Tager wrote, urban "progressives" of all kinds in the early twentieth century agreed that a principal aim of society was "to revitalize the concept of civic responsibility and to inculcate high standards of citizenship in the American urban dweller." See Tager, *The Intellectual as Urban Reformer: Brand Whitlock and the Progressive Movement* (Cleveland, 1968), 78.

18 "Keep on the Right Side," *Memphis Chamber of Commerce Journal*, V (August, 1922), 51; Knoxville *Journal and Tribune*, December 20, 1920; Charleston *News and Courier*, September 29, 1926. See also "Not Birmingham—But You," *Birmingham*, I (September, 1925), 2; and Birmingham *Labor Advocate*, April 2, 1926.

19 John R. Hornady, *Atlanta: Yesterday, Today and Tomorrow* (New York, 1922), 5, 322;

That some citizens failed to demonstrate this kind of total commitment required of the bona fide city booster was a source of concern to many urban spokesmen, even in Atlanta. "Citizens are inclined to accept as a matter of course the benefits which they derive from community life," the Birmingham *Age-Herald* lamented, "and, like spoiled children, to regard their community as a poor kind of affair." [20] Whether or not such apathy and passivity existed, dozens of local advertising campaigns were initiated during the decade to drum up civic spirit and buttress local pride. A positive and active attitude toward the community, defined in commercial-civic terms, was expected and demanded of the "good citizen."

In Nashville, for example, the Commercial Club Forum designated May 26, 1920, as "Know Nashville Day" and distributed a special "primer" containing pertinent facts about the city. In June, 1924, the *Tennessean* began an editorial feature entitled "This Is Our Town," consisting of bits and pieces of information about the local area. On October 5, 1925, the chamber of commerce began a thirty-nine-week-long "Sell Nashville to Itself" campaign that featured a variety of activities including the posting of special slogans on street corners, in streetcars, and on business and city stationery. In the first week of 1926 alone, local Boy Scouts handed out thousands of lapel buttons reading "Smile with Nashville," and thousands more were distributed through the mails. The chamber of commerce then attempted an advertising campaign aimed at outsiders, and the organization's president suggested that "a considerable part" of the expense be borne by city taxpayers "so that every man and woman would be required to aid in the campaign." [21]

In March, 1925, "Know Birmingham Week" was acclaimed "a tremendous success" by the chamber of commerce. The chamber and the Birmingham Real Estate Board distributed thousands of booklets about the city; speakers addressed large crowds in theaters, motion-picture houses, and clubs; and preachers reminded their congregations about the virtues of the city and the superiority of Birmingham religious institutions. The regimen of civic

Walter O. Foote, "The 'Spirit of Atlanta,'" Atlanta *Christian Index*, CII (December 7, 1922), 10; Edna Baker, *My City: A Workbook for Geography of Atlanta* (Atlanta, 1932), 15.

20 Birmingham *Age-Herald*, April 2, 1922.

21 Nashville *Tennessean*, May 14, 1920, May 21, 1920, June 19, 1924; *Nashville This Week*, I (September 21–28, 1925), 5; I (January 11–18, 1926), 7; I (April 19–26, 1926), 10. "If all of us believed in Nashville as we should," the *Banner* stated (November 26, 1922), "the carrying of the story to the outside world would take care of itself."

patriotism involved concerted attention to the virtues and foibles of the local community, a paramount concern for its welfare, an abiding interest in its past, present, and future. "In order to understand more intelligently this institution called a Town," the *Memphis Chamber of Commerce Journal* commented, "to know its origin, growth, structure and activities one must develop an interest in its every movement. One must study its progress and regress."[22] To do anything less, this rhetoric implied, was to abrogate the responsibilities of citizenship. In practice, it was not so much a search for truth as a renewal of faith, an introspective self-appraisal necessary to the spirit of civic loyalty.

Perhaps the greatest challenge to the city, in the view of commercial-civic spokesmen, was an increasing urban complexity which fragmented human endeavor to the point where great numbers of citizens had little in common with each other in terms of their everyday activities or interests. On the one hand, this was a sign of economic progress. On the other hand, social, economic, and ideological divisions were seen as undermining community spirit and the achievement of commercial-civic goals. Concern on this score was manifested explicitly in the urban literature of the time, both in discussions of urban problems and the need for community solidarity. "With the rapid growth of a city," the *Constitution* observed, "there is a tendency to break into sections or classes, so that team work, denied team thinking as its logical predecessor, becomes ragged or impossible." The chamber of commerce, for its part, lamented that "Atlanta has its groups, each pursuing its own objects, thinking its own ideas and acting on its own prejudices." The greatest need, according to one writer, was for a leader "who can raise these various groups [which were, regrettably, not identified] out of a class consciousness into the larger social and civic consciousness."[23] Social solidarity and urban consensus were indeed difficult to achieve in a heterogeneous community. In the face of increasing complexity and multiplying socioeconomic interests, southern urban spokesmen looked primarily to a revival of psychological unity in the city—a type of unity which, when viewed in the context of commercial-civic

22 *Birmingham*, I (April, 1925), 12; "How Well Do You Know Your City?" *Memphis Chamber of Commerce Journal*, VII (April, 1924), 44.
23 Atlanta *Constitution*, December 31, 1920; W. W. Orr, "The Spiritual Needs of a City," Atlanta *City Builder* (October, 1924), 10, 52; Valerie Farrington, "Awakening a new Civic Consciousness," *Memphis Chamber of Commerce Journal*, V (September, 1922), 24.

priorities and the desire to retain existing social and economic patterns, assumed clearly manipulative overtones.

One means of promoting psychological unity, of course, was to call attention to common interests and to encourage awareness of the widespread interdependence in the modern city. "No man can live unto himself, now," the *Tennessean* observed. "Each is dependent upon others and each must play his part in the city's progress." Similarly, the Atlanta *Independent* concluded: "The various and varied phases of community life are interdependent; what is healthy for one, is healthy for all; what is hurtful or destructive for one, is hurtful and destructive for all."[24] Innumerable editorials stressed that the individual was becoming less and less viable apart from the social unit; that cooperation between individuals, and between various groups of individuals, was the essence of "community"; and that community, with its consensus of opinion on urban priorities, was essential to the survival, growth, and progress of the modern city.

The "good" community, as elaborated in southern urban literature in the 1920s, was thus founded on a cooperationist ideal, in which the individual was important for promoting the common good (defined, of course, according to standards of the commercial-civic elite). "The keynote of Nashville's prosperity," a business publication concluded in 1925, "is PROGRESS harmonized with CO-OPERATION." Business writers, in fact, contributed most significantly to this vision of the community, scorning—at least in theory— the very competitive spirit that supposedly lay at the heart of the free-enterprise system. They heaped ridicule on those who placed "selfish interest above all—and know nothing of what is going on around them," who persisted in "selfishly thinking" of their "own little affairs and pleasures." Competition, as described by a Nashville business spokesman, was "nothing in the world but war," a "wholly destructive" adventure dangerous to all concerned. "But from the very dawn of civilization," he added, "we have been climbing out of the pit of competition toward the splendid goals of non-wasteful co-operation." And a Memphis writer agreed: "Competition can be the death as well as the life of trade."[25]

The type of cooperationism advocated by the commercial-civic elite was

24 Nashville *Tennessean*, May 26, 1920; Atlanta *Independent*, November 29, 1923.
25 *Nashville This Week*, I (August 24–31, 1925), 3; *New Orleans Association of Commerce News Bulletin*, X (October 16, 1928), 2; *Nashville This Week*, I (March 15–22, 1926), 3; *Memphis Chamber of Commerce Journal*, I (April, 1918), 51.

the product of a merging of private and public interests under business middle-class auspices. And the role of the business leaders in the life of the community was expanded accordingly. As the president of the New Orleans Association of Commerce expressed it in 1924, "The executive who is successful today looks upon his business as an institution created for public service. He does not seek his own selfish advantage at the expense of others." This was a social solidarity and community spirit which rested firmly on commercial-civic values and goals; it was, in fact, accomplished by the complete acceptance of commercial-civic priorities and leadership. The city itself was often equated with the business corporation, and government became little more than the application of management skills to urban problems. The city "is nothing other than a big corporation," the *Constitution* declared in 1921, and "its affairs must be managed by men who are acquainted with at least the rudimentary elements of business." In the same year, the *Banner* recommended: "A municipal government should be run on practical business principles." [26]

The doctrine of business efficiency, so central to much of the business ideology of the 1920s, also played a central role in shaping this vision of the urban community. "Individual efficiency is the foundation of all constructive effort," a New Orleans writer explained, "and when merged with mass-efficiency, whether it be a corporation or a community, the sum total of the result is reflected in achievement. The close kinship between efficiency and cooperation thus manifests itself." Equally important was the dependence of

26 William Pfaff, "Is Yours a Money Machine?" *New Orleans Association of Commerce News Bulletin,* VI (February 5, 1924), 2; Atlanta *Constitution,* April 20, 1921; Nashville *Banner,* August 2, 1921. The city-commission and city-manager forms of municipal government were, of course, attempts to operate government according to business methods and principles. As James Weinstein has suggested, business and political leaders throughout the country were in the process of forming, in the early twentieth century, a "liberal corporate social order" in which public and private agencies increasingly cooperated to achieve social peace and maintain basic institutional arrangements. The emphasis was on "cooperation and social responsibility" rather than on unrestrained competition, and business spokesmen were principal advocates of this "ideal of a responsible social order in which all classes could look forward to some form of recognition and sharing in the benefits of an ever-expanding economy." The prevalence of such views among the commercial-civic elite in southern cities during the 1920s suggests that they were more widespread than even Weinstein believed. See his *The Corporate Ideal in the Liberal State, 1900–1918* (Boston, 1968), ix–xiv. The Lynds noted a similar tendency in Muncie in the 1930s "toward the liquidation of the traditional right to 'go as you please' in matters importantly affecting the public interest; and toward the closer coordination of city government, civic clubs, and other value-carrying and -forming agencies under its business agencies to present a united front to the world." See *Middletown in Transition,* 439.

progress and efficiency on *social order*, since change, innovation, and growth were considered destructive if they fundamentally shifted the boundaries of the general urban status quo. "What we have," the *Age-Herald* observed, "we owe to the conditions of a well-ordered community life." [27]

What this cooperationism, social solidarity, and efficiency would actually mean in practice was, in one instance, suggested by commercial-civic spokesmen themselves. The local controls and coerced uniformity of the domestic mobilization during World War I—the focusing of the economy on the war effort and the lack of resistance to commercial-civic leadership—was regarded as a clear demonstration of the possibilities and advantages of "cooperative effort" toward "common goals." Industrial production rose, efficiency prevailed, and domestic and industrial peace stood in stark contrast to the normal political squabbles, labor discontent, and disagreement over priorities. It was here that the manipulative overtones of urban boosterism, the emphasis on social control in the urban ethos, became most obvious. "The war spirit that is among Memphians," one business writer commented in 1918, "has brought to us forcibly a realization of the imperative necessity of co-ordination, of the real, genuine 'community spirit,' of working together unselfishly for the great cause. So, having felt our power and the good that can be accomplished by such combined effort well directed, I do not believe that when the war shall have ceased. . . . that this spirit will be permitted to die." And the "great cause" following the war would be replaced with the unifying spirit of the urban ethos. "Frivolous and purposeless living" and "unambitious indolence" seemed to vanish under the pressures of domestic mobilization, "and people of all ranks and stations, of all conditions, of wealth and poverty, are working together side by side to carry on this greatest of all world enterprises." [28] This was, precisely, the commercial-civic ideal of

27 *New Orleans Association of Commerce News Bulletin*, II (October 5, 1920), 6; Birmingham *Age-Herald*, December 3, 1920. As George B. Tindall wrote, the term "progress" was, in the South during the 1920s, "more closely associated with the urban middle class, with chambers of commerce and Rotary clubs. It carried the meaning of efficiency and development rather than of reform. . . . The 'progressive' community was the community that had good governments, great churches, improved schools, industry and business, real estate booms. . . . Progressivism in the age of normalcy had become almost synonymous with the Atlanta spirit." See Tindall, "Business Progressivism: Southern Politics in the Twenties," *South Atlantic Quarterly*, LXII (Winter, 1963), 94–96; and his *The Emergence of the New South, 1913–1945* (Baton Rouge, 1967), 233, 254.
28 Robert R. Ellis, "Why I Believe in Memphis," *Memphis Chamber of Commerce Journal*, I (April, 1918), 52; "War's Compensations," *ibid.*, I (September, 1918), 252; "Civic Pride in War Time," *ibid.*, I (March, 1918), 24. (The last article encouraged the assigning of residents to

community—a corporate order with priorities set and direction provided by the commercial-civic elite.

The wartime experience had provided, in the words of the Atlanta *Constitution* in 1920, a most vivid "idea of community service" not soon to be forgotten.[29] Commercial-civic spokesmen largely rejected the idea that basic social and economic divisions had been mitigated only temporarily by the demands of wartime; they seemed to believe that, with sufficiently compelling urban goals, the populace could be similarly united in peacetime for a virtually indefinite period. Such unity was, undoubtedly, especially desired by urban leaders in light of those racial and economic disturbances that wracked many American cities in the immediate aftermath of the war.

The call for social harmony and cooperation was echoed in most urban newspapers and among blacks and labor spokesmen as well as white middle-class entrepreneurs. According to the Norfolk *Journal and Guide,* "There is nothing cooperation cannot accomplish for the community," and the 1923 Labor Day edition of the Memphis *Labor Review* was emblazoned with a slogan stressing the necessity for cooperation between business and labor. William L. Harrison, a labor spokesman on the Birmingham City Commission, declared in 1921: "There is too much selfishness, too much jealousy of the motives of others, too much attention to personal advantage and too little vision of the larger needs of the city. United effort will be to the advantage of all." Whatever its source, cooperation carried increasingly favorable connotations throughout the 1920s and constituted a principal editorial theme in both major and minor urban papers. The good citizen may have been a thorough capitalist and a back-slapping Rotarian, but he was expected, at least by the "community ethic" of the time, to submerge his "personal predilections where the benefit of all is concerned."[30]

"local" units in the military to foster a continued spirit of civic loyalty.) As William Lloyd Warner noted in *The Living and the Dead: A Study of the Symbolic Life of Americans* (New Haven, 1959), 274–75, "It is in time of war," when normal intra-community antagonisms were directed at a common, outside enemy, with all persons in the community sacrificing in pursuit of a common goal, "that the average American living in small cities and towns gets his deepest satisfactions as a member of his society."

29 Atlanta *Constitution,* February 13, 1920.

30 Norfolk *Journal and Guide,* March 5, 1927; Memphis *Labor Review,* September 3, 1923; Birmingham *Age-Herald,* September 20, 1921; Charleston *News and Courier,* October 15, 1920. The concept of social harmony was hardly new to American cities in the twentieth century. As Christopher Tunnard noted in *The Modern American City* (Princeton, 1968), 12, "The concept of the common good is never far away from the American urban mind, a condition that should not seem strange even in the light of much violent and irrational urban

The emphasis on cooperationism also reinforced what is, by any measure, a rather curious phenomenon: the critique of self-interested materialism and "commercialism" by businessmen. "There can be no substantial growth commercially and industrially," the *Commercial-Appeal* warned, "unless back of it is a deep-rooted desire to rise above purely material things." The publicity secretary of the New Orleans Association of Commerce even boasted to Atlanta businessmen that "New Orleans is—thank heavens—one of the few cities in which it is virtually impossible for a man to devote his whole life to sordid commercialism." The profit motive occupied a central place in urban business enterprise, and few businessmen forgot their commitments either to themselves or to their stockholders. But even in a decade in which business activity was looked upon as a high calling, the accepted rhetoric included a heavy emphasis on "public service," "community welfare," and similar phrases and slogans of the corporate community ideal. "A city cannot grow solidly in business," a Memphis writer suggested, "unless there is a corresponding growth in civic consciousness, cultural development and community welfare. A one-sided development can never equal a well-rounded development."[31]

The solution offered for urban fragmentation and conflict was not to lower class barriers, discourage occupational specialization or industrial development, promote pluralistic neighborhoods, or fundamentally rearrange and alter urban institutions. The key to community spirit was not the imposition of common backgrounds and tasks, but the pursuit of large, common goals and priorities on which everyone could presumably agree. And the largest, most noncontroversial goal of all was, of course, the "growth and progress" of the city. The reasoning had come full circle: "growth and progress" could only be achieved with community spirit and civic loyalty, and community

---

history. After all, both religious and nonsectarian groups have sought to build the ideal or communal city in all periods of American life." And the notion had clear antecedents in the South. *Scott's Monthly Magazine* of Atlanta, for example, called in June, 1868, for urban unity in the pursuit of the common good: "The club, the guild, the coterie, the fraternity, the corporation, the church, the State—if, indeed, all these shall not be merged into one full orb of society, normal, organic, adjusted, [they] shall all work together with a harmony consistent with speciality [sic] of purpose and a proper subordination to the good of the whole." Quoted in White, "The Self-Conscious City", 324.

31 Memphis *Commercial-Appeal*, May 13, 1924; Wilson S. Callender, "New Orleans—Where the World Comes to Play," Atlanta *City Builder* (November, 1925), 10; W. C. Headrick, "Memphis: City of Commerce and Industry," *Southern Magazine*, I (June, 1924), 72.

spirit depended on uniting the urban community behind the compelling goal of expansion and city development. Thus, the answer to social and economic fragmentation was "psychological" unity in pursuit of the "common aim" of city growth. Citizens "working in harmony with a common purpose" would give birth to the kind of "solidarity of thought and action" regarded as "among the most important and desirable of community assets." Faith in the city, belief in its destiny, commitment to its growth would, almost by themselves, create the social cement to bind diverse groups together and insure social peace. And the benefits from expansion would accrue to all groups and classes and provide tangible evidence of the wisdom of civic spirit and the efficacy of the urban ethos.[32]

Southern Urban Blacks and the Ideal of Community

White commercial-civic spokesmen talked about the city in relatively comprehensive terms," but their frame of reference—the focus of their attention—was not all-inclusive. Their concerns were centered in the downtown business areas and in the white middle-class sections of the city. When they did focus on lower-class areas—the run-down boarding-house neighborhoods and outlying factory districts—their perspective was shaped by their particular social and economic status. And their interest was largely in those conditions—crime, vagrancy, immorality, and disease—that appeared to threaten the health and stability of the city as a whole.

This was especially apparent in their attitudes toward black neighborhoods. The white commercial-civic ideal of community called upon all citizens—including blacks—to cultivate civic loyalty and support the priorities of growth and stability. But white commercial-civic spokesmen did not regard blacks as equal partners in this enterprise. They believed, in fact, that blacks required special control and guidance. Negro entrepreneurs could promote their business interests, blacks could maintain their own churches, schools, and civic organizations, and develop their own racially separate neighborhoods—but only to the extent that these activities did not imperil the established racial patterns or threaten the interests of the white commercial-civic elite. When blacks were unruly, disorderly, or defiant, the response of

32 "Why Is Atlanta?" Atlanta *City Builder* (December, 1923), 43; Birmingham *Age-Herald*, November 23, 1922.

white authorities was usually swift and often severe. White commercial-civic groups sometimes supported black schools and public health projects, but on the whole black neighborhoods lay within an acute blind spot of the white conception of the urban community—an affliction dictated by age-old racial attitudes.

Southern urban blacks thus found it difficult to wax eloquent on the prosperous and unified metropolitan community envisioned in the white media, largely because they could not participate fully or equally in it. Prevailing white attitudes—and the increasing separation of white and black communities in the late nineteenth and early twentieth centuries— encouraged blacks to concentrate their attention—socially, economically, and conceptually—on their own urban neighborhoods. Most southern black commercial-civic leaders of the 1920s maintained a racially particularistic view of the urban community.[33] But they also shared with their white counterparts notions of social solidarity, community consciousness, civic pride, business middle-class leadership, and urban growth and prosperity that were consistently emphasized in the major urban Negro newspapers of the 1920s.

The patterns of black ideology and leadership in southern cities during the 1920s are extremely complex, and cannot be treated adequately here. Southern urban Negroes engaged in a variety of social and economic activities, including those of traditional religious organizations, small and large businesses, social service agencies, and groups like the newly formed Urban League; and they held a variety of political opinions, from those of the National Negro Business League to the National Association for the Advancement of Colored People and Marcus Garvey's Universal Negro Improvement Association. Our attention will be directed almost solely to the largely business and professionally oriented black elite, which tended to sympathize with the ideas of self-help, racial solidarity, economic chauvinism, and bourgeois economic nationalism as Booker T. Washington

33 Southern urban black spokesmen seemed especially interested in the activities in Negro communities in other cities. News of such activities was frequently carried in regular features in the black press entitled "Chicago Notes" or "Baltimore Notes," etc. Blacks apparently felt an ever greater sense of identity and kinship with other urban communities—especially those outside the region—than did whites, which undoubtedly contributed a fairly high level of urban consciousness among black spokesmen in southern cities. Though this black urban awareness may have been more inclusive in a spatial sense, however, it was nevertheless racially particularistic on the whole.

had expressed them, and as they were enunciated by the National Negro Business League.[34] If members of the Negro commercial-civic elite were not the only leaders in southern black communities, they were certainly the most influential ones, especially in an economic sense.

Commercial-civic spokesmen—black and white—tended to view the city as an arena for commercial enterprise and business opportunity. Nashville's growing black sections offered, as the *Globe* observed in 1911, "exceptional opportunities for the Negroes who are commercially inclined to do business." Black writers constantly extolled "the fire of enthusiasm, cooperation, go-get-it, faith to do or die that beget appreciable business progress." The collapse of a large or promising black business, such as the Standard Life Insurance Company of Atlanta in 1924, was considered a major economic and psychological blow to the entire black urban population.[35]

This type of economic chauvinism was—like the notions of self-help and racial solidarity—a century-old theme. And black ideals of community were shaped not only by desires for growth, material progress, and order, but also by the exclusion of Negroes from many aspects of the larger, white-dominated culture and by the racial consciousness that had always been rooted in most black urban settlements. What gave these themes a particular cogency for southern Negro commercial-civic leaders during the 1920s, perhaps, were the heralded economic opportunities of the "business decade" and the continuing adjustments of Negro neighborhoods to the growth and flux of the first years of the century.

The principal need in the eyes of most Negro commercial-civic spokesmen was the creation of stability and prosperity in black communities through black control of their own institutions. Their notions of urban community were therefore focused fairly precisely, and most Negro leaders found a significant outlet for their energies in the commercial and noncommercial affairs of their own neighborhoods. In Atlanta alone, for example, the Neighborhood Union, organized on the model of the settlement house in 1908 by Mrs. John Hope, wife of the president of Atlanta University,

34 I am indebted for the term "bourgeois economic nationalism" to John H. Bracey, Jr., August Meier, and Elliott Rudwick, (eds.), *Black Nationalism in America* (Indianapolis and New York, 1970), 235–45, xxvii–xxviii. As they observe, the idea that blacks should support black business enterprises was "not inherently part of an accommodating philosophy" and was "very marked in the militant decade of the 1920s."

35 Nashville *Globe*, August 4, 1911; Norfolk *Journal and Guide*, August 16, 1924; Ridgely Torrence, *The Story of John Hope* (New York, 1948), 248–49.

sponsored a variety of civic activities, including investigations of sanitary conditions in stores and meat markets, neighborhood "clean-up" campaigns, demands on city government for additional services, and general social work. The main emphasis was on "home improvement and the development of community spirit on each block" throughout the city's black sections. The appearance of the Atlanta Urban League in 1919 increased the services available to Negroes—from improved nursing care to vocational training— and its work was characterized by the *Independent* as "phenomenal." In addition, scores of church groups and women's clubs sought to improve the conditions in black neighborhoods and doubtless also increased the degree of urban and racial consciousness in the process.[36]

The growth and rising prosperity of the urban black community was a source of considerable satisfaction to many in the black elite. Even with the disadvantages attendant to southern racial policy, the tangible advances made by Negroes in business, housing, and self-awareness were encouraging. "When I walk over Atlanta and see the different stores and nice office buildings built and operated by colored people, it makes my heart rejoice," a regular columnist for the *Independent* wrote in 1921. "When I came here fifty-four years ago there was not a decent colored house in Atlanta of any kind, but thank God, I have lived long enough to see my people in the city living in homes as magnificent as [those of] any race." Similarly, James C. Napier could marvel at the "progress" and business growth in Chattanooga's black sections. Through hard work, thrift, social peace, and civic conscious- ness these achievements could be consolidated and greater development begun. The Norfolk *Journal and Guide* expressed a consistent theme in much of the black press, encouraging its readers to "continue the industrious and thrifty life . . . the pathways of which lead constantly to the home, the work place, the church and the savings banks."[37]

Most southern black papers decried factionalism, and called for a new

36 Anne Lavinia Branch, "Atlanta and the American Settlement House Movement" (M.A. thesis, Emory University, 1966), 58–60; Louis Delphia Shivery, "History of Organized Social Work Among Atlanta Negroes, 1890–1935" (M.A. thesis, Atlanta University, 1936), 40–42, 204; Atlanta *Independent*, February 7; 1924, April 21, 1921, October 23, 1924, December 15, 1921.
37 Atlanta *Idependent*, December 22, 1921; James Carroll Napier, "Presidential Address" to the annual meeting of the National Negro Business League in Chattanooga, Tennessee, August, 1917 (Typescript in James Carroll Napier Papers, Special Collections, Fisk University), 1; Norfolk *Journal and Guide*, January 1, 1921.

unity of purpose among Negroes. "Our numbers... are sufficient," the *Journal and Guide* advised in 1927, "if imbued with a civic consciousness and a sane group consciousness to bring us almost unimaginable advantages." In the same fashion, the Nashville *Globe* had asked in 1913 "that Negroes who have the welfare of the race at heart should get together, lay aside all selfish ambition and work for the general good of the people." A fundamental prerequisite for the creation of civic spirit and the laying aside of assorted jealousies and disagreements was the achievement of social peace. The Richmond *Planet*, for example, praised both the NAACP and Garvey's UNIA for their contributions to racial consciousness but lamented the almost incessant controversy between them. More important than the substantive issues of this disagreement, in the editors' view, was the advent of racial solidarity that would pave the way for progress. Thus, they appealed for an end to the conflict "to permit those of us, who are dying to do business in a business way, [to] live in peace."[38] The black commercial-civic ideal of urban community was quite similar in some respects to that put forth in the white media: stable, orderly, prosperous, expanding, and unified in thought and action on basic community priorities set, preferably, by the black commercial-civic elite.

For middle- and upper-class blacks, however, this community ideal was always infused with a painful awareness of social injustice, racial discrimination, and economic oppression. Many black commercial-civic spokesmen largely accepted the notion, or at least the reality, of racial segregation and the development of a separate black community, but the great majority also protested vigorously and angrily against racial segregation in public facilities, the job ceiling, and poor Negro schools and health care. Aside from lynching (which was most prevalent in smaller towns and rural areas), the inequitable distribution of municipal services—streets, sewers, street lights, law enforcement, and transportation—was the subject of perhaps the greatest black discontent in southern cities during the 1920s. When city officials stated that

38 Norfolk *Journal and Guide*, January 1, 1927; Nashville *Globe*, June 6, 1913; Richmond *Planet*, March 29, 1924. Among the projects proposed by the editors of the *Globe* were the creation of a Negro "civic center" in Nashville (January 10, 1913), and the removal of "slum" areas in black sections along the lines of later urban renewal projects. "Black Bottom has been an eyesore to this city for many years," the paper commented (September 2, 1910), "and the only hope of redemption is to wipe it out, and build where now stand numerous old, delapidated buildings, occupied by people who have no regard for themselves or respect for other people, a beautiful park."

services were allocated on the basis of property-tax contributions, black leaders could only respond, as did the Richmond *Planet* in 1928, that "Negroes constitute the laboring class of this community and add more to the wealth of this municipality than the official records show." [39]

Black commercial-civic leaders were also disheartened when denied a role in city-wide efforts to encourage trade or development. Black entrepreneurs were barred from participating in a "Made in Richmond" exposition in 1922 to promote the city's products, and the *Planet* termed this, with some understatement, a "thoughtless oversight." The *Independent* refused full support of Atlanta's million-dollar national advertising campaign because it thoroughly ignored black community aspirations for population growth and economic advancement: "how can we enter heartily into the movement," the editors asked, "when the million dollars are spent among white folks only, and the invitation extended through advertisements are [sic] to white people only [?]" Given this white insensitivity to Negro problems, the *Independent* angrily denounced the Atlanta spirit as only so much "soft soap and blah": "When Atlanta boasts, all the braggadocio west of the Mississippi assembled into one vast and airy mass would be as a mole hill in comparison." [40]

Mixed with these protests, however, was a full measure of urban boosting. The *Planet* encouraged Richmond blacks to become "'boosters' for home people, for home institutions, and for home enterprises." For the *Journal and Guide*, "Boost Norfolk late and early must be the sign by which we conquer." The Nashville *Globe*, "first of all things," the editors explained in 1908, "is a 'Booster.' We want to make of every Negro in Davidson County a 'Booster' of Greater Nashville and its Negro enterprises. . . . We believe this city to be one of the best in the country for any live, energetic man." The *Independent*, at other times contemptuous of hypocritical braggadocio, announced in 1921 that "when the Atlanta spirit is aroused, no obstacles or difficulties can stand in her way." [41] Even when municipal projects were initiated with little attention to black needs, most Negro publications adopted many of the slogans advocated in the white media and offered their support out of "civic

39 Richmond *Planet*, April 14, 1928.
40 Richmond *Planet*, February 25, 1922; Atlanta *Independent*, December 16, November 27, 1926.
41 Richmond *Planet*, December 24, 1921; Norfolk *Journal and Guide*, February 18, 1922; Nashville *Globe*, September 4, 1908; Atlanta *Independent*, March 3, 1921.

spirit" and the realization that blacks stood to derive some benefit—if only marginal—from general urban improvement.

The cooperationist ideal was most frequently advanced by black commercial-civic leaders with reference to their own communities, but it was also employed as part of an effort to demonstrate the essential interdependency of black and white sections of the city—a theme noticeably absent from the white commercial-civic ideal of urban community. Southern Negro publications thus called attention to the fact that blacks were very much a part of the whole metropolis, important to its growth and interested in its progress. The *Journal and Guide* characterized Norfolk's blacks as "forming an integral part of our citizenship, realizing at all times that what is good for the whole is in like manner good for all of its parts." "The interests of our group," the editors wrote on another occasion, "are so wrapped up in Norfolk and its well being as to be inseparable from the interests of other groups." [42]

Significantly, cooperation between blacks and whites in the city was often couched in terms of a distinct class analysis. The *Planet* expressed a fairly common viewpoint in the black press by suggesting that genuine cooperation was possible only between the "better" classes in both the black and white populations. The "better" class of white people, according to this analysis, descended from the benevolent plantation owners of antebellum times, while those who resisted black improvement resembled plantation overseers and "poor whites." The Ku Klux Klan and similar groups were destructive primarily because they tended "to disturb the bond of friendship that now exists between white and colored people in this... community." If class distinctions were preserved among both whites and blacks, racial distinctions would be eased, and a union would then become possible between the two populations in terms of their ultimate urban goals. [43]

Most black commercial-civic spokesmen, like their white counterparts,

---

42 Norfolk *Journal and Guide*, September 1, 1923, February 18, 1922.
43 Richmond *Planet*, April 21, April 28, May 24, 1923, September 25, July 17, 1920; Norfolk *Journal and Guide*, March 22, 1924. Many black writers also desired to improve the local reputation for harmonious race relations. The *Journal and Guide* contended (January 12, 1929) that a minor racial disturbance in the city in 1919 had been played up by the northern press, whereas in reality amicable race relations were preserved in Norfolk through "the will and the wisdom of leaders of both races to confer and cooperate for the common good." Similarly, Nashville editors asked their readers (August 7, 1908) to join "with the Globe in presenting the bright side of the race question in our home city to the whole world."

saw no necessary contradiction between psychological solidarity and a maintenance of socioeconomic class barriers. In any event, the "best" people—*i.e.*, those members of the business and the professionally oriented elite in both the white and black sections of the city—did share much the same social and economic ethic and many conceptions of the urban community. But for blacks the ideal urban community was one based on social justice without racial barriers and with full opportunity for the expression of black cultural and economic aspirations. As the *Independent* said of Atlanta: "Let us build the greatest city in the south where race relations are most cordial and employment most abundant for every man who is willing to work; where the enforcement of all laws is the slogan of every citizen without regard to race, color or previous condition of servitude." And the editors declared full support for the city's goal of 500,000 population by 1930.[44]

Not surprisingly, black commercial-civic spokesmen were somewhat ambivalent in their conceptions of the urban community—an ambivalence born of their position as participants in the larger patterns of southern urban life whose activities and aspirations were constricted by white racial repression and exclusiveness. Racial loyalty and civic patriotism were not, however, mutually exclusive: racial and civic consciousness were generally joined in a concern for the development of the local black community, and in this context black leaders attempted to make some contribution to the larger urban society. By concentrating on improving conditions in their own sections of the city, blacks would contribute to the growth and progress of the metropolis. The first necessity of social unity, according to the *Independent*, was "to develop a consciousness of kind" within various social groups, and this would be followed, the editors believed, by an adjustment of these groups to one another within the city as a whole.[45]

The key to such city-wide interracial solidarity was, for many Negro writers, cooperation between the commercial-civic elite in both black and white communities, an alliance of the "better" people of both races in pursuit of common objectives. For others, it was enough just to be rid of institutional discrimination, so that blacks could make their own way. What the black commercial-civic elite seemed to desire, in either case, was an urban

44 Atlanta *Independent*, March 6, 1920.
45 *Ibid.*, December 6, 1923.

community characterized by cooperation, unity, stability, material progress, and growth. But no matter how much they shared in these elements of the white commercial-civic community ideal—and the similarities here are often striking—they steadfastly opposed those means of social control which whites directed at the black population on racial grounds. And their allegiance to the ideal was always qualified by their sense that, somehow, they had been terribly wronged by it.

The Corporate-Expansive City

The city which lay at the heart of the southern urban ethos was essentially corporate in form. It was envisioned as "an organized corporation" composed of many distinct elements, which "fulfills its functions only when its organization is harmoniously developed, the all essential element being that of harmony."[46] It was thoroughly committed, at the same time, to growth and expansion.

The kind of urban community that most commercial-civic spokesmen sought, in other words, was *corporate-expansive*, unified in spirit, harmonious in social and economic relations, and capable of almost infinite growth. It was rarely drawn in comprehensive terms during the decade, but it was nowhere better portrayed in all its typical dimensions than in an advertisement sponsored by twenty-nine Knoxville businesses in the *Journal and Tribune* in 1920:

Can you visualize Knoxville with neighborly houses following one another closely until they press upon the ridges to the north and east, can you see an expansion far into the country on the west; can you see that beautiful country south of the Tennessee river built up into a closely knit community?

Can you see hundreds of new factories operating at capacity in Knoxville?

. . . .

Can you see the streets of Knoxville thronged all day by men and women and children whose faces reflect prosperity and contentment, which indicate universal enjoyment of these blessings by all within the boundaries of this city?

. . . .

We must have faith in our city, we must work together for the common good, each of us giving a little time and a little effort.[47]

46 Felix Z. Wilson, "Our City," *Nashville Review*, III (September 15, 1921), 2.
47 Knoxville *Journal and Tribune*, March 1, 1920.

Such a goal was not unworthy of an idealist or utopian philosopher; a goal sufficiently compelling, it was thought, in its material and social promise, to gain the allegiance of all groups in the city. In this sense, the urban ethos not only portrayed the city as an entity clearly distinct from agricultural areas and small towns, confronted with an array of uniquely urban problems and challenges, inherently dynamic and expansive, and essentially corporate in form—it also posited an ideal, yet ultimately attainable, metropolis that was orderly, growing, smoothly functioning, anabatic, and prosperous. The urban ethos thus synthesized—or attempted to synthesize—growth and stability, complexity and neighborliness, industrialism and contentment, expansion and a sense of community. Here the theories of growth and progress, civic patriotism, and urban community came together in a vision of a city almost limitless in potential extent, expanding in territory and increasing in population, yet still a "closely knit community" through the widespread commitment to its own realization.

The urban ethos promised an efficient and unified city without fundamental socioeconomic reorganization. It assumed that social, economic, ethnic, and ideological divisions in the city could be meliorated by an expanding awareness of urban interdependence, by a revivification of local loyalties and a deference to business middle-class leadership. It proposed a sort of "virtual representation" for the urban masses, whereby the best interests of the entire city population would be protected and advanced within the existing social and economic framework by those with vested interests in the city. And it emphasized responsibility and citizenship for members of the white middle and upper classes, and social control for blacks and lower-class whites. Conflict in the city would not, then, be exacerbated by growth; rather, expansion and its benefits would serve to unite urban interests behind commercial-civic priorities and preserve the dominance of the commercial-civic elite. Business middle-class spokesmen therefore sought to promote a city-wide allegiance to their concept of the community by constantly emphasizing various aspects of the urban ethos and by calling for harmony and consensus.[48]

48 The call for urban unity has apparently always been a common theme in the city press. The Lynds noted in *Middletown in Transition*, 445, the tendency of Muncie newspapers to "minimize differences in their effort to spread the idea that the community was just a big happy family." Similarly, William Lloyd Warner and Morris Janowitz both recognized the "integrative symbols" and "emphasis on common values" in the community press. See

The urban ethos appears, at first glance, as a historical curiosity. Business and civic spokesmen continually and insistently called for unity, stability, expansion, and progress during the very decade when commercial-civic leadership seemed most secure, when voices of opposition to the established order were frail and hesitant, when rising prosperity, technological innovation, and economic opportunity promised, more than ever before, a fulfillment of the American Dream. Certainly, the possibility that the masses would increasingly share in material prosperity seemed very real, even to many of those on the farms and in the factories who could not yet point to any relative improvement of their condition. These illusions would, of course, be shattered in the Depression; but during the 1920s the established order seemed capable of meeting, in the near future if not in the present, the most important social and economic needs.

A labor periodical might occasionally hail the benefits of the Single Tax, a black paper might protest racial injustice, and members of the urban elite could, and did, disagree from time to time on specific municipal projects. But these were hardly serious threats to the principal tenets of the urban ethos or to the commercial-civic elite, especially since even these few dissenting voices were generally also raised in support of urban expansion, stability, and material progress. This apparent inconsistency cannot be explained by reference to any significant challenges to business middle-class goals in southern cities during the 1920s, for such challenges simply did not exist. The motives behind the urban ethos may remain forever obscure, but they most likely arose not out of class conflict or political struggle but out of a more general and pervasive apprehension that the process of twentieth-century urbanization, and the changes it entailed, threatened to undermine the legitimacy, stability, and socioeconomic order of the city itself.

Warner, *The Living and the Dead*, 231; and Janowitz, *The Community Press in an Urban Setting: The Social Elements of Urbanism* (2nd ed.; Chicago, 1967), 60. Anselm Strauss, *Images of the American City*, 148, also suggested that perhaps "the most widely appealing urban symbols abroad in a given city must function to bridge the gap among the many different populations, thus to give some appearance of homogeneity to these populations and some feeling that everyone has a share in the city, a common residence, and a more or less common history."

VI The Urban Ethos and Municipal Policy

A plan is only a means to an end, and that end is a stable and well-balanced physical structure so designed as to secure health, safety, amenity, order and convenience, and, generally, to promote human welfare.

—Thomas Adams, *Outline of Town and City Planning* (1935)

The phenomenal growth and expansion taking place in Memphis demanded the services of a body of public spirited men to plan for the future, and correct present defects in our past growth.

—*Memphis Chamber of Commerce Journal* (1922)

MUNICIPAL improvements were invariably enumerated in chamber of commerce advertising, like the features of automobiles or radios. Commercial-civic leaders pointed to the tangible economic values of street paving, education, recreation, law enforcement, and transportation—for such things attracted new business and additional customers. The expansion and improvement of urban institutions and services were also necessary, they believed, to meet the demands of growth and to enable the city to absorb new populations and business enterprises without upheavals in its social and economic structure. Members of the commercial-civic elite supported improvements and institutional adjustments which tended to fulfill the goals of the urban ethos—control of the city's population, the inculcation of "proper" notions of citizenship, the protection of life and property (especially in the downtown and white middle- and upper-class sections), and continued city expansion, both geographic and economic.

The commercial-civic elite, especially as it was organized in chambers of commerce and civic associations, has been acknowledged by historians as the single most influential group in formulating municipal policy in southern

157

cities during the 1920s. Members of this group disagreed on specific aspects of particular policies and on the precise arrangement of urban priorities, and they were by no means all-powerful. But behind the priorities of municipal budgets, the attempts to deal with problems of air pollution, housing, and welfare, and the efforts to preserve order among the lower classes lay a clear pattern of commercial-civic goals and values. These policies were, after all, some of the specific responses by urban elites to the problems of the deteriorating urban environment and the potentially disorderly, wayward population. Particularly revealing of commercial-civic concerns in this period were policies relating to urban transportation, to the challenges and dilemmas posed by the automobile. And the movement for comprehensive city planning in the major regional cities in the 1920s was a direct product of the commercial-civic elite and represented what was thought at the time to be the ultimate solution to the problems of the modern metropolis and the fulfillment of the urban ethos.

In retrospect, the policies adopted during the period to overcome urban difficulties appear barely adequate if not wholly ineffective. Compared with large cities elsewhere in the country, some southern municipalities exhibited low rates of taxation and bonded indebtedness, left many needs of the population—such as housing and aid to the poor—for private agencies to fill, and failed to give adequate authority to those charged with abating air pollution or regularizing the physical arrangement of the metropolis. The commercial-civic elite—no matter how much they talked about the interdependence and collectivism of urban society, no matter how much they sought more effective means of social control and increased the powers of local governments—were hesitant to abandon the principle and habit of voluntarism. Yet this was the pattern which prevailed in the great majority of American urban areas in the 1920s. Judged by the standards of the time, rather than by those of a half-century later, southern urban policies constituted real efforts to deal with city problems and especially mirrored the fears, prejudices, and aspirations of the commercial-civic elite.

The Priorities of Urban Policy: Growth and Social Control

Commercial-civic leaders called constantly for improved and expanded municipal facilities—schools, streets, water works, street lighting, sewers—

which would be adequate for both present and future needs and draw new citizens and business to the city. Facilities and services were the tangible signs of vital, "progressive" cities and of active, enlightened civic leadership. The lights which brilliantly illuminated the "great white ways" of downtown business districts were not only impediments to petty street crime but symbols of urban wealth, power, and superiority.

To a considerable degree, commercial and civic groups were able to achieve public support for expanded city facilities in a series of bond issues enacted in virtually all regional urban centers during the decade. Their efforts were not, however, always successful: some bond issues were defeated (though they were usually revised, reintroduced, and eventually passed), and southern urban electorates maintained a stubborn resistance to increased taxes, especially for civic centers, auditoriums, airports, and some park projects which were often considered mere amenities for the upper classes. Even with this kind of potential resistance, though, southern cities acted to provide more adequate municipal facilities and services through increased urban expenditures.

Per capita municipal spending increased substantially in most major southern cities during the 1920s and almost doubled in New Orleans and Birmingham between 1921 and 1928. In an era when private enterprise and an ever-expanding economy were rarely questioned as the surest means to social progress, rising municipal expenditures revealed a growing commitment to the solution of many urban ills through the agencies of government, and the joining of public and private interests under commercial-civic auspices as suggested in the corporate community ideal. Municipal budgets emphasized education, the protection of life and property (at least for the white middle and upper classes), and law enforcement—to the extent that most southern cities devoted more than half of their financial resources to schools, police forces, and fire departments. Sanitation, health, streets, recreation, and charities received smaller portions of city funds, though the appropriations in these categories were thought to be generally adequate to meet the needs of growth. So also with efforts to cope with air pollution, which were regarded in their time as progressive steps to insure a better quality of urban environment.

The major item in all southern city budgets was public education, which ranged from 26.3 percent of all municipal outlays in New Orleans in 1928 to

43.8 percent of those in Birmingham.[1] A considerable financial commitment was obviously required in a region where public education had been virtually nonexistent through most of the nineteenth century, and national urban standards demanded respectable school systems. Education was regarded as a significant pathway of upward mobility, a prime attraction for new citizens and industry, and an effective means of imparting useful skills in a technologically oriented urban society. For members of the commercial-civic elite, it was also a bulwark of urban stability.

From the earliest beginnings of American public education, schools were viewed not simply as repositories of truth or knowledge but as fundamental training grounds for "responsible" citizenship—and this conception clearly dominated the thinking of the southern urban commercial-civic elite.[2] Students learned the rules and expectations of the community as well as rudimentary language and mathematical skills. Pamphlets and text materials stressed local patriotism, the ideals of good citizenship, and the values of urban order and growth. Students in elementary and secondary schools recited facts and figures of city population, industry, and trade and learned the names of notable urban pioneers. The city was presented to its youth as essentially unified, with little attention to class or ethnic diversity. Thus, education was viewed both as a source of individual opportunity and an additional guarantee of community stability, and it apparently enjoyed the support of virtually every group and class in the southern urban population.

Second only to education in the allocation of city funds was the general category of protection of life and property—the combined outlays for police and fire departments. Downtown merchants were especially vocal in demanding fire protection for the rich central business districts, and commercial-civic spokesmen in general demanded strict law enforcement to prevent burglaries and street crime and preserve order among the less "responsible" of the city's

1 Unless otherwise noted, all statistics on municipal budgets are taken from the U.S. Bureau of the Census, *Financial Statistics of Cities Having a Population of Over 30,000: 1921* (Washington, 1922), 96–99, and U.S. Bureau of the Census, *Financial Statistics of Cities Having a Population of Over 30,000: 1928* (Washington, 1931), 325–27, 333–35. One reason for the relatively low percentage of funds expended for education in New Orleans was, undoubtedly, the prevalence of Roman Catholic parochial schools in the Crescent City.
2 For a brief, perceptive analysis of early American public education as an attempt by urban elites "to secure social order in a disorderly age," see Stanley K. Schultz, "Breaking the Chains of Poverty: Public Education in Boston, 1800–1860," in Kenneth T. Jackson and Stanley K. Shultz (eds.), *Cities in American History* (New York, 1972), 306–23.

residents. The expenditures for fire departments rose in every southern city during the decade and even exceeded the outlays for police forces in New Orleans in 1921 and in Birmingham, Memphis, Nashville, and Knoxville in both 1921 and 1928. By the latter date, combined expenditures for police and fire protection ranged from 15.9 percent of the budget in New Orleans to 26.2 percent in Nashville and 27.5 percent in Charleston.

Municipal police departments found it particularly difficult to keep pace with the rising demands of city expansion, especially automobile traffic control, and with the expectations of commercial and civic groups. Atlanta's police chief complained in 1928 that his force was woefully undermanned, with a ratio of one department employee (including clerical workers) to 761 citizens—as compared with ratios of 1 to 363 in Boston, 1 to 367 in New York, and 1 to 690 in Chicago. But the Georgia metropolis almost doubled police appropriations between 1920 and 1930, from $468,900 to $903,525 annually, and some regional city budgets accorded a priority to law enforcement second only to that for education.[3] Actual expenditures for police departments nearly doubled in Atlanta, Birmingham, and New Orleans and declined only in Memphis. By 1928 outlays for law enforcement amounted to 14.5 percent of the city budget in Charleston, 12.8 percent in Nashville, 11.7 percent in Atlanta, 10.5 percent in Birmingham, 9.5 percent in Memphis and Knoxville, and 8.7 percent in New Orleans.

Street construction and improvements consumed significant portions of city funds, from 7.9 percent in Charleston to 18.2 percent in Memphis in 1921. Though these percentages generally dropped in later years, additional state funds for roads became available. Expenditures for health and sanitation increased in most cities during the decade, accounting for 9.3 percent of the overall budget in Birmingham in 1928, and for 9.6 percent in Nashville, 9.9 percent in Knoxville, 10.3 percent in New Orleans, 10.9 percent in Atlanta, 11.2 percent in Charleston, and 12.2 percent in Memphis. Almost all regional cities increased their per capita outlays for hospitals, charities, and corrections during the period from 1921 to 1928, though such increases were generally meager and occasionally constituted an actual decline in their percentage of the overall municipal budget. Birmingham alone among major southern urban centers experienced a decrease in such expenditures, from an

3 *Annual Report of the Chief of Police of the City of Atlanta* (Atlanta, 1928), 7–8; *Annual Report of the Chief of Police of the City of Atlanta* (Atlanta, 1930), 40.

already low twenty-five cents per capita to twenty cents. Actual outlays in Atlanta rose by about a third, while Memphis and Nashville increased their expenditures by about 20 to 25 percent.

The need for parks and recreational areas, partly to turn the energies of youth into constructive and orderly channels and partly to relieve the tensions of urban overcrowding, also received attention during the period. Actual expenditures increased in all large regional cities for recreation, though these accounted in most cases for no more than 4 percent of overall municipal budgets. Birmingham more than doubled its spending in this category between 1921 and 1928, and Atlanta and New Orleans approximately doubled their appropriations in the same period. Nashville and Memphis devoted 7.2 and 7.1 percent, respectively, of their total budgets to parks and recreation in 1921, but actual outlays declined later in the decade. And in all southern cities, commercial-civic spokesmen pointed to the recreational possibilities in surrounding suburbs and rural hinterlands.

Several initial efforts were made during and just prior to the 1920s to contend with problems of air pollution. Nashville passed ordinances in 1912 and 1914 creating a Smoke Abatement Commission and appointing a Smoke Inspector. By 1917 Birmingham had a fairly elaborate ordinance on the books which officially prohibited the emission of "black smoke" by any train or factory except for a short period each day. The ordinance provided for a city smoke inspector, a regulatory commission of three mechanical engineers, and a set of standards to measure air pollution. Atlanta enacted a smoke abatement law aimed especially at locomotives (and exempting private homes); and Memphis passed similar legislation in February, 1923, and created a City Smoke Commission and appointed a Smoke Prevention Marshall in October, 1925.[4]

Measures to regulate air pollution might well have disrupted commercial groups by setting the downtown merchants who complained of air pollution against the manufacturers who contributed to it, except for the fact that those charged with enforcing such statutes usually had no real powers, and some large industries—as in Birmingham— were beyond the jurisdiction of munici-

4 *Digest of the Ordinances and Resolutions of the City of Nashville* (Nashville, 1917), 467–73; *The Code of the City of Birmingham, Alabama* (Birmingham, 1917), 713–16; *The Charter and Ordinances of the City of Atlanta: Code of 1924* (Atlanta, 1924), 554–55; City of Memphis, Board of Commissioners Minutes, Book H, 358, Book I, 593.

pal authorities. (And, in any event, most air pollution at this time was apparently attributable to residential coal furnaces.) The Memphis Chamber of Commerce did oppose an ordinance enacted unanimously by the city's board of commissioners in June, 1926, providing for fines and jail sentences for violators of the smoke statute, on the grounds that such a law would discourage new businesses from locating in the area. But Mayor Rowlett Paine explained that such action was required immediately to control a serious "smoke menace."[5] There is no evidence to indicate that any business was dissuaded from locating in the city, or that any violators were ever fined or sentenced to jail terms.

The urban housing shortage and high rents were perceived as inimical to both city growth and order, but the proposed remedies for these difficulties were decidedly voluntaristic. Commercial-civic bodies issued public appeals for reasonable rents, and some even advocated the creation of municipal mediation boards to encourage the cooperation of local landlords. More drastic action would have run counter to the grain of private capitalism. Efforts to contend with the consequences of housing shortages were similarly restrained. Municipal authorities and chambers of commerce looked to local financial institutions to resolve the crisis by increasing the flow of home mortgage capital, and virtually all spokesmen saw in suburban development a promising means of easing urban tensions. In New Orleans, the housing committee of the civic bureau of the Association of Commerce was instrumental in arranging for an extensive development of new medium-priced housing near the downtown area in 1920. But even this ambitious scheme relied completely on private resources and initiative, and was premised on the widespread belief that individual home buying was the only real solution to the postwar housing shortage.[6]

For dealing with the problems of a wayward urban population, southern cities placed major emphasis on control rather than relief. Only the most destitute of the population were provided the meager public assistance that was available during the decade. In Birmingham and Jefferson County, for example, expenditures for relief (primarily for the maintenance of alms houses) were reported at only $29,563.03 in 1924, though they did rise to $67,497.47 in 1928. Before the crisis of the Depression, most of those on

5 City of Memphis, Board of Commissioners Minutes, Book J, 179.
6 *New Orleans Association of Commerce News Bulletin*, II (August 16, 1920), 3.

public assistance were black (about 90 percent in 1925) in large part because many private assistance agencies refused to take them. At one time the city even abolished the local "welfare department" and appointed a member of the city health department as a special "welfare secretary" to act as liaison with the Community Chest. In Nashville, a provision in the city charter prohibited the municipal government from allocating more then $10,000 annually to the Charities Commission.[7]

The major efforts to provide food, shelter, clothing, and basic subsistence to the urban poor were initiated through private agencies, especially religious organizations and the Community Chests, which consolidated many of the local voluntary charities in cities across the country. Churches offered aid to the unemployed and to struggling families and occasionally joined together in projects to protect young women in the labor force or unfortunate children from the vicissitudes of city life. Chambers of commerce created employment bureaus when the jobless rate mounted, and Memphis even organized a public employment office in July, 1928, at the behest of a number of local civic groups.[8]

Policies concerning public assistance and housing were shaped in part by traditional habits of thought which resisted the full intervention of municipal government into certain areas of city life. Commercial-civic groups tended to regard welfare and public housing as undermining prevailing wage scales and the private construction industry, not to mention moral standards and material ambition. If their ideal of the urban community was corporate, it was also largely voluntaristic. A great deal was written in the public prints during the 1920s on the responsibilities of well-to-do citizens to their less fortunate brethren and of the necessity for aiding the "deserving" poor. But since unemployment and poverty were usually considered mainly the results of moral infirmity, laziness, or social irresponsibility, private charity was believed to be best, particularly in distinguishing between the deserving poor and mere "loafers." For the latter, harassment and arrest would serve well

7 E. M. Henderson. Jr. "Relief in Jefferson County: A Brief Survey" (MS in Birmingham Public Library, 1934), 9–11; Birmingham *Post*, November 23, 1925; *Charter of the City of Nashville* (Nashville, 1923), 25; *Charter of the City of Nashville* (Nashville, 1928), 44.

8 Floyd Hunter, "Community Organization: Lever for Institutional Change?" in Rupert B. Vance and Nicholas J. Demerath (eds.), *The Urban South* (Chapel Hill, 1954), 254; Birmingham *Age-Herald*, April 28, 1920; City of Memphis, Board of Commissioners Minutes, Book K, 433.

enough. Urban stability would be insured neither by allowing large numbers of citizens to exist in a state of poverty and desperation nor by rewarding shiftlessness.

The most obvious means of controlling lower-class elements was strict enforcement of the vagrancy laws. Blacks were, by all indications, the principal victims of such arrests, and—in Birmingham—often found themselves sentenced to convict labor in nearby mines or to street work-gangs. As Carl V. Harris noted, Birmingham whites "believed, first, that the Negro was a useful, indeed necessary, menial laborer; but, second, they regarded him as an irresponsible and unreliable worker; and, third, they considered him menacing, prone to commit crime." Vagrancy laws were "steadily broadened and strengthened" in the Alabama metropolis between 1890 and 1918, and in 1920 city and county officers initiated another effort to round up "every negro loafer, male and female," in the area. In March, 1927, the Birmingham police chief and the Jefferson County sheriff launched what was billed as "the greatest offensive against vagrants in the history of Alabama." The law officers emphasized that all "loiterers" and persons without gainful employment were potential criminals.[9] Such campaigns were recurrent throughout the urban South during the decade and only lapsed when massive numbers of unemployed during the Depression rendered strict enforcement, except with regard to blacks, impossible and politically unwise. In the 1920s, the commercial-civic response to unemployment was partly one of genuine sympathy for innocent victims caught in a temporary recession; but it was characterized to a much greater degree by strictures against idleness and the disorderly tendencies of those removed from the discipline of work.

Arrests for vagrancy were a means of harassment as well as of regulating the urban labor force. More than 7,000 arrests for "loitering" were recorded in Atlanta during the economic setback of 1920–1922. But of these persons only 396 were actually bound over for vagrancy and only 69 were actually

9 Carl V. Harris, "Reforms in Government Control of Negros in Birmingham, Alabama, 1890–1920," *Journal of Southern History*, XXXVIII (November, 1972), 568, 580, 582; Birmingham *News*, December 6, 8, 1920; Birmingham *Age-Herald*, March 2, 1927. Harris' article also contains information on other means by which whites exercised control over the city's black population, such as the regulation of Negro saloons and the county fee system, and a useful analysis of the disagreements within the city's white leadership—and within what I have designated the commercial-civic elite—over the theory and implementation of such policies.

convicted. The total arrests for idleness and loitering in the Georgia metropolis during the decade exceeded 20,000—only 400 of which resulted in convictions. The same was true in Memphis, where some 16,673 cases of vagrancy were brought before the municipal court between 1919 and 1925. Arrests for drunkenness and disorderly conduct also struck hardest at the city's lower classes—probably most severely at blacks—and constituted another means of social control available to municipal authorities. Though Charleston's population declined during the decade, for example, arrests for drunkenness and disorderly conduct while under the influence of alcohol rose from about 400 in 1919 to almost 1,500 in 1929.[10]

The fact that lower-class citizens generally, and blacks in particular, received far less than their share of urban facilities and services merely pointed up the degree to which lower-class groups were *potentially*, rather than actually, disruptive elements of the population during the 1920s. It also reveals the extent to which the commercial-civic elite relied on law enforcement and the public schools as institutional means of social control, rather than on the alleviation of sources of lower-class and black discontent. Urban expansion and its attendant economic growth, according to the urban ethos, would eventually ease the pangs of poverty and unemployment among those who worked hard to help themselves.

Some southern cities were at least partially hampered in their responses to urban problems by relatively low rates of taxation and bonded indebtedness, indicating a lack of necessary public financial resources. In 1925, for example, the final adjusted per capita tax rates for every $1,000 of assessed

10 *Annual Report of the Chief of Police of the City of Atlanta* (1930), 37–38; Andrew A. Bruce and Thomas S. Fitzgerald, "A Study of Crime in the City of Memphis, Tennessee," *Journal of the American Institute of Criminal Law and Criminology*, XIX (August, 1928), 11; *Year Book, City of Charleston: 1929* (Charleston, 1929), 152–53. Comments on police harassment were not usually preserved for the historical record, though virtually every Negro newspaper mentioned it as a source of considerable discontent in black neighborhoods. One of the most interesting observations, from the perspective of a resident of New Orleans' Vieux Carre in 1927, described "utterly outrageous" arrests of the "non-criminal poor" by a "splendidly corrupt" police force. "These cops," Oliver La Farge wrote, "were required to keep their records up by making a certain number of arrests per month, and this they did by picking up anyone who looked like easy game. Because of them all New Orleans dined early, since it was not safe for a coloured maid to walk home after the police began its night prowling." Oliver La Farge, "Completely New," in Etolia S. Basso (ed.), *The World from Jackson Square: A New Orleans Reader* (New York, 1948), 366, 370. As Harris noted, white middle-class elements in Birmingham came to oppose the county fee system because it provided economic incentive for deputies to arrest the "easy game" among the city's lower classes, and thus corrupt law enforcement officers and direct attention away from more serious crime. Carl V. Harris, "Reforms in Government Control of Negroes in Birmingham," 593.

valuation ranged from lows of $14.40 in Birmingham and $17.05 in Atlanta to highs of $30.81 in New Orleans and $31.10 in Charleston. Tax rates in southern cities tended to be lower on the whole than those in many nonregional urban centers. Atlanta and Birmingham also compared very poorly with cities of similar size elsewhere in the country in their rates of bonded indebtedness. But New Orleans placed fourth out of nine cities of its size in the country in per capita net bonded debt in 1925, while Memphis and Knoxville ranked very high nationally in their respective categories.[11] Given the fact that southern cities generally had a far less lucrative tax base to draw upon than many cities in the Northeast and Midwest, these figures suggest a relatively considerable financial commitment to the alleviation of urban problems in the South.

Furthermore, the priorities in southern city budgets were about the same as those in most nonregional urban areas, though actual outlays were often less per capita. The proportions of expenditures for education, recreation, and police and fire protection compared favorably with those in cities like New York and St. Louis and also with the expenditures in municipalities like Youngstown, Ohio, a midwestern city similar in size to Atlanta, Birmingham, and Memphis in this period.

The range of possible motivations for any particular set of urban priorities is, of course, virtually endless, and the justifications for various policies differed somewhat from group to group. The different circumstances in southern cities—the size of the black population, the relative severity of unemployment, the mix of industrial and commercial economies, and the quality of existing facilities and services—suggests that these motivations were hardly uniform throughout the region. Significantly, however, the character and dimensions of municipal policy during the 1920s—whether in Atlanta or New Orleans—corresponded quite closely with the concept of the corporate-expansive city, and clearly reflected the desires of the white commercial-civic elite for urban order, stability, and expansion,

Urban Transportation: An Imperative of Progress

The city was like an organic body, the familiar explanation ran, with muscles of industry, commerce, and labor and a brain of enlightened civic administra-

11 C. E. Rightor, "The Comparative Tax Rates of 215 Cities, 1925," *National Municipal Review*, XIV (December, 1925), 756–59; C. E. Rightor, "The Bonded Debt of 207 Cities as of January 1, 1925," *ibid.*, XIV (June, 1925), 370–71.

tion. And the body required an uncluttered and efficient circulatory system to function properly. Without urban transportation—of goods and people—the urban organism would degenerate and perhaps pass away altogether. Without adequate urban transportation, the city's circulatory system would literally be poisoned and choked by urban growth. This seemed, for members of the commercial-civic elite, to be one of the most important lessons of history, a lesson any city could ignore only at its extreme peril.

The consideration of street improvements, street assessments, highway financing, paving projects, and the extension and widening of roads constituted the single most time-consuming item on the agendas of southern city governments throughout the decade. When traffic regulations and parking provisions were added, the total demands upon the time and resources of urban governments grew to almost overwhelming proportions. The Nashville City Council, for instance, took action on nineteen separate parking ordinances alone between 1921 and 1923. This time and effort was, according to commercial-civic spokesmen, very well spent. Whatever the mode, transportation was to be preserved, promoted, and improved at all costs; for the ideal of the corporate-expansive city was, in many respects, tied to the new technological capacity to unite a potentially fragmented city while concurrently insuring its geographical and population growth.

A major priority of most commercial-civic groups in the urban South in the 1920s was the improvement of city streets. The incoming president of the New Orleans Association of Commerce in 1920, for example, rated street repair as a major goal of his administration.[12] Most commercial, and many civic, bodies maintained special committees concerned with local roads and interurban highways, and downtown merchants constantly demanded that central pathways be cleared for more and more motorcars and greater parking space. At the same time, existing streetcar systems had to be shored up to withstand the threat of declining patronage, because many residents could afford neither a private car nor the generally higher taxi, jitney, and motor-bus fares.

Many cities initiated transportation surveys during the period in an effort to improve the efficiency of streetcar routing, maximize the number of potential customers, and separate trolleys from the main flow of motor traffic. Commercial and civic groups usually banded together in support of streetcar

12 *New Orleans Association of Commerce News Bulletin,* II (January 26, 1920), 1.

fare increases, both to offset new challenges to mass transportation and underwrite new equipment—though they also expressed concern that higher fares would force patrons to experiment with other forms of transportation. In Atlanta and Birmingham, jitneys were removed as a significant source of competition with the street railways, with the full support of local commercial-civic groups. And some spokesmen even suggested similar restrictions on private cars. [13]

City governments responded to the automotive challenge by enacting a wide variety of vehicle regulations, installing traffic signals, increasing the size and technological capacity of police forces, constructing streets and bridges, and initiating studies and surveys to improve traffic circulation. By 1920 the five major southern cities—Atlanta, Birmingham, Memphis, Nashville, and New Orleans—had enacted comprehensive traffic codes providing for motor vehicle speed limits, specific "rules of the road," some parking restrictions on major streets, and a host of other policies calculated to regularize vehicular movement. These codes were revised and expanded in the course of the decade, and by 1930 all five urban centers had designated one-way streets and at least a single "thoroughfare" on which traffic had the right-of-way through the city core. Birmingham's traffic regulations were more or less typical. The new code of 1921 required city driver's licenses (a provision later voided by the state supreme court), imposed a wider range of precise speed limits, established sixty-four "safety zones" to protect streetcar passengers, prohibited parking on at least one side of the most heavily traveled streets and intersections, introduced a one-way street, and designated seven intersections where left turns were prohibited. The provisions were extended by 1930 to include specific parking areas with one-hour and thirty-minute limits, more precise speed regulations, and eight additional one-way streets. [14]

Southern cities also moved early to take advantage of new technology by installing modern control devices. Atlanta and New Orleans provided signal

---

13 See Blaine A. Brownell, "The Notorious Jitney and the Urban Transportation Crisis in Birmingham in the 1920s," *Alabama Review*, XXV (April, 1972), 105–18.

14 *Traffic Code, City of Birmingham, Alabama* (Birmingham, 1921), 10, 40, 19–30, 31–36, 47, 14; *Laws Governing Traffic, As Provided in the Birmingham Code, .1930* (Birmingham, 1930), 25–32, 10–12, 38–39. Also see *The Charter and Ordinances of the City of Atlanta: Code of 1924; Memphis Digest: 1931* (Memphis, 1931), I; "Ordinances Enacted by the City Council, City of Nashville" (Office of the Metropolitan Clerk, Nashville, Tennessee), I, II; Department of Public Safety, City of New Orleans, *Ordinances Concerning Traffic, Corrected to December 1, 1925* (New Orleans, 1925).

lights at the most congested intersections in 1922, and a year later Birmingham established a new traffic-control system composed of a dozen signals coordinated from a central traffic tower. In June, 1926, the Memphis Board of Commissioners approved the purchase of automatic signals, which were installed the following year.[15]

The 1920s was a transitional period during which law enforcement agencies slowly began to close a troublesome gap between their own limited technology and equipment and that available to traffic violators and enterprising law-breakers. The Memphis police department created a bicycle squad in 1908 and purchased its first motor vehicles in 1910—an ambulance and a patrol wagon. New Orleans had a special "auto patrol" in the downtown district as early as 1915. But Nashville did not acquire its first police motorcycles until 1920; Memphis possessed only seven squad cars as late as 1930; and Birmingham persisted in equipping most of its patrolmen with bicycles even late in the decade. Police radios were not pressed into service in most southern cities until the 1930s.[16]

Even with the problems involved in enforcing the traffic ordinances, however, the number of arrests for such violations skyrocketed during the decade. Between 1919 and 1929, arrests for traffic violations rose from a mere 431 in Charleston to 2,309. In Atlanta arrests increased from 3,972 in 1920 to 10,921 in 1929 and 7,413 in 1930. Eventually, most larger regional municipalities were forced to create special traffic courts to relieve the judicial system of its new burdens (such as those formed in New Orleans in 1925 and in Memphis in 1927) and to detail additional men to traffic duty.[17]

Paved streets, ample thoroughfares, adequate downtown parking, efficient traffic control, street safety, and modern streetcar lines were all aspects of that

15 City of Atlanta, "Council Minutes" (Offices of the City Clerk, Atlanta, Georgia), XXVII, 658; Harland Bartholomew to the New Orleans Commission Council, *Official Proceedings of the Commission Council of the City of New Orleans* (City Archives, New Orleans Public Library), October 4, 1927, p. 2; Birmingham *Age-Herald*, October 30, 1923; City of Memphis, Board of Commissioners Minutes, Book J, 175.

16 Memphis Police Department, "History of the Memphis Police Department" (MS in Memphis Public Library, 1964), 5–6; City of New Orleans, *Annual Report of the Police Department* (New Orleans, 1915), 42; *Commissioners' Minutes, City of Nashville* (Office of the Metropolitan Clerk, Nashville, Tennessee), XX, 164, 202; Birmingham *News*, November 16, 1921.

17 *Year Book of Charleston: 1919*, 292–93; *Year Book of Charleston: 1929*, 152–53; *Annual Report of the Chief of Police of the City of Atlanta* (1930), 39; *Official Proceedings of the Commission Council of the City of New Orleans*, September 29, 1925; *Memphis*, II (March 30, 1927), 2.

vision of a united, orderly, prosperous, and expanding city in which suburbs reinforced the commercial strength of the downtown business district and larger populations were absorbed by demographic decentralization and technological efficiency. Commercial-civic spokesmen were not content, however, to tackle the problems of urban transportation piecemeal. They demanded the development and implementation of a coordinated transportation system through comprehensive city planning—a proposed panacea for urban ills that most clearly reflected their desires for social control and most certainly promised the fulfillment of the corporate-expansive urban ideal.

Planning the City Efficient

The first city planning commission in the United States was established in Hartford, Connecticut, in March, 1907. Quickly, cities across the country moved toward planning as a means of alleviating blight, population density, poor transportation, and confusing patterns of land use. By 1915 the comprehensive plan—which took virtually every phase of the city's life into account, including railroads, streets, housing, recreation, subdivisions, buildings, and civic art—had become the fashion. It was not until the 1920s, however, that a significant number of American urban areas contracted for comprehensive plans, and this trend was reflected in the South as it was in other regions of the country.[18]

Most urban leaders thought, as far as we can judge by their public remarks, that it was essential that the forces which were both so promising and troubling during the decade—population immigration, technological innovation, and larger and more complex industrial and commercial enterprises—be somehow correlated, controlled, and directed. Comprehensive city planning was an obvious response to such concerns, a nostrum which seemed to herald an orderly evolution for the sprawling twentieth-century metropolis.

18 The best overall survey of modern city planning in the United States is Mel Scott, *American City Planning, Since 1890* (Berkeley and Los Angeles, 1969). See, especially, Chapters 3 and 4. An excellent brief overview is John L. Hancock, "Planners in the Changing American City, 1900–1940," *Journal of the American Institute of Planners,* XXXIII (September, 1967), 290–304. The eleven former Confederate states contained 71 of the 786 official planning commissions reported by the U.S. Department of Commerce in 1930. Some thirty-six towns and cities in the South had enacted zoning ordinances by the end of the 1920s. See Lester G. Chase (comp.), *A Tabulation of City Planning Commissions in the United States* (Washington, 1931), 1–2, 7–39.

The influence of commercial-civic groups in promoting city manager and city commission forms of muncipal government in the early twentieth century—as a means of consolidating their own social, economic, and political power and insuring efficient municipal administration on business principles—is well known.[19] But such groups were perhaps even more prominent and influential in the early attempts to solve urban ills and direct future growth through systematic, comprehensive city planning. In every major southern city, commercial-civic organizations—especially chambers of commerce and real estate boards—were in the forefront of the planning movement, impressing it with their values, goals, and motives, and providing in most cases its earliest talent and resources. City planning, more than other municipal efforts and policies, was regarded by the commercial-civic elite as the premier means of fulfilling the promises of the corporate-expansive ideal, of implementing the urban ethos.

In North Carolina, for example, local chambers of commerce, with the assistance and support of other civic groups, spearheaded the state's planning movement in the period just before and during World War I. An earlier emphasis on the "city beautiful," stressed by local women's clubs and focusing on civic art, architecture, and amenities, was rapidly replaced by a concern for the "city efficient," for functionalism rather than aesthetics. In January, 1919, the general assembly passed legislation enabling North Carolina municipalities to establish official planning bodies. Of the twelve towns and cities which formed planning commissions in the state during the 1920s, local chambers of commerce were, according to one authority, extremely influential in at least seven. And members of the commercial-civic elite were prominent in virtually every city planning effort in the state.[20]

City planning committees appeared in Atlanta and Memphis in 1920 and in Nashville a year later. In some cases, mayors appointed advisory bodies even before they received legislative approval. Thus, the first "official" commission in Nashville was not established until 1925. Knoxville and New Orleans created authorized planning commissions in 1923, and the Crescent City committee was reorganized in 1927. Charleston established a city

19 See especially James Weinstein, "Organized Business and the Commission and Manager Movements," *Journal of Southern History,* XXVIII (May, 1962), 166–82; and Samuel P. Hays, "The Politics of Reform in Municipal Government in the Progressive Era," *Pacific Northwest Quarterly,* LV (October, 1946), 157–69.
20 Kay Haire Huggins, "City Planning in North Carolina, 1900–1929," *North Carolina Historial Review,* XLVI (Autumn, 1969), 389–90, 392–93.

planning and zoning commission in 1929. Though Birmingham failed to initiate a comprehensive urban plan during the decade, the city did create a zoning board and adopt a traffic plan recommended by an outside consultant in 1927. In all cases, the predominance of the local commercial-civic elite in city planning was evident from the beginning.

In November, 1925, at a meeting of the Nashville Exchange Club, "Colonel" Luke Lea, owner of the *Tennessean*, and representatives of the Chamber of Commerce and other civic bodies formally suggested the formation of an official planning commission. Lea further recommended that the commission be composed of noted civic leaders. The long-standing interest of local commercial-civic groups in city planning was culminated in August with the appointment of two commissions by the City Council, one for city planning and one for zoning.[21]

In Knoxville, interest in the movement was aroused by the board of commerce, which sponsored a 125-member committee on city plans that brought in outside speakers and publicized the need for systematic planning. These efforts resulted in the formation of the first local planning body in 1923 and in a comprehensive plan completed in 1929 by the noted St. Louis planning consultant, Harland Bartholomew.[22]

Formal attempts at city planning began in Atlanta under the auspices of the Chamber of Commerce in 1909. With the city's real estate board, the chamber organized a joint committee on civic improvement which solicited plans to renovate the city. The chamber and the city council sought legislative approval in 1912 for a proposal by Haralson Bleckley, a local architect, to construct a civic center and plaza of shops, hotels, and office buildings over the maze of railroad tracks which frustrated the flow of traffic and commerce in the city's center. The railroads, however, anxious to protect their charter rights, opposed the plan and ultimately prevailed with the state road commission, which rejected the proposal and its subsequent modifications in 1917.[23]

21 *Nashville This Week*, I (November 9–16, 1925), 5; Nashville City Council Minutes, August 18, 1925, XXII, 360–61; *The Charter of the City of Nashville* (1928), 148–54; *Nashville Review*, III (September 15, 1921), 9; Lyndon E. Abbott and Lee S. Greene, *Municipal Government and Administration in Tennessee* (Knoxville, 1939), 27–28.
22 Abbott and Greene, *Municipal Government and Administration in Tennessee*, 27; Knoxville *Journal and Tribune*, March 25, 1920.
23 Thomas M. Deaton, "Atlanta During the Progressive Era" (Ph.D. dissertation, University of Georgia, 1969), 405–407; Walter G. Cooper, *Official History of Fulton County* (Atlanta, 1934), 441; *Atlanta City Builder* (January, 1917), 9, (May, 1920), 22–24; Robert R. Otis,

The chamber of commerce, however, did not relax its efforts for city planning. William J. Sayward, who opened his architectural practice in the Gate City several years after the Bleckley Plan was first submitted, headed a chamber committee devoted to city planning and housing conditions in 1919 and consistently promoted the notion of an "official" municipal planning body. On December 29, 1919, in an address to a chamber gathering, Mayor James L. Key asked the organization's help in creating a city plan. It was at this meeting that the first full-scale Atlanta city planning commission was organized. Composed of twenty-four members—eight appointed by the president of the chamber of commerce, eight by the mayor, and eight by the Fulton County Board of Commissioners—the planning commission elected John W. Grant, a former alderman and chairman of the city finance committee, as chairman. Louis P. Marquardt, an attorney and labor spokesman, and Mrs. Samuel Lumpkin, a local civic leader, were designated as vice-chairmen. Other members of the body included the permanent head of the President's Club, a group of Atlanta civic association leaders; two other former presidents and several former officers of the chamber of commerce; representatives of the three major daily papers; the president of the Rotary Club and a member of its board of directors; the president of the Georgia Automobile Association; and two women civic leaders. All in all, fifteen of the twenty-four commissioners were members of the chamber of commerce, and the planning body was endorsed by all major commercial-civic groups. No blacks were appointed to the commission. This initial body proved too large and unwieldy, however, and within six months it passed into obscurity.[24]

On October 12, 1920, Mayor Key appointed a new, smaller commission authorized by the state legislature. Of the six members, only Robert R. Otis, a prominent real estate developer and broker, had served with the initial twenty-four-member group. Other members included a railroad president, a contractor, a labor representative, a real estate broker and developer, and Hoke Smith, U.S. Senator from Georgia and a former governor and secretary

---

"Atlanta's Plan, 1909–1932" (Mimeographed diary, Georgia State Library, Atlanta), 1, 4–5. My account differs somewhat from Deaton's, which relies primarily on Franklin B. Garrett, *Atlanta and Environs: A Chronicle of Its People and Events* (New York, 1954), II, 684–86.

24 Atlanta *City Builder* (May, 1919), 8, (January, 1920), 5–6, (February, 1920), 7; *List of Members: Atlanta Chamber of Commerce* (Atlanta, 1918); Atlanta *Journal*, February 10, 14, 1920; Atlanta *Constitution*, February 10, 1920.

of the interior who had considerable real estate interests and business connections in Atlanta. Though the mayor was an ex officio member and temporary chairman, Otis emerged as the active leader of the new commission.[25]

The leading commercial-civic groups in Memphis also demonstrated significant interest in city planning by 1919. Under the leadership of Wassell Randolph, a local attorney and businessman, the chamber of commerce established an active city planning committee of more than twenty members drawn from various civic organizations. The Memphis City Club created several committees concerned wtih various aspects of city planning which met with similar groups from the Lions Club, the Kiwanis Club, the Rotary Club, the Engineers' Club, the Memphis Art Association, the Nineteenth Century Club (a large women's organization), and the Chamber of Commerce. In December, the City Club and Engineers' Club approved a resolution calling for a joint civic effort in establishing a municipal planning board and sponsoring a comprehensive city plan. After several meetings with Mayor Rowlett Paine, these advocates of city planning achieved their initial goal: an ordinance of March 30, 1920, creating a nine-member city planning commission. A year later the commission was "constituted" as an official municipal body by state law, and the original members were reappointed to staggered three-year terms. Serving as ex officio members were the city engineer, the chairman of the park commission, and two commissioners whose responsibilities included public utilities and streets. Bartholomew was engaged to prepare what became the most elaborate and ambitious of those city plans to appear in the South during the decade.[26]

"It may be said with becoming modesty," Wassell Randolph wrote, that the chamber of commerce city planning committee "is the forerunner of the City Planning Commission—that through the activities of this Committee resulting in several conferences with the City Commissioners, the Commissioners were influenced to give the City Planning Movement very careful consideration, with the result that the need for a City Planning Commission

25 Garrett, *Atlanta and Environs*, III, 95, 127, 572–73; Dudley Glass (ed.), *Men of Atlanta* (Atlanta, 1924), pages not numbered; Atlanta *Journal*, October 12, 1920.
26 Memphis Chamber of Commerce, *Annual Reports, 1919–1920* (Memphis, 1920), 33; *Memphis Chamber of Commerce Journal*, II (January, 1920), 294; City Club of Memphis *Bulletin*, November 4, December 30, 1919; City of Memphis, Board of Commissioners Minutes, Book G, 78.

became a conviction." The first annual report of the new commission attributed the origins of that body to the election, in 1920, of "a new administration of progressive business men" who had been "elected on a business administration platform," who "drew largely from the civic organizations which had City Planning Committees" in determining the commission's membership. Indeed, Randolph was not only chairman of the city planning commission but also a former president of the City Club and an active member of the chamber of commerce board of directors. Other members of the commission included Charles J. Hasse, a real estate and insurance broker, financier, and member of the Rotary and City clubs; Edward B. LeMaster, a major realtor and developer who had helped organize the Memphis Real Estate Board in 1910 and served as its first president; Samuel E. Ragland, president of the First National City Bank and founder of a real estate mortgage firm; Dan Wolf, owner of a commercial printing company and a member of the City Club; Mrs. Irby Bennett, a civic leader especially active in the Nineteenth Century Club; and Mrs. Eleanor O'Donnell McCormack, a former school superintendent, Red Cross director, and advisor to important figures in state and local government.[27]

In New Orleans, the story was very much the same. The Association of Commerce appropriated $7,500 for city planning in 1917. Since most planning consultants were involved in war work, however, it was not until 1919 that the association's Civic Bureau, headed by Charles A. Favrot—a local engineer and architect descended from one of Louisiana's oldest families—was able to engage Philadelphia planner Milton B. Medary to prepare an initial survey and publicize the importance of city planning. Medary's series of fifty-two articles began appearing in the Sunday issues of local papers in August, 1919, and were later credited with increasing the interest of civic leaders in planning projects. Finally, in January, 1923, the association's city planning committee met with the New Orleans Commission-Council and shortly thereafter submitted an ordinance creating an official municipal planning body which became law in May.[28]

27 Memphis Chamber of Commerce, *Annual Reports, 1919–1920*, 33; Memphis City Planning Commission, *First Annual Report: City Planning Commission, Memphis, Tennessee, 1921* (Memphis, 1921), 9; "Memphis, The South's Paris," *Memphis Chamber of Commerce Journal*, VII (October, 1924), 31; Biographical Files, Memphis Room, Memphis Public Library.
28 *New Orleans Association of Commerce News Bulletin*, II (October 12, 1920), 10; II (June 21,

The New Orleans City Planning and Zoning Commission was, from the beginning, dominated by commercial and civic interests. Thirteen of the twenty members were appointed—as required by the ordinance—as representatives of the thirteen "leading commercial and civic organizations," including the Association of Commerce, the Board of Trade, the Cotton Exchange, the Contractors and Dealers Exchange, the Real Estate Agents Association, the New Orleans Federation of Clubs, the Young Men's Business Club, and the Central Trades and Labor Council. Of the seven commissioners appointed "at large" by the mayor, virtually all were drawn from the commercial-civic elite. Furthermore, the commission's work was initially funded by contributions of local individuals and interested organizations. Favrot was named chairman of the new commission, and General Allison Owen—an architect and builder who belonged to most of the city's major civic groups—was appointed vice-chairman. By 1927 the commission had included among its members a number of engineers, architects, real estate agents, and contractors, and fifteen persons who were members of the Association of Commerce. Owen, in fact, served as president of the association in 1927 and again in 1932. When the commission was reorganized to fifteen members in 1927, seven of the original commissioners were reappointed. Favrot and Owen were retained as chairman and vice-chairman, and representatives were added from various municipal officers and agencies. In 1926 Bartholomew was engaged to prepare a comprehensive plan, and the city assumed primary responsibility for funding the commission. The Association of Commerce justifiably took credit for many of these developments; it expended close to $20,000 on various city planning projects between 1917 and 1923.[29]

Visions of the "city beautiful" had given way by the 1920s to notions of the "city efficient." The aesthetic was superseded by the practical and the utilitarian. Considerations of cleanliness and artful symmetry remained, to be sure, but these were clearly secondary to matters of urban transportation, land use, and subdivision controls. This was due not only to the functionalist movement among professional planners themselves, but to the interests and

---

1920), 1; V (January 16, 1923), 1; V (January 23, 1923), 2; V (February 6, 1923), 1, 8; New Orleans *Times-Picayune*, August 22, 1919.
29 *New Orleans Association of Commerce News Bulletin*, V (May 8, 1923), 1, 4; V (July 24, 1923), 1; New Orleans *Times-Picayune*, May 2, 1923; New Orleans City Planning and Zoning Commission, *Major Street Report* (New Orleans, 1927), 8; New Orleans *Times-Picayune*, June 7, 8, 1927.

priorities established by their clients—the commercial-civic elite. "City planning," the Memphis *Commercial-Appeal* observed in 1922, "really is given to making things useful, efficient and convenient." Rather than focusing on civic decoration, "real" city planning dealt with streets, zoning, and "many other things connected with the economy of population in the mass." Perhaps William J. Sayward of Atlanta said it best: "The city beautiful . . . is a very commendable ideal and one which should be assured its place; but we must not forget that the city beautiful must absolutely be founded upon the 'city practical'; otherwise, there is no justification for any procedure along this line." It was more important, in other words, that the city function properly than that it be aesthetically pleasing.[30]

Frequent annexations in the late nineteenth and early twentieth centuries swelled city boundaries and populations and escalated the demands on municipal authorities for streets, water and gas lines, sewers, police and fire protection, and trolley service. Neighborhoods were uprooted or transformed, industries moved into residential areas, and businesses coveted desirable properties along heavily traveled thoroughfares. Growth by annexation was not usually "organic"—in the parlance of the time—but resulted from the addition of seemingly indigestible chunks of land and people, some of which were organized into fairly autonomous communities. This was urban growth on a grand scale, but it was often without visible design.

In facing the consequences of this growth, established commercial interests became less enamored of the "boom or bust" enthusiasm that vaulted small towns into great metropolises and more concerned with protecting property and consolidating gains in the mature city. With their faith in efficiency, organization, and businesslike methods, and their interest in social control, members of the commercial-civic elite were appalled by the haphazard waste and chaos they perceived in uncontrolled urban expansion. They were disturbed that many municipalities took their basic shape, not from the decisions of enlightened community leaders, but from the random meanderings of Indian trails and cow paths: "instead of being laid out by the highest rate of intelligence," Sayward complained, the modern city "has in most cases been laid out, strange as it may seem, by the most primitive of minds." Few propertied citizens stood to gain from haphazard, unpredictable,

30 Memphis *Commercial-Appeal*, February 18, 1922; William J. Sayward, "City Planning Committee Urges Survey," Atlanta *City Builder* (January, 1920), 12.

and unregulated urban expansion—whether they were bankers or real estate speculators—and commercial-civic spokesmen increasingly began to emphasize not only growth but "the economic value of a well ordered city."[31]

Matters of street transportation and zoning dominated the planning movement in the urban South during the 1920s. They comprised the bulk of those comprehensive plans drawn by Harland Bartholomew. Beginning his career in 1912 as an assistant engineer for the Newark, New Jersey, plan directed by Ernest P. Goodrich and George B. Ford, Bartholomew became the engineer for the city planning commission of St. Louis in 1916 and started his private consulting practice three years later. His firm, Harland Bartholomew and Associates, was exceptionally active during the 1920s, completing comprehensive plans for thirty-two cities, including Kansas City, Pittsburgh, Toledo, and—in the South—Memphis, New Orleans, Chattanooga, Knoxville, and Orlando. His Memphis Plan of 1924 became the prototype of his later efforts. Housing and other "social" concerns were eliminated from his plans in the 1920s, according to one authority, "leaving . . . a planning portfolio confined to the more acceptable objectives of the community's physical and functional reordering." His clients, in other words, were not interested in such things.[32]

The two major documents of the Memphis City Planning Commission, prepared by Bartholomew, reflected the major concerns of the commercial-civic elite. A 42-page *First Annual Report*, issued in 1921, contained a preliminary major street plan, a transit proposal, and initial zoning studies; and Bartholomew's *Comprehensive City Plan* of 1924 was organized with principal attention to (1) major streets (2) transit (3) transportation (4) recreation (5) zoning, and (6) civic art—with the most detailed and extensive portions dealing with streets and zoning. Likewise, the 1922 annual report of

31 Sayward, "City Planning Committee Urges Survey," 12–13; Birmingham *Age-Herald*, May 15, 1926.
32 Norman J. Johnston, "Harland Bartholomew: His Comprehensive Plans and Science of Planning" (Ph.D. dissertation, University of Pennsylvania, 1964), 7–24, 98–99, 122, 144, 154–55, 158. Johnston also notes (143, 150) that the commercial-civic influence on early city planning efforts prevailed among other Bartholomew clients. In Wichita, Kansas, city planning was initiated through efforts of the Rotary Club and the Board of Commerce, and in Hamilton, Ohio, the first planning studies were paid through subscriptions from the chamber of commerce. Bartholomew's firm accounted for almost a quarter of all those comprehensive plans drawn in the nation in the first six years of the decade, and he served as the sixth president of the American City Planning Institute (the forerunner of the American Institute of Planners) in 1927–29.

the Atlanta City Planning Commission listed zoning as the top priority item of business, followed closely in importance by a comprehensive traffic plan.[33]

The street system was usually designated, as in Memphis, "the fundamental element" of the city plan, the "skeleton or framework of the city structure." A viable street network would include "main arterial thoroughfares" to carry the heaviest loads of motor vehicle traffic, "secondary (crosstown) thoroughfares" to funnel traffic into the main arteries, and "minor streets" to serve specific areas. A primary goal was to widen existing streets and construct new "links" between them. As the Atlanta planners put it, "The central business section of the city should have an approximate rectangular street layout, every street constituting the central portion of a main arterial thoroughfare." Bartholomew, in his New Orleans plan, noted that not all streets "are of equal value and importance in the city." The main emphasis now, he suggested, should be placed on "major streets" which bore the heaviest burden of traffic. "Almost all metropolitan centers find it necessary," he wrote, "to designate major streets and devise plans for bringing them all into coordinated use."[34]

Furthermore, the downtown business district would be a central "focal point" linking the main traffic arteries. "The aim," Bartholomew wrote, "is to create a series of wide, direct and well paved arteries radiating from this primary objective." Reconstruction of the city's street system was both "a costly process of correcting errors of omission and commission in the upbuilding of the city" and an encouragement of efficient, economical, and orderly expansion. "The circulation of the urban body must be kept alive," Bartholomew recommended. "Structural weaknesses in the arterial system, whatever their cause, bring about disorders which affect every phase of city life."[35]

The street plan was designed to facilitate travel toward the central city, to centralize the patterns of urban mobility and vitalize the downtown business district that lay at the heart of the urban ethos. It was also calculated to promote expansion, especially into previously undeveloped areas. Here the

33 Harland Bartholomew, A *Comprehensive City Plan: Memphis, Tennessee* (Memphis, 1924); Atlanta City Planning Commission, *Annual Report . . . 1922* (Atlanta, 1922), 5.
34 Memphis City Planning Commission, *First Annual Report*, 11, 19–28; Atlanta City Planning Commission, *Annual Report . . . 1922*, 6; New Orleans City Planning and Zoning Commission, *Major Street Report*, 56.
35 New Orleans City Planning and Zoning Commission, *Major Street Report*, 56.

contradictory tendencies of the time—centrifugal and centripetal—were resolved in the paved street which linked the center with the periphery, and the automobile allowed each to reinforce the other. New Orleans planners, for example, were particularly interested in exploiting regions on the urban periphery by means of the major street system as well as "underdeveloped" areas near the city's core. Bartholomew discovered that the "principal area of New Orleans" contained twenty-eight thousand acres of land, of which only twelve thousand were sufficiently developed. Of the remainder, fourteen thousand acres "have incomplete drainage, sewerage and water services." He suggested that initial concern had to be with correcting past faults in the system; but the street plan should look toward the eventual development of these areas, toward a decentralization of population over a large territory.[36]

The street system was considered essential to the realization of the corporate-expansive city. "Birmingham . . . must plan for an almost completely motorized community," a local paper commented in 1926. "It must plan for a population in its immediate trade territory of more than a million persons within a comparatively short time." Without adequate thoroughfares this massive population—and the accompanying commercial and industrial enterprises—would simply compound the confusion that large numbers of people and motor vehicles already created in the central city. It was through a coherent street plan that such consequences were, at least in part, to be avoided. With the eventual adoption of the Memphis plan, the commissioners fully expected in 1921 that "orderly development will have been made certain for the future. The ultimate in city progress, which in January of 1920 was merely discussed, will have become a reality."[37]

Zoning was a fundamental feature of city planning during the 1920s, and usually the first coercive power obtained by local planning bodies. It was commonly applied to preserve the integrity of residential districts against the influx of industry and commerce; but it was much more than this. Zoning was, in a very real sense, the principal tool both for stabilizing and fashioning the metropolis, for fixing spatial arrangements and facilitating orderly expansion. Through the designation of specific "use" districts, zoning plans separated various kinds of economic activity as well as residential and work

36 *Ibid.*, 36–37.
37 Birmingham *Age-Herald*, January 4, 1926; Memphis City Planning Commission, *First Annual Report*, 10.

functions. Through height regulations, zoning encouraged a gradual population dispersal outward from the central urban core. And in subdivision
ordinances planning and zoning committees sought to direct the development
of the city into peripheral areas—even beyond the municipal limits.

The Memphis zoning ordinance, drawn by Bartholomew, went into effect
in November, 1922, without great difficulty; but in New Orleans and Atlanta
zoning laws were held up in the courts. New Orleans obtained zoning
authority in the Louisiana constitution in 1921, but it was not until July,
1923, that the city won the first major court test of its powers. Not until
1929—after two years and seven months of public hearings—was Bartholomew's revised comprehensive zone ordinance adopted by the commission-
council. Atlanta's first zoning ordinance, passed in April, 1922, was successfully challenged in the courts, and an amendment to the state constitution was
ultimately required to grant zoning authority to Georgia municipalities.
Finally, in December, 1928, a zoning law based upon the earlier statute was
approved by the city council.[38]

Zoning was put forth in southern cities as a means of stabilizing property
values, protecting investments, easing the blight and confusion of "transitional" and "mixed" areas, segregating the races, and encouraging orderly
expansion and the decentralization of the urban population. Real estate
interests initially opposed zoning efforts in some cities, especially Atlanta, but
a majority of real estate spokesmen praised city planning and zoning for
stabilizing property values and guarding land investments. The Memphis City
Planning Commission, for example, argued that "Areas now occupied or
expected to be occupied for residential purposes . . . should most certainly be
given the protection essential to their permanency of development through
exclusion of industrial or commercial intrusions." The social and economic
chaos of changing neighborhoods, and the uncertainty of unregulated
development, were to be avoided if at all possible. As the chairman of the

38 New Orleans City Planning and Zoning Commission, "Handbook to the Comprehensive
Zone Law, New Orleans, Louisiana" (1929–33) (Bound mimeographed volume in City
Archives, New Orleans Public Library), Chap. IV, 3–4, 7–8; New Orleans City Planning and
Zoning Commission, "Factors Involved in Carrying Out the City Plan" (November 30, 1931)
(Mimeographed report in City Archives, New Orleans Public Library), 29; Bartholomew, A
Comprehensive City Plan: Memphis, 117–19, 127; Wassell Randolph, "Municipal Zoning:
Proposed Ordinance," *Memphis Chamber of Commerce Journal*, V (May, 1922), 37–38;
Garrett, *Atlanta and Environs*, II, 839; Robert Whitten, "Atlanta Adopts Zoning," *American
City*, XXVI (June, 1922), 541–42; Atlanta *Constitution*, December 22, 1928.

Memphis commission noted, the "modern view" of city planning "is that the public can control the private use of realty as to prevent an owner making a use of his lot which will depreciate the value of his neighbor's lots." By fixing certain spatial arrangements, zoning plans sought to buttress social order and foster confidence among investors and businessmen.[39]

The Memphis zoning plan set out to avoid the blight associated with older "transitional" residential areas on the periphery of commercial and industrial regions. Such areas were zoned for both single-family residences and apartments in order to "fix the character of these transitional districts." Social dislocation and fluctuating land values inevitably characterized "mixed" areas, and zoning was one way to "give stability and character, as well as encouragement, to the proper development of the city"—especially in those neighborhoods on the verge of chaotic transformation.[40]

Spatial stability in the South also meant racial segregation. Like most American cities, southern urban areas reflected informal patterns of spatial separation along racial lines. Randolph noted that most black neighborhoods in Memphis were found "in the lower ground bordering on the drainage courses." While no law demanded residential segregation, "the rule is that the colored population is found exclusively in the cheaper, less desirable sections of the city. Thus we have a sort of natural zoning of the races." Birmingham did not provide for statutory residential segregation until 1926, when the city's zoning ordinance mandated the rigid separation of white and Negro residential areas (though it did permit property ownership by one race in districts allocated to members of the other race, thereby protecting white landlordism in black areas). The city commission considered the petition of white citizens who protested the construction of Negro housing contiguous to white neighborhoods, and on at least one occasion the zoning commission revoked the permits of several of the contractors involved.[41]

The first zoning law in Atlanta changed informal Jim Crow arrangements into a formal pattern of residential segregation. Residential areas were divided

39 Memphis City Planning Commission, *First Annual Report*, 15–16; Randolph, "Municipal Zoning: Proposed Ordinance," 37. Also see Huggins, "City Planning in North Carolina, 1900–1929," 392.
40 Bartholomew, *A Comprehensive City Plan: Memphis*, 123; Memphis City Planning Commission, *First Annual Report*, 16.
41 Memphis City Planning Commission, *First Annual Report*, 7; Carl V. Harris "Reforms in Government Control of Negroes in Birmingham," 571; *Zoning Ordinance of Birmingham, Alabama* (Birmingham, 1926), 12–15; Birmingham *News*, June 15, 1926.

into white, black, and undetermined zones, while black servants' quarters in white neighborhoods were legally protected. The plan, devised by consultant Robert Whitten of Cleveland, was, according to *Survey* magazine, "the first to embody in an outspoken form segregation along the line of social composition of the population" and a potential precedent for separating immigrants and other ethnic groups in the American metropolis. Whitten defended the concept on the grounds that it was neither undemocratic nor antisocial. The creation of "colored districts" provided adequate area "for the growth of the colored population," and encouraged blacks to develop "a more intelligent and responsible citizenship." Separation lessened the possibility of race riots, he claimed, and stabilized the property values in transitional racial areas. "Hundreds of acres of land were left undeveloped or poorly developed in various parts of the city," Whitten wrote, "because of uncertainty." He observed "that whenever you have a neighborhood made up of people largely in the same economic status, you have a neighborhood where there is most independence of thought and action and the most intelligent interest in the neighborhood, city, state and national affairs."[42]

Zoning was both a tool for fixing existing spatial arrangements and a method of promoting urban expansion, of extending the city into surrounding territory and encouraging economic development. Height restrictions discouraged the rise of skyscrapers since, according to the planning theory of the time, such structures were "uneconomical" and "injurious to the community." By limiting building heights population density would be lessened and urban residents dispersed over a larger area. In his Memphis plan Bartholomew wrote that "the primary purpose of city planning and zoning is to regulate and distribute the population of a city for the protection of health, safety and general welfare." New Orleans was particularly anxious to populate those areas of the city which had only recently been rendered habitable by sewer and drainage improvements, and Atlanta planners devised their zoning ordinance to promote "the spreading out of the population" and prevent "excessive overcrowding in the tenement house areas." In addition, zoning could set aside large areas for industrial and commercial development.

42 "The Atlanta Zoning Plan," *Survey*, XLVIII (April 22, 1922), 114–15; Robert Whitten, letter to the editor, *ibid.*, XLVIII (June 15, 1922), 418–19. According to the Atlanta City Planning Commission's *Annual Report* . . . *1922*, 4, residential segregation was adopted for "the promotion of public peace, order, safety and general welfare."

Sizable tracts of Memphis were allocated for industry, and the major thoroughfares were zoned for commercial use, creating a "ribbon" pattern of business expansion throughout the city.[43]

City planning was likened to the process in "every large industry" of "logically planning the arrangement of its plant and equipment." The fact that planning and zoning interfered with individual, private decisions concerning the uses of property was momentarily disturbing to some business interests; but it was generally accepted as necessary to secure the public good, as defined by the commercial-civic elite. "Zoning will interfere with the plans of individuals," the *Memphis Chamber of Commerce Journal* noted in 1922, "the same as other phases of city planning will temporarily discommode some of the people whose property is affected. But this is the cost of progress, and today's loss, in any program of permanent improvement, is compensated by tomorrow's gain." The "obstacles and precedents surviving from earlier times . . . must give way in the public interest."[44]

The city planning adopted with such alacrity by the urban commercial-civic elite was hardly an unqualified success: it was fraught with problems and difficulties that deepened during the 1920s and into the Depression years. Municipal governments and state legislatures were reluctant to grant power or autonomy to city planning commissions, and the advocates of city planning were themselves soon caught up in the policy wrangles which accompanied ambitious schemes of this sort.

City planning commissions were usually empowered to survey existing

43 Bartholomew, *A Comprehensive City Plan: Memphis*, 124, 126; New Orleans City Planning and Zoning Commission, "Handbook to the Comprehensive Zone Law," Chapter II, p. 2; New Orleans City Planning and Zoning Commission, *Major Street Report*, 34; Atlanta City Planning Commission, *Annual Report* . . . 1922, 4; Johnston, "Harland Bartholomew," 163–64. Johnston writes that "much of the zoning chapter in the firm's 1940 restudy of Memphis is used for recommending a reduction in these excessive areas zoned commercial and industrial. But it was in the nature of the circumstances that to get zoning in at all would mean buying off the business interests and the boosterism of their confident expectations of the times."

44 *Memphis Chamber of Commerce Journal*, V (September, 1922), 27; "Zoning," *ibid.*, V (August, 1922), 51. Johnston, "Harland Bartholomew," 158, maintains that, by the time of the 1924 Memphis plan, "the whole idea-concept of community over private right as expressed by Bartholomew's earlier reports is obscured." Johnston is misled here by his reliance on Frederick Lewis Allen's portrait of the decade, for such an "idea-concept" is indeed found in contemporary urban newspapers—at least in the South—and in Bartholomew's plans for southern cities. The point is that the reordering and structuring of the city, the prevalence of community over private rights, was made to conform to commercial-civic interests and priorities and to their notion of the corporate-expansive city.

conditions, draw up plans and ordinances, review street projects and land subdivisions, and make recommendations—but they were always under the shadow of the elected municipal bodies from which they drew their authority. They possessed coercive powers only to the degree that city governments acquiesced in their policies. Bartholomew noted that the Memphis commission passed judgment on land subdivision plans and sat as an administrative board to interpret the zoning ordinance: but without persuasive and politically astute leadership neither the general public nor elected officials would abide by the substance of the comprehensive plan. New Orleans planners warned that without "general acquiescene" in planning policies "individual and local interests will gradually bring about changes and amendments for selfish reasons until the entire scheme has been vitiated." And this, of course, was "the very sort of practice that has brought American cities to their present state of physical deficiencies." To preclude this possibility, the city planning and zoning commission recommended the formation of citizens' committees to actively and publicly support the comprehensive plan and its enforcement.[45]

Atlanta never did adopt a comprehensive plan during the decade, although local planning advocates could boast of a working zoning ordinance. Bartholomew lamented in 1939 that the Gate City lagged twenty years behind other urban centers in the progress of its planning efforts. Planning bodies complained constantly of inadequate financial support, public misunderstanding, and the intransigence of public officials. Carrying out the major features of the major street plans, and especially the time-consuming and politically delicate enforcement of zoning laws, drained many planning commissions of their energies and prevented a genuinely comprehensive approach to urban ills. From the beginning, Atlanta's commission "became immersed in zoning matters," according to one of its principal leaders, "which forced a separation of the two into distinct boards." Long range planning gave way, in other words, to immediate, piecemeal changes. The formation of city planning commissions was heralded throughout the urban South, at least among the commercial-civic elite, as ushering in a "new epoch" in city development. But these expectations were not to be fulfilled during the 1920s.[46]

45 See Bartholomew, A *Comprehensive City Plan: Memphis*, 137–38; *The Charter and Ordinances of the City of Atlanta: Code of 1924*, 132–33; New Orleans City Planning and Zoning Commission, "Factors Involved in Carrying Out the City Plan," 26–27.
46 Otis, "Atlanta's Plan, 1909–1932," 19–20; Garrett, *Atlanta and Environs*, II, 820; Atlanta

Though city planning during the 1920s was not entirely successful, it did reveal in its purposes and justifications the aspirations and concerns of the commercial-civic elite who fashioned and supervised it. Cities, "like all living organisms," Bartholomew wrote, "must either progress or decay." And unregulated growth, given the increasing complexity of the modern metropolis, could lead inevitably to deterioration. Unless cities provided adequate facilities for traffic, education, recreation, and public health "its very progress will become a penalty." "Material expansion," the Atlanta *Journal* put it, "is worthwhile only to the extent that it is accompanied by inner civic advancement." Again, in city planning as in other areas of concern, emphasis was placed on the relationship between the physical city and civic spirit. "When people begin to feel the ties that bind them together as citizens and which attach them to the place which they inhabit," one planner noted, "when they shall understand that their prosperity, that their dignity, that their happiness are bound up with the welfare of the city; when they have learned to cherish their home town... this expansion of civic consciousness is not the least of the benefactions that we can expect from the adoption of comprehensive programs for future civic development."[47]

Planners appealed for some measure of control over areas beyond the city limits, since "only in this way can uniformity in the growth of the city be preserved." Unbridled individualism was synonymous with anarchy, and a state of "disorderly development" that may have been tolerable in the early stages of a city's existence became unacceptable in the mature metropolis. Atlanta's "pioneering days are over," a local chamber of commerce planner wrote, "its future is assured and its continued commercial supremacy cannot be doubted. This is the time for Atlanta, as it has been for all progressive cities, to take stock of herself with particular regard to those values which exist beyond the mere supply of bread and butter for our stomachs or clothes for our backs." Earlier necessities had dictated a chaotic urban arrangement that "has not kept pace with our commercial progress." All of this led to the question: "Shall we permit ourselves to go down in history as a nation of traders simply like the Phoenicians or the Carthaginians, or shall we aspire to

Constitution, December 13, 1939; Huggins, "City Planning in North Carolina, 1900–1929," 396–97; New Orleans *Times-Picayune*, July 22, 1923.

47 Bartholomew, *A Comprehensive City Plan: Memphis*, 137; Atlanta *Journal*, February 13, 1920; Warren H. Manning, "Introduction," *Warren H. Manning's City Plan of Birmingham* (Birmingham, 1919), pages not numbered.

something like the measure of Athens and Rome?" References to antiquity aside, the principal concern of the commercial-civic elite and their planners in the 1920s was that "uncontrolled growth invites chaos and economic disaster."[48]

Order, unity, and expansion, the principal tenets of the urban ethos, attracted new industry and population, insured stable property values, curtailed threats to the established order from below, and, of course, continued control of urban affairs in the hands of the commercial-civic elite and their chosen professional "experts." And the pressures of city growth could be channeled through city planning to acceptable ends. A comprehensive plan would insure "not only a bigger city," a Charleston editorialist remarked, "but a more beautiful and more healthful city, and a city in which there will be no 'slums,' nor congested insanitary areas, and where living and housing conditions for the average family will be vastly improved." Decentralized cities, with healthy economic cores and efficient transportation—"one-street cities twenty miles long with business nucleuses at the center"—seemed to be just the answer to a whole range of urban ills. City planning commissions were thus called upon "to correlate and to harmonize the various interests of the city," as the Atlanta *Constitution* put it, "and to bring them together in a working whole in pursuit of a definite general plan, concurred in by all, whereby to bring the city up to the required standard of efficiency in all of its departments and activities."[49]

Harland Bartholomew suggested, in a 1933 St. Louis speech, that "Our boastful slogan of 'Bigger and Better' must yield to a new slogan which implies balanced design, unity and satisfaction for all groups comprising the urban poplulation."[50] He realized that the urban masses had actually gained very little from the comprehensive plans of the 1920s. But he failed to see that, for

48 Wassell Randolph, "City Planning: Its Relation to the Environs of the City," *Memphis Chamber of Commerce Journal*, VI (September, 1923), 1; New Orleans City Planning and Zoning Commission, "Handbook to the Comprehensive Zone Law," Chap. I, p. 2; Comment by Sayward in Atlanta *City Builder* (May, 1918), 13; Bartholomew, *A Comprehensive City Plan: Memphis*, 6.

49 Charleston *News and Courier*, September 17, 1926; Birmingham *Age-Herald* April 3, 1927; Atlanta *Constitution*, February 10, 1920. Also see Huggins, "City Planning in North Carolina, 1900–1929," 389.

50 Quoted in Johnston, "Harland Bartholomew," 187. Johnston notes (183) that Bartholomew's plans failed to reflect some of his larger apprehensions: "The impact... of his thinking on central issues is lost in the much larger body of his practice which appears to institutionalize some of the very palliatives that, outside the confines of his business contracts, he criticizes."

most of his southern clients at least, the goals of urban growth and order—of 'Bigger and Better' and "balanced design"—were firmly joined in the corporate-expansive ideal. If these goals were contradictory, they refused to believe it. According to most southern commercial-civic spokesmen, in fact, the urban ethos had been the consuming motive behind their cities from the very beginning.

VII The Uses of Local History

The dream of the founders of Birmingham has been more than fulfilled. Its history rests on the hardy frontiersmen, the farsighted engineers and city builders, the resourceful pioneers, the men of muscle and ambition, the loyal service of the generations which have come after. Today, too, there are those of vision who see this city four-fold in numbers, in size, in worth to the state and the nation. And, viewed in the light of what has gone before, who shall say their vision is idle?

—Birmingham *Fiftieth Anniversary Announcement* (1921)

BIRMINGHAM'S fiftieth anniversary was celebrated in 1921 with more hoopla and historical romance than even a visit by President Warren G. Harding could dampen. Fireworks, fancy dress balls, and a baloon race seemed fitting companions to that glorious version of the city's past written especially for the occasion. The way local people told it, the story of Birmingham was merely the unfolding of a spectacular drama, an inevitable response to a call of destiny.

No wonder that scholars have usually dismissed local history for its antiquarianism, its distortion of historical reality, its dwelling on the insignificant or peculiar, and its lack of anything in the way of serious interpretation. Much local history was quite deserving of this indictment. While such criticisms have revealed much about the content and style of local history, however, they have equally obscured a great deal concerning its role in formulating and elaborating concepts of the local community. For the great majority of people the accuracy and precision of history—even its "objective" truth—was less important than the additional perspective which

191

notions of the past cast on contemporary life. Interpretation of local history has, not surprisingly, been one of the many ways in which men have sought to explain, justify, understand, and cope with their communities. It was important that the city's place be established not only in space but also in time. Ascertaining the city's role within the larger patterns of regional or national history was just as crucial, probably, to a well-rounded urban consciousness and a viable urban identity as the awareness of its problems and concern for its growth.

Popular historical accounts, recollections, and celebrations were prominent in the urban South throughout the 1920s, especially as they pertained to the local area. Wit, drama, romance, and a cast of bold, if somewhat implausible, characters were all features of the historical story most likely to engage the popular mind; but urban history also served to explain contemporary conditions, enrich local traditions, and bolster civic pride. Most important, it was an interpretation of the city's past thoroughly shaped by the concerns and values of the present, an expression of the temporal dimension of the urban ethos. Surely, this ethos would have languished in a vague and distant future without some measure of historical dimension. Local history was also significant because, as R. Richard Wohl and A. Theodore Brown have noted, "what people believe about the history of their locale may shape their notions of how they ought to live in it and of the values they may hope to realize in their community."[1] The substance of local history can provide— regardless of its accuracy or inaccuracy—additional insight into contemporary life and thought and also suggest why men act as they do.

Local historical accounts supported the elements of stability and permanence so important to the southern urban ethos of the 1920s and helped to further confidence in the city's future by recalling past accomplishments. In addition, comercial-civic spokesmen tended to discern in the local past those very values and trends that constituted the urban ethos and defined the ideal of the corporate-expansive city. Though often differing widely in their substance and emphasis, recollections of the local past established a body of knowledge, tradition, and precedent primarily useful in illuminating the successes and failures of contemporary urban life, and served as a vehicle for the expression of present hopes and apprehensions.

1 R. Richard Wohl and A. Theodore Brown, "The Usable Past: A Study of Historical Traditions in Kansas City," *Huntington Library Quarterly*, XXIII (May, 1960), 259.

The Dilemmas of Past and Present

In an urban society which worshipped progress as both a means and an end of a successful civilization, the dead past was not usually an object of particular reverence. This was especially true of southern urban blacks, for whom the antebellum years hardly represented a "golden age." The fulfillment of black social, economic, and cultural aspirations neccessarily existed more in the future than in either the past or the present. The white business booster could also be virtually reckless in resisting—at least rhetorically—the voice of tradition and the security of habit.

A business spokesman in New Orleans proudly escorted a group of visitors through the commercial labyrinth of the downtown sections west of Canal Street, pointing out "the big department stores with their smart window displays and their revolving doors sucking in the tide of women shoppers as whirlpools gobble jetsam." The languid city of French and Spanish antecedents seemed almost a threat to this new, promising reality. " 'She is modern,' he assured us, time and time again, 'absolutely modern. The old New Orleans is dead. Of course,' shrugging his shoulders and spreading out his hands, 'we regret the passing of so delightful a creature. But you know, my friends, she was perverse; she was dreadfully dangerous.'" [2] Other observers agreed that there were fundamental conflicts between past and present but found the modern age and all its implications both disconcerting and undesirable. And still others clung to the notion of local history as an organic unity, with future events flowing naturally from what existed and what had gone before.

A strictly organic view of local history was, however, rarely advanced in southern cities during the 1920s. The realities of Civil War and Reconstruction simply made it too difficult to portray the patterns of regional history as continuous and unbroken, and the same kinds of discontinuity marked the experience of most southern cities. On the other hand, many spokesmen successfully maintained some connection between past, present, and future through an "evolutionary" or "progressive" interpretation of the local past which not only preserved a sense of historical continuity but fully embodied the ideals of optimism, growth, and constant improvement.

2 Mildred Cram, *Old Seaport Towns of the South* (New York, 1917), 269–70, 273–74. Mrs. Cram undoubtedly exercised a bit of literary license in reporting these remarks, but the basic idea is clear enough.

Such an interpretation was hardly novel. As Strauss observed of popular historical views in the nineteenth-century Midwest, societies were assumed to have "progressed from earlier stages to later, higher ones; and thence to the highest stage of all: industrialization and commerce." If change was often disconcerting, southern city dwellers could console themselves, as the Nashville *Tennessean* suggested, "with the fact that the civilization of the world is constantly being builded [sic] on the wrecks of former glory and noble achievements." In the context of a progressive-evolutionary interpretation, the contrast between modern Nashville and the full-scale replica of the Athens Parthenon which stood in a nearby park became especially instructive: "Thus the broken stones of a decayed civilization, revived by the subtle hand of a new civilization, have become the stepping-stones upon which genera-tions unborn may ascend to heights yet unscaled by any civilization."[3] If history was indeed a stairway on which men journeyed ever upward, then neither the past nor the future was particularly threatening.

One variation on the progressive-evolutionary theme was the view that societies, and cities, were confronted with periodic challenges—natural disaster, war, economic collapse, social turmoil—the responses to which not only determined the city's survival but fundamentally shaped its destiny. The more serious the problem, the more significant the solution; the more severe the challenge, the more heroic the response. Such an interpretation hardly suggested continuity, but the city's history was at least unified by a thread of recurrent crises. This view was generally joined firmly to the notion that the city emerged from each of these encounters triumphant, strengthened, and improved. The challenge-response interpretation was, in a way, simply a more dramatic punctuation of the progressive-evolutionary development of the city through time. It not only contributed an element of drama to the urban story but also lent itself perfectly to the contemporary requirements of the urban ethos.

For some writers the course of history was neither an upward spiral nor a succession of conquests over great difficulties but a fragile pattern all too easily disrupted and despoiled by tragedy and conflict. This view was especially compelling for southern conservatives like Donald Davidson, who felt very ill-at-ease amidst the instability and materialism of the twentieth-century

3 Anselm Strauss, *Images of the American City* (New York, 1916), 161; Nashville *Tennessean*, July 12, 1926; George B. Moulder, *The Parthenon at Nashville, Tennessee* (Nashville, 1930), 1.

South. It was in the classic antebellum southern civilization—"tragically interrupted" by the Civil War—that Davidson found the self-sufficiency, independence, and "high-minded" provincialism by which all later regional history was to be judged. By this standard, he could praise Nashville for its stability and cultural eminence, for its refusal to be totally dominated by the expansionist fervor of other cities; but it also aroused fears that Nashville was on the verge of succumbing to the siren call of false and dangerous gods. [4]

Though this interpretation prized an organic, continuous past, it also emphasized the discontinuities which had torn the fabric of tradition and threatened even more damage in the future. The pattern of regional, and local, history was sometimes seen as a slow decline from a "golden age." It was an interpretation most congenial to academics, artists, literary figures, and hidebound traditionalists, however: while it was one of the most articulately expressed it was also one of the least popular. Most southern spokesmen, if they saw major breaks in the local past, tended to divide history, as did a 1923 Baton Rouge pageant, into "the dead past," "the living present," and "the golden future." [5]

Ellen Glasgow, from her perspective on Richmond's Main Street, captured the subtleties and ambiguities of change with greater sensitivity than perhaps any other southern writer of her generation. Though she could write to Hugh Walpole at the beginning of the 1920s that "Richmond is just the same, and I hope that it will be the same," she was only too well aware of the urban transformation which surrounded her. Emotionally attached to the values and cultural standards of the past, she was also convinced that the older ruling gentry were incapable of reacting positively to the future. In *One Man in His Time*, published in 1922, she presented perhaps her most complete statement on the conflict between the "evasive idealism" of the fading urban aristocracy and the newer pace and vitality of urban life after World War I. Stephen Culpeper, the principal character of the novel, returned from service in the Great War to find the secure traditions of his aristocratic Richmond family so suffocating that he was eventually driven

4 Donald Davidson, "Here or Nowhere!" Nashville *Tennessean*, May 29, 1927. Social change itself could, of course, inspire and reinforce a penchant for tradition and familiar customs. As Kevin Lynch, *The Image of the City* (Cambridge, 1960), 42, observed of modern Boston, "Perhaps because so much of the environment is new or changing, there was evidence of widespread, almost pathological, attachment to anything that had survived the upheaval."
5 New Orleans *Times-Picayune*, April 1, 1923.

"like a hunted creature out into the streets." The war had not freed him from tradition, Culpeper said on one occasion; "it only made me restless and dissatisfied. It destroyed my belief in the past without giving me faith in the future. It left me eager to go somewhere; but it failed to offer me any direction. It put me to sea without a compass." Richmond was likewise poised uncertainly between past and future. "Long ago the village had disappeared. Long ago the spacious southern homes, with their walled gardens of box and roses and aromatic shrubs in spring, had receded into the shadowy memories of those whom the modern city pointed out, with playful solicitude, as 'the oldest inhabitants.'" The village had been replaced by a "city which was outgrowing its youth, outgrowing the barriers of tradition, outgrowing alike the forces of reaction and the forces of progress." The city, like Culpeper, was finally confronted with the realities of maturity and stricken with ambiguity and uncertainty. Large, metallic, expansive—the new Richmond was driven by necessity toward the future yet for the first time quite unsure of its direction or purpose. And it was the lack of direction and purpose, not the recent dynamism of Richmond's history, that Miss Glasgow found so disconcerting.[6]

Few writers pondered the implications of history with the intent serious- ness and genius of Ellen Glasgow; and fewer still struck such an artful balance between the legacies of the past and the realities of the present. For most spokesmen, though, interpretations of local history were definitely linked with attitudes toward socioeconomic and cultural change. The ideal of the corporate-expansive city—the desire to participate fully in the larger American dream of growth and material prosperity—precluded any genuine worship of a genteel, static antebellum society. Even the term "New South," regardless of perfunctory rituals to the Lost Cause, was an explicit recognition that the present and future had been somehow wrested forcefully from the grasp of a distant, dying past. But southerners, perhaps even more than most Ameri- cans, insisted on retaining some sense of security and stability in the history of their communities.

Notions of history either wholly organic or completely fragmented were thus rarely put forth during the 1920s. Instead, the progressive-evolutionary view was by far the most popular, whether expressed in a somewhat subdued

6 Ellen Glasgow to Hugh Walpole, November 9, 1920, in Blair Rouse (ed.), *Letters of Ellen Glasgow* (New York, 1958), 67; Ellen Glasgow, *One Man in His Time* (New York, 1922), 69, 83, 57–58, 377.

fashion or enlivened by the theme of challenge-response. These various approaches to local history were not, of course, mutually exclusive, and most popular accounts of the time included features of both organic unity and significant change. The particular emphasis of popular histories also inevitably depended to some extent on the actual facts of a specific city's history as well as on the requirements of contemporary boosterism, so that the substance and theme of urban historical accounts differed from city to city. The connection of such accounts with the values and priorities of the prevailing urban ethos remained remarkably consistent throughout the urban South, however, especially in the region's younger and most rapidly growing cities.

The Usable Urban Past

Local history was partly, of course, an antiquarian venture with genealogical overtones. But it was also employed as something more—a device for promoting contemporary socioeconomic and cultural views. As such, it went beyond the usual dimensions of presentism and historical relativism and became an additional resource for shaping conceptions of the city and urban society during the 1920s. Just as business-oriented middle-class spokesmen promoted the ideal of the corporate-expansive city, so also did they emphasize growth, civic cooperation, business leadership, and local patriotism in the urban past. The basic priorities of the urban ethos thus tended to infuse historical views of the city just as they dominated urban policy.

Though there have been few studies of the subject, it is clear that the practical application of urban history to achieve contemporary ends was hardly a novel device of the twentieth century. Robert Thompson Van Horn, in his efforts to encourage Kansas City's growth in the 1850s, constructed a "community ideology" which predicated future greatness on the strength of prior accomplishment. Urban development was, in Van Horn's view as in William Gilpin's, essentially progressive-evolutionary, with cities arising in answer to a call of destiny. History became "but a fulfillment that might have been predicted far back in time. The proof offered was that such prophecies had indeed been made." In Kansas City and elsewhere a "dominant tradition" of written local histories in this and later decades derived "from conceptions of what the city was supposed to *be* and what it was supposed to become." Aspirations for the future were invariably reflected in interpretations of the past, to the extent that history itself became an additional means of fulfilling those aspirations.[7]

In most southern cities the historical record was presented as proof of the city's claim to greatness and of the validity of the urban ethos. The local past became a continually unfolding success story of an essentially monolithic urban community, in which all citizens, regardless of their socioeconomic standing, were united in meeting challenges and resolving common problems. The avid city booster of the nineteenth century, probably considered a bit mad in his own time, emerged as an early prototype of the latter-day business progressive. This popular view generally held sway throughout the urban South during the 1920s, though it did not go unchallenged in the region's older cities where the pull of tradition was strongest. In Charleston and New Orleans, especially, the conflict among varying views was mirrored in interpretations of local history.

The new buildings, roads, and dock facilities which marked Charleston's somewhat belated commitment to business progressivism stood starkly against the backdrop of delicate, pastel structures of the old city. And those persons of a literary bent were quick to seize upon the symbolic implications. A new bridge represented more than just an improvement in transportation; it was, as Katherine B. Ripley described it, "a complicated spider-web of steel against the sky, dwarfing the old town, throwing the solid brick buildings out of scale, and showing up the church steeples thin and papery." Many older citizens recoiled in anger at the disturbing specter of modernity. "The skyline of the city suited them as it was, and before the bridge went up, the church steeples were tall. The bridge is new; it will always be new and shiny with the crude, beautifully balanced strength of the machine age." It was, most certainly, a tangible confrontation between the past and the present. The engineers, builders, and city planners who perpetrated such things on the community were portrayed by DuBose Heyward as thoughtless destroyers, even as he begged them to preserve at least the semblance of historical integrity.

> Trading new lamps for old, you storm the street.
> Then, heedless of the magic of the old,

---

7 Wohl and Brown, "The Usable Past," 242, 238. Also see Charles N. Glaab, *Kansas City and the Railroads: Community Policy in the Growth of a Regional Metropolis* (Madison, 1962), 1. As the Birmingham *Age-Herald* put it (January 5, 1927), "The record of the past is the most convincing proof of what will happen in the future."

> You leave them strewn in fragments at our gate.
> Oh, pause before the ruin is complete.
> For that which stands have pity, and withold.
> Leave for your sons these walls inviolate.

Heyward lamented the passing of the "beautiful city that time had forgotten before it destroyed," the city whose streets "lay like nothing else upon Earth." [8]

Charleston's commercial-civic elite, however, battled strenuously against this image of their community. For the *News and Courier,* much of the city's history had been little more than "a long stagnant period" in which Charleston was forgotten not only by time but by progress as well. The remnants of antiquity and history—which many believed responsible for stifling the city's expansion—were primarily useful for their potential in increasing the tourist trade. The editors argued that such a glorious and interesting past "could be capitalized and made immensely valuable to the present and the future Charleston, and that this would be wholly consistent with a practical, progressive, and forward-looking spirit." In identifying their city, however, even business-minded Charlestonians could hardly fail to note those qualities which set the city apart, especially the "vital, glowing history . . . saturated with authentic story that springs like grass from her soil . . . weaving a golden thread of romance through the years of her existence." [9]

Stripped of this heritage, this local folklore and tradition, Charleston would indeed have been left with few distinguishing features. Though the urban ethos was constantly emphasized by commercial-civic spokesmen, it never drew significantly from Charleston's past, and it never achieved the ascendancy it enjoyed in other regional cities. Thus, Charleston remained somewhat divided in its allegiances to the past and the present.

In New Orleans, too, the local past seemed "a record to test the chronicler, to furnish material to poet and romancer . . . a mine from which great epics might be wrought." And the old Latin city certainly had its defenders against intrusions of the modern metropolis. William Faulkner,

---

8 Katherine B. Ripley, *Sand Dollars* (New York, 1933), 172, 174; DuBose Heyward, "Chant for an Old Town" in *Skylines and Horizons* (New York, 1924), 65, 69–70; DuBose Heyward, *Porgy* (New York, 1925), 11.

9 Charleston *News and Courier*, June 7, 1921, March 24, 1920; Harriette Kershaw Leiding, *Charleston: Historic and Romantic* (Philadelphia, 1931), 285.

briefly a member of the small coterie of writers and artists in the city during the
1920s, saw the Vieux Carre from his window as "an aging yet beautiful
courtesan in a smokefilled room, avid yet weary of too ardent ways." One could
hardly have said the same thing of the bustling commercial district to the west.
Lyle Saxon, who placed the city's "Golden Age" in the years between 1830 and
1860, was emotionally drawn to the old New Orleans and its landmarks and
recalled bitterly how he and a group of fellow citizens had vainly tried to save
the Hotel Royal from destruction and "were laughed at for our pains." The
presence of the old amidst the new was in some ways reassuring to those who
despised modernization, but in other ways it was distressing. "You can see how
sad it is on the street where I used to live," one of Hamilton Basso's characters
lamented. "The world has moved on since then and the street was like an old
piling that marks the place where the river used to run before it changed its
course." Indeed, these devotees of ancient New Orleans were stranded in a
quiet backwater, distant from, yet within earshot of, the roar of the mainstream.
Faulkner could write with literary disdain in his New Orleans sketches of the
"automatic food and bathtubs per capita" that, more than luxuries and vices,
led to "imaginative atrophy," but this was doubtless a rather discordant note for
the average reader of the *Times-Picayune*.[10] After all, artists and writers were
supposed to say such things. The Vieux Carre was prized by the business
community as a commercial resource and a reminder of past grandeur, but for
many in the commercial-civic elite it was simply an esoteric appendage to the
twentieth-century metropolis.

Unlike Charleston, however, New Orleans was the largest city in the
region, a bustling entrepot with an active and vocal business elite. The city's
history was widely interpreted as progressive-evolutionary, and as a story of
dramatic urban success in the face of adverse circumstances. "This city, 206
years old," an Association of Commerce president declared in 1924, "has been
through more trials and vicissitudes than any other city in the nation. It has
fought determinedly and has come through all triumphant." Disaster was,
according to another writer, "the meat on which our New Orleans had fed. It
has grown great on calamity." In the context of such a history no contemporary

10 Edward Alexander Parsons, *The Latin City: A Plea for Its Monuments* (New Orleans, 1925),
   5,.2; William Faulkner, *Mosquitoes* (New York, 1927), 10; Lyle Saxon, *Days Before Lent*
   (New York, 1939), 39; William Faulkner, "Damon and Pythias Unlimited," New Orleans
   Times-Picayune, February 15, 1925. For the collected essays, see William Faulkner, *New
   Orleans Sketches*, ed. Carvel Collins (New York, 1958).

problem could be perceived as insurmountable, no future challenge impossible to meet. "As the past is index to the future, we know it [New Orleans] will continue to still greater accomplishments." In the wake of Reconstruction, the city "was flat on its back and as nearly 'out' as New Orleans has ever been." A half-century later, however, the Crescent City was proud mistress of all she surveyed: "Such has been the astonishing development of a city that has had to fight for every minute of its life."[11]

But the triumph of New Orleans over the natural hazards of its location, the troubles of war, and the fierce competition of other cities was not the result of chance. The progress of the city was, as Mayor T. Semmes Walmsley said, "inevitable in its ultimate results." The historical record demonstrated fully that "Our true greatness lies ahead." The 1920s seemed to many spokesmen a crucial, transitional period, a watershed during which the city was challenged to consolidate its past achievements and move forward toward greater expansion. "It may be said," a prominent business leader stated, "that we are now passing through the most important period of our history; upon the present generation rests, in a large measure, the material, constructive future of New Orleans." Faced with this new challenge, the city could ill-afford backsliding, helpless antiquarianism, or social disunity: "a city to be notorious has only to outrival her sisters in brazenly proclaiming her weaknesses and short comings."[12]

Nashville also had the reputation of a traditional regional urban area, an image which Donald Davidson and some of his Vanderbilt colleagues eagerly articulated. Neither a major manufacturing center nor one of the very largest southern cities, Nashville was presented in local historical accounts with primary attention to its stability and cultural eminence rather than to its spectacular growth or economic power. Many commercial-civic spokesmen even considered the "Athens of the South" an "old-fashioned southern city," for many years "the political, cultural and social center of life in the South." Most writers were quick to add, however, that the city did not place

11 *New Orleans Association of Commerce News Bulletin*, VI (February 5, 1924), 3; Thomas Ewing Dabney, *The Indestructible City: The Story of New Orleans' Battle with Nature, and How, in Overcoming the Obstacles with Which It Was Faced, It Has Set a Superb Record of Progress and Development* (New Orleans, 1929), 9, 27.
12 T. Semmes Walmsley, "Forward," *Thirty-Five Years of Progress in New Orleans: "The City of the Future"* (New Orleans, 1931), 3; B. C. Casanas, "Presidential Report," *New Orleans Association of Commerce News Bulletin*, II (January 19, 1920), 3.

"unnecessary emphasis" on the past—"rather... the Past is appreciated." Conflict between reverence of the glories of an earlier era and the values of the urban ethos were not nearly as pronounced in the Tennessee capital as it was in either Charleston or New Orleans, and business spokesmen frequently enunciated the popular phrases of the "New South." Though Nashville's history lacked a dramatic theme of postwar resurgence or the exotic cultural background of New Orleans, it did contain the imposing figure of Andrew Jackson and appeared, to most local residents, just as "romantic" and exciting as that of other regional urban areas. The urban ethos was, in fact, widely accepted as a means of making the city "a place worthy of its illustrious beginnings." [13] Still, given the inherent limitations of its history, the themes of stability, continuity, culture, permanence, and consistency were generally stressed over those of exceptional growth and large size.

In Charleston, New Orleans, and Nashville, conflicting interpretations of the local past mirrored the larger conflict over urban priorities. But it was largely on the battlefield of local history, rather than in the realm of urban policy, that the urban ethos and the ideal of a corporate-expansive city were seriously contested. There was little in Charleston's past which could be fully exploited to demonstrate the validity of the corporate-expansive city; therefore, most business middle-class spokesmen dismissed local history altogether as a significant resource for the elaboration of the urban ethos. In New Orleans, past commercial growth and physical expansion made possible the full development of a progressive-evolutionary interpretation that was certainly as pervasive as those lamentations from artists in the French Quarter. And in Nashville the conflict between past and present was comparatively muted. In younger southern cities like Atlanta and Birmingham—and even in Memphis—the progressive-evolutionary view of the local past had assumed, by the 1920s, the status of historical orthodoxy.

Though the founding of Atlanta could be traced back to the first simple farmstead in the 1830s, the dramatic history of the city began with the Civil War, when General Sherman's torch set the stage for the most spectacular urban revival the region ever witnessed. The fabled "Atlanta spirit" was, according to popular histories of the 1920s, born not in the flames of war but

13 Nashville *Tennessean*, October 5, 1925; Maude Weidner, *Nashville Then and Now*, 1780–1930 (Nashville, 1930), 39, 73.

during the city's rebuilding. As seventh graders at the East Atlanta School recorded it, local citizens in the war's aftermath "showed a spirit of determination and pluck by building upon the ruins a new city, finer, greater, and more beautiful than the old one." Atlanta was invariably characterized as the Phoenix arising resolutely from the ashes of its own destruction. By 1880, Atlanta began to assume its modern proportions, defying not only Sherman's designs but the pull of the antebellum South. "Muddy thoroughfares were transformed into Great White Ways and paved streets radiating in all directions. The store of general merchandise, the vine-covered cottage, the small school house, and the simple church have been replaced by big business houses, palatial homes, graded schools, colleges, universities, and beautiful edifices of worship." All of this was achieved only by struggle and sacrifice, to be sure; but without great challenges the city's accomplishments would have been far less impressive and its destiny far less obvious. That Atlanta "was destined inevitably to become a great metropolis," the *Constitution* commented, "has been apparent since the days when it was a crossroads village." [14]

According to contemporary accounts, the spirit of progress, growth, and expansion was a consistent feature of local history and the crux of the city's "wonderful heritage of ideals" which remained vital during the 1920s. The Atlanta Historical Society, chartered in 1926, was one notable effort to expand community awareness of the local past, and the chamber of commerce launched a "Hall of Fame" to commemorate the contributions of early Atlanta residents to the city's development. Praising the chamber's activities, the *Constitution* agreed that "Future generations should know of the indefatigable courage, and of the indomitable plodding toward a goal by which the Atlanta of today was brought into being." This was an effort to initiate a rebirth of historical consciousness, to focus attention not only on commercial affairs but also on all those individuals who, in the chamber's view, had helped shape the "personality" of the city. Atlanta should "remember other phases than the whir of wheels and the clash of machinery, other phases than the rustle of bank notes and the click of adding machines," the *City Builder* wrote. An appreciation of the city's past was, like the de-

14 *City of Atlanta by Seventh Grade Pupils of the Atlanta Public Schools* (Atlanta, 1921), 7, 14; Atlanta *Constitution*, March 13, 1921.

velopment of civic loyalty, not simply a "pleasant pastime" but a "bounden duty."[15] The antebellum South played a very abbreviated role in the Atlanta story, and the burning of the city during the war was looked upon in retrospect more as a great and fortuitous opportunity than a tragic loss. In a very real sense, Atlantans of the 1920s were satisfied that Sherman's fire had fully consumed whatever debt the city owed to the Old South.

In Memphis and Birmingham the themes of urban unity and expansion were extensively elaborated in anniversary celebrations as well as in the usual spate of popular historical accounts. It was especially evident in these celebrations that, as one scholar has observed, "reenactment has absolutely no meaning except in its relevance to the present." Not only was the local past called upon for answers to questions of contemporary interest, but it was itself enlisted in defense and support of the prevailing urban ethos. The commemoration of anniversaries has always been, as William Lloyd Warner argued in his study of Newburyport, Massachusetts, "a vast exchange of understanding between the living and the dead," in which "secular rites" express "symbolically what the collectivity believed and wanted itself to be." As reaffirmations of community solidarity and purpose, such celebrations were more a reflection of contemporary concepts of the city than they were of historical reality. In Memphis and Birmingham, certainly, the local past was thoroughly manipulated to meet the conceptual needs of the present.[16]

On May 21–22, 1919, Memphis celebrated the hundredth anniversary of its founding and also the initial exploration of the region by Hernando De Soto in 1541. The title of the centennial spectacular, "The Blossoming of the Century Plant," appropriately reflected the organicism employed throughout the pageant to describe the city's development. At a cost of $30,000, the play was the central feature of a celebration which included an impressive fireworks display, a $25,000 floral parade, an industrial exposition, military exhibits, and community dances and festivities. According to an "official" historical account by Annah Robinson Watson, Memphis' heritage began in

15 Frederic J. Paxon, "A City of Friendships," Atlanta *Christian Index*, CII (December 7, 1922), 12; Franklin M. Garrett, *Atlanta and Environs: A Chronicle of Its People and Events* (New York, 1954), II, 836; Atlanta *Constitution*, January 17, 1921; Atlanta *City Buidler* (February, 1921), 14.

16 Cortland P. Auser, "The Viable Community: Redirections Through Applied Folklore," *New York Folklore Quarterly*, XXVI (March, 1970), 6; William Lloyd Warner, *The Living and the Dead: A Study of the Symbolic Life of Americans* (New Haven, 1959), 4, 107–109, 120–21, 126, 130.

an exotic and romantic foray by the Spaniards into the lush, wild forest of north Alabama and west Tennessee (a story told in the meter and style of Longfellow's *Hiawatha*). Attention then shifted to the city's founding in 1819 by John Overton, associate and confidant of Andrew Jackson. Though Overton wished to name the new town for his friend, the hero of New Orleans gallantly dissented: "I see another river, a sacred river. I see a mighty city upon its banks, queen of ancient Egypt, Memphis, it was. Memphis shall be the name of our city! Here in primeval forests, here among the aboriginal savages shall we rear a glorious city,—Memphis it shall be!' A solemn silence had fallen upon his companions. Their hearts were stirred by his vision, and a decision quickly reached."[17]

The major emphasis in Watson's history was on the De Soto expedition and the city's founding. The years from 1820 to 1919, in fact, were recalled in only two brief paragraphs! The floral parade explored the city's past in a bit more detail, though it was essentially the same in spirit. Separate floats commemorated De Soto, the founding of the city, and the exploits of Davy Crockett in 1850. Memphis' Civil War experience was definitely played down, though a float did call attention to Nathan Bedford Forest's cavalry raid in the city in 1864. The parade also included floral displays honoring King Cotton, Transportation, and Economic Diversification. The twenty-third and final float concluded the triumphal procession, on a note of modernity as well as organicism. "All that has been shown of Memphis," Watson wrote, "has led up to this climax: all that it has accomplished during the hundred years is here suggested. A great Century Plant rises in the center of a green hillock, the leaves reach out and upward toward the highest point, where the magnificent blossoms appear, and shows all, in electric lights, the name 'MEMPHIS.' "[18]

Throughout the festivities the city's origins were presented as not only fortuitous but exotic, romantic, and even mysterious. The founding of Memphis was linked directly to one of the great heroes of American, southern, and Tennessee history, and also with the spirit of frontier business enterprise which both Overton and Jackson represented. The foundations of the Memphis economy were likewise celebrated, and the unpleasant memories of war and the massive yellow-fever epidemic of 1878 were significantly erased

17 E. P. MacNicol, "Centennial Plans Maturing," *Memphis Chamber of Commerce Journal*, II (April, 1919), 52, 57; Annah Robinson Watson, *The Blossoming of the Century Plant: Memphis Centennial Celebration, 1918–1919* (Memphis, 1919), 5–7.
18 Watson, *Blossoming of the Century Plant*, 7–8, 15–17.

from the slate of official memory. Memphis was associated with major patterns of regional history, though more with the early frontiersmen and recent businessmen than with prominent figures of the Old South or the Civil War. Like floats in the centennial parade the flow of local history appeared uniform and inexorable, predestined to a great end, unbroken by a doubt or tragedy or failure—a joining of the past, present, and future. As local judge J. P. Young expressed it at an official ceremony in 1926 commemorating the centennial of the city's incorporation, the founders had been possessed of a "prophetic vision" that was fully realized in the reality of twentieth-century Memphis. "They dared to think of Memphis not as a small Indian trading post, but as a city, the greatness of which would far exceed the greatness of Memphis on the Nile. May generations yet unborn hold steadfast to the ideals of the founders."[19]

The notion that the city's development had been inexorable, that its growth was the result of powerful natural forces, did not preclude contemporary warnings that the solution of new problems was crucial to continued advance. If the flow of local history was securely within the channel of progress, to change the metaphor, then challenges of the present did at least threaten to slow the stream or possibly divert it. In the same words used earlier by a New Orleans Association of Commerce president, a business writer in Memphis declared: "Memphis now is in a state of transition." In many respects, the present decade was the most important of the city's history, and progress depended, more than ever, on the efforts and dedication of the present generation of citizens.[20] An inevitable feature of local historical interpretation during the 1920s was that it almost always led eventually to some call for renewed civic fervor and commitment.

The most memorable and elaborate celebration of local history during the decade occurred in the Birmingham semicentennial in 1921. The predominant theme of these festivities was, not surprisingly, the city's spectacular growth rather than its accumulated traditions or stability—neither of which the city possessed in large measure. Virtually since Birmingham's founding, in

19 *Special Meeting of the Board of Commissioners of the City of Memphis, December 9, 1926, in Commemoration of Hundredth Anniversary of the Incorporation of the City* (Memphis, 1926), pages not numbered.
20 *Memphis Chamber of Commerce Journal,* V (January, 1923), 23. The precise similarity of these remarks suggests, also, the degree to which chamber of commerce spokesmen relied upon one another for ideas and methods.

fact, residents had remarked on the city's size in relation to its short span of existence. "The country town has been swept to oblivion in the whirlwind rush of progress. Upon the cornfields which surrounded it, a modern city, lighted by the fires of many furnaces, now proudly rears her head. The muddy streets of forty years ago have changed to arteries of rushing traffic." "Birmingham has done in 50 years," one resident declared, "what it has taken most other towns 150 to do. Today our city is the biggest one in the United States for its age." [21]

In Birmingham, as elsewhere, the prescience of the founders seemed as remarkable as the result of their vision. "With a series of indifferent farms to start with," a former city commissioner wrote, "they planned a vast metropolis. The sky and the horizon were their limits, and they laid out a colossus." Given Birmingham's brief history and the dramatic strides of its growth, the semicentennial celebration was perhaps destined to become not so much a survey of the past as a broad, emphatic commentary on the comtemporary city. "Birmingham's growth has been largely a romance of industry, of pioneers who built furnaces, steel mills and skyscrapers and burrowed into the earth for coal and ore," the *Age-Herald* observed. "That phase of the city's history can be made spectacular and interesting in a pageant."[22] And the "Birmingham Pageant" was the central feature of the semicentennial celebration in October, 1921.

A special committee of local notables, with the aid of the state's congressional delegation, organized a series of events which included the pageant, a preliminary balloon race, parades, special street decorations, public dances, country club festivities, and a visit by President Harding. In a bedlam of factory whistles, with flags and bunting strewn across most of the business section, Harding rode in a motorcade along downtown streets lined with cheering school children, attended several gala functions, and delivered what was at least intended as a speech conciliatory to the South. Though originally scheduled to occupy a special presidential box to witness the pageant at Avondale Park, he found it necessary to return to Washington earlier than anticipated. Local citizens were apparently unaffected by the president's ab-

21 *Forty Years of Birmingham and the Birmingham Trust and Savings Company, 1887–1927* (Birmingham, 1927), 4; Brimingham *Age-Herald*, January 10, 1921.
22 John R. Hornady, *The Book of Birmingham* (New York, 1921), 1–2; Birmingham *Age-Herald*, September 14, 1921.

sence, however, and enjoyed a street carnival in the central downtown park and a ball at the country club, which lasted far into the night. The tone of the entire celebration was summed up accurately in the official semicentennial announcement, in which past, present, and future blended together almost as a single moment: "The dream of the founders of Birmingham has been more than fulfilled. Its history rests on the hardy frontiersmen, the farsighted engineers and city builders, the resourceful pioneers, the men of muscle and ambition, the loyal service of the generations which have come after. Today, too, there are those of vision who see this city four-fold in numbers, in size, in worth to the state and the nation. And, viewed in the light of what has gone before, who shall say their vision is idle?"[23]

Undaunted by unseasonably cold and disagreeable weather, large crowds turned out on the three nights of the pageant. "Fifty years of seeking and finding, of trials and success, were on display," James F. Sulzby wrote, "celebrating with words and music, the founding of Birmingham." The play was presented by more than sixty members of various special committees (history, costumes, dances, music, and drama) and included four musical selections, ten choral numbers, and nine dances. The pageant featured scenery imported from Chicago and entailed the services of virtually every vestige of local talent, including some well-known representatives from the local business community.[24]

As was the case in Memphis, Birmingham was clearly anxious to trace the city's origins as far back as possible, even to the precolonial days of the north Alabama region. The Birmingham pageant thus opened with scenes of Indians and the discovery of Alabama by De Soto. The Spaniard's steel sword was symbolically presented as a prophecy of Birmingham's later industrial prowess, and even the impressionable Indians were made to seem aware of the region's ultimate destiny. The scene then shifted abruptly to 1871. No homages to the Old South, no sentimental memoirs of the War Between the States marked the history of Birmingham. With the exception of a brief prologue, in fact, the events occurring between 1539 and 1871 were totally

23 Birmingham *Age-Herald,* October 25, 1921; James F. Sulzby, Jr., *Birmingham Sketches, from 1871 through 1921* (Birmingham, 1945), 188, 186, 182; *1921 Fiftieth Anniversary Announcement* (Birmingham, 1921), 14.

24 Sulzby, *Birmingham Sketches,* 181; Wallace Rice, *The Pageant of Birmingham: Presented in Avondale Park on Monday, Wednesday, and Thursday Evenings, October 24, 26, and 27, 1921, in Connection with the Semi-Centennial Celebration of the Founding of the City of Birmingham* (Birmingham, 1921), 2.

ignored. The main act of the play centered on the election of 1871 in which Birmingham displaced Elyton as the Jefferson County seat. The large numbers of blacks who attended the election-day outdoor barbeque (and who were played by whites in blackface makeup) were presented as ignorant children, easily tricked into voting for Birmingham by the clever ploys of early civic leaders. (Among other things, the Negroes in the play were advised that General Ulysses Grant was attending the barbeque and had cast his ballot for Birmingham.) Multiple voting among blacks was portrayed as rampant, and this easy manipulation of Negroes by whites hardly suggested any widespread white anxiety concerning Reconstruction. The possibility that Birmingham was born in the midst of electoral corruption and misrepresentation only further delighted the audience.

The dramatic apex of the play was reached with the grand entrance of "Colonel" James R. Powell, the most famous early city father, played by prominent local businessman John C. Henley. The "colonel" delivered an inspiring speech which, along with the playful manipulation of ballots, supposedly insured Birmingham's electoral victory: "Fellow citizens, this is the Magic City of the World, the marvel of the South, the miracle of the Continent, the dream of the Hemisphere, the vision of all Mankind! Within fifty years we shall have a hundred thousand people here, the best people on earth. Within a hundred years there'll be a million in the metropolis of the Globe."[25]

In this spirit the pageant moved onward. The symbolic "Anglo Saxon iron maker" drew together coal, limestone, and iron ore to create steel in Scene iv, and toward the end an Indian prophet, who had presented the prologues to each new scene, invited the "downtrodden" of Europe to join in the freedom and prosperity of the new city. The production concluded with personifications of all the world's nations paying homage to a resplendent figure symbolizing Birmingham. "There was a moment of silence," Sulzby recalled, "and then applause burst forth and echoed through the hills of Avondale Park. It was agreed without reservation that the story of the glorious first half-century of Birmingham had been faithfully and superbly told in the pageant."[26]

One would think that a city so audaciously new, so bereft of urban

25 Rice, *Pageant of Birmingham*, 5–16.
26 *Ibid.*, 23, 27; Sulzby, *Birmingham Sketches*, 185.

tradition, would suffer at least a few pangs of doubt about its legitimacy. "A few cities are so new," Anselm Strauss has observed, "that they and their residents share little in common with the rest of the region, in history or in taste, and so are constrained to build some sort of urban history, however flimsy, or to engage in other ceremonial gestures to reaffirm their association with their region." [27]

But Birmingham's links to the South were clearly forged with the future rather than the past. The lack of an extensive local history was a source not of regret but of pride, and made it easier for business middle-class spokesmen to identify Birmingham with the dynamic, modern currents of American life.

"The founding of a new community, one without history and without memory," wrote John C. Henley, Jr., "meant to young men and women a place where a new life could be begun, away from an environment where opportunity seemed hopeless." Urban boosterism in Birmingham was thus enlivened by the rhetoric of an urban frontier rather than by memories of a grandiose past. "It is the more to Birmingham's credit," the *Age-Herald* commented in 1923, "that it is breaking prior records at a time when reports of a slowdown come from other cities. But it is the Birmingham way. Somehow we are always 'just starting' here. Birmingham is always developing." And the prevailing image remained one of newness. No matter how much Birmingham might suffer in specific comparisons with other cities, it would always emerge quite superior in comparison with its recent and modest beginnings. "One marvels," a writer observed on the city's fifty-sixth anniversary, "how so huge and wonderful a city could have been a wilderness such a short time ago." [28] In the battle of history, Birmingham could be truly victorious.

The Urban Ethos and the New South

By virtually any standard of assessment during the 1920s, the "golden age" of southern cities came after the Civil War rather than before—and, more specifically, in the years after 1880. Most commercial-civic spokesmen

27 Strauss, *Images of the American City*, 114–15. Wohl and Brown, "The Usable Past," 252–53, also noted Kansas City's efforts to "extend its historical base" and relate regional—and even national—history to the local past.

28 John C. Henley, Jr., *This Is Birmingham: The Story of the Founding and Growth of an American City* (Birmingham, 1960), ii; Birmingham *Age-Herald*, March 29, 1923; Birmingham *News*, November 6, 1927.

maintained an attachment to the New South rather than to the Old and felt much more comfortable with the business initiative, commercial expansion, and sectional reconciliation of recent times than with the provincial, agricultural, slavery-dominated society and economy of the antebellum period. Especially in younger cities like Birmingham and Atlanta, the decade of the 1920s was itself considered the most promising period of regional urbanization.

The affinity of the business-oriented middle class for the values and aspirations of the New South was by no means coincidental. In a very real sense, the cities of the region had been the keys to that compelling vision of an industrialized, prosperous, and economically independent South espoused by Henry W. Grady, James D. B. DeBow, Daniel A. Tompkins, Richard Hathaway Edmonds, Henry Watterson, and Walter Hines Page. The "essential plank" in their "New South program was that wealth and power flowed from machines and factories, not from unprocessed fields of white cotton." Thus, Paul M. Gaston noted, "The crusade for an urban, industrialized society was their absorbing concern." Their vision was frankly materialistic and substituted the ideal of "the hardworking, busy, acquisitive individual" for the "Old South patriarch." It was in this "New South Creed" of the 1870s and 1880s, in fact, that the urban ethos probably first began to emerge in the region. [29]

The call for economic diversification, the leadership of a rising business elite, and an infusion of northern capital to support regional industrialization came in a period when the psychological wounds of war still festered. The New South ideal appeared, in fact, to be a wholesale acceptance of that Yankee business ethic which southern apologists had so severely condemned during the 1840s and 1850s. New South spokesmen were therefore in no position to renounce the past or totally recast southern history in their own particular mold. They "understood instinctively that no program of reform could do violence to a universally cherished past and hope to succeed." Their literature was thus, as Gaston observed, "permeated with a sense of the organic relationship between the old and the new." They attempted in every way possible to link their aspirations for a strong and economically self-sufficient South with popular notions of the struggle for southern independence in

29 Paul M. Gaston, *The New South Creed: A Study in Southern Mythmaking* (New York, 1970), 54, 68, 107.

1861–1865. Of necessity, the New South creed joined the myth of the Old South with dreams of the New.[30]

By the 1920s, however, the Civil War and the Old South myth were far less crucial to regional consciousness than they had been a half-century before. Popular notions of the near-perfection of antebellum society had in some ways assumed even greater proportions, of course, but they were generally far more removed from day-to-day social, economic, and political activities. After so many years, the Old South had become encased in legend and sentiment rather than in memory and was expressed more through periodic ritual than in practical affairs. This is not to suggest that the Old South had lost its usefulness. It was often resorted to in discussions of race relations and remained a tool for the maintenance of regional identity. But it was far less potent as a commanding ideological force by the beginning of the twentieth century, and members of the urban, commercial-civic elite—in a very real sense the New South spokesmen of the 1920s—were less bound by the necessity to support the romantic legend of the Lost Cause.

The organic connection between the Old South and the New which the first New South spokesmen fashioned in the wake of Reconstruction was alive and well in some quarters during the 1920s. The *Southern Magazine*, published in several regional urban areas including Nashville and Atlanta during the decade, carried a regular series of articles entitled "Through Southern Cities" and provided information on industrial development and commercial growth. Its editors portrayed the new industrial South very much as Henry Grady had pictured it, a South "irrevocably linked with the old," which carried on "the finer and nobler institutions of by-gone days" while also "adding to them the strength of vast resources and undeveloped industries." Likewise, the Nashville *Tennessean* believed that a "flawless skein of sentiment is woven into the industrial fabric which replaces the war-torn fabric which was a people's only shelter." As a writer for the Birmingham *Age-Herald* put it, the region of the 1920s was "no new south. Let's never call it that. It is the same old south grandly reasserting herself after the prostrating effect of war. The seed has always been there in southern manhood and womanhood." This view bears resemblance to the interpretation of southern history put forth by Wilbur J. Cash two decades later. Behind the din of skyscraper construction in southern towns Cash could hear "the gallop of Jeb

30 *Ibid.*, 153, 160, 189.

Stuart's calvarymen," for this new commerical expansion basically derived, he wrote, from "the native genius of an incurably romantic people, enamored before all else of the magnificent and spectacular." Whatever the sources of this New South spirit, the necessity for coupling commitments to a new order with protests of loyalty to the old, which C. Vann Woodward observed of the late nineteenth century, was no longer so profound by the third decade of the twentieth.[31]

Even those scholars who have recognized the existence of prourban views in the region have been puzzled by their origins in a pattern of "defensive agrarianism." According to Anselm Strauss, a "post-bellum roseate mythology developed which supported the view that life at the planter's big house had been cosmopolitan and urbane, something less like 'farming' than like gentlemanly leisure. If true," he concluded, "the South could claim a tradition of urbane agrarianism—an urbaneness perhaps more cosmopolitan than that of many a northern or western city." John K. Bettersworth, who articulated this thesis in 1957, held that since "the whole plantation South was a city," southerners could incorporate their expanding metropolises into their conservative, agrarian heritage.[32]

This theory is not, however, supported by the evidence. The progressive-evolutionary interpretation became, by the twentieth century, the most popular means of linking past, present, and future—and of virtually excluding the legend of the Old South and the "urban plantation" from most local history. In Memphis and Birmingham the spirit of the twentieth-century metropolis was traced back to the adventurous frontiersman rather than to the patriarchal planter. And the same connection was made in the cover illustrations of popular historical accounts in Nashville and Atlanta. Maude Weidner's brief history of the Tennessee capital carried on its cover an illustration of Indians around a campfire and a lonely cabin in the wilderness—and in the background gigantic and resplendent skyscrapers of a modern metropolis (far grander than those which Nashville possessed at the time). Similarly, the cover of an Atlanta centennial publication in 1937 was

31 *Southern Magazine* [Nashville], I (March, 1924), 61; Nashville *Tennessean*, December 20, 1925; Richard A. Johnston, "For Good of the Community," Birmingham *Age-Herald*, June 19, 1922; Wilbur J. Cash, *The Mind of the South* (New York, 1941), 225; C. Vann Woodward, *Origins of the New South, 1877–1913* (Baton Rouge, 1951), 155.
32 Strauss, *Images of the American City*, 126; John K. Bettersworth, "The Urbane Bourbon," *Mississippi Quarterly*, X (Spring, 1957), 84.

composed of a photograph of the contemporary city upon which drawings of Indians, a buckskin-clad frontiersman, and a log cabin were superimposed.[33]

Between the two extreme "symbolic stages" of urban history depicted in these illustrations—the wilderness and the modern city—it was the early pioneer rather than the Confederate cavalryman or Old South statesman who received a place of honor. This version of local history is significant for a variety of reasons, not the least important of which is the primarily national rather than regional connotation of the pioneer symbol. But the principal value of the frontiersman was probably his identification with qualities much prized in the contemporary city—boldness, pride, an adventurous spirit, and a determination to establish a new and more perfect community. In the context of a progressive-evolutionary interpretation, the early urban pioneers began a tradition of growth, progress, and local loyalty of which the corporate-expansive city was but the inevitable and perfect culmination. The early frontiersman not only served as a link between past and present but also became a symbol of the post–Civil War New South.

A chorus of New South sentiment was sounded throughout the region in scores of various publications and especially by the commercial-civic elite. "For thirty years before the War Between the States," the Charleston *News and Courier* declared, "the best energies of the Southern people were devoted to a vain effort to maintain the status quo. For fifty years after that struggle they contended for the right of existence. Now beyond a doubt a new day has come. The South no longer dreams of the past. Her eyes are to the future." Even Katherine Ripley was happy that a "new South of industry and bustle and optimism" had replaced "the indolent, slovenly, romantic South of insolvent colonels wistfully dreaming of departed glories." In the region's largest city, some spokesmen felt compelled to explain that age posed no threat to progress: "With 206 years to its credit," one writer commented in 1924, "New Orleans is one of the oldest cities in the land. But its ways are young." After all, its citizens were "no older than the citizens of other communities."[34]

Any undue emphasis on the pleasures and security of the past was likely to be interpreted as expressing a lack of faith in the city's destiny. "Frequent-

33 Weidner, *Nashville Then and Now*, cover; *Atlanta Centennial Year Book, 1837–1937* (Atlanta, 1937), cover.
34 Charleston *News and Courier*, March 27, 1920; Ripley, *Sand Dollars*, 49; *New Orleans Association of Commerce News Bulletin*, VI (February 19, 1924), 2.

ly some discontented persons refer feelingly to the so-called 'good old days' and express a longing for their return," the *Tennessean* observed. But "we are so far ahead of the good old days that the improvement is almost unbelievable." In Atlanta, also, the past was regarded less as example than as a prelude to a future in which the new must inevitably replace the old. "There is no more certain indication of progress than the extent of destruction," the *Constitution* commented in 1923. "The city which has ceased to grow and to improve is satisfied with the old, and sees no need for tearing down to make way for the new." According to Carter Helm Jones, pastor of the city's Second Baptist Church, who spoke at the grand opening of the Biltmore Hotel in 1924, "Atlanta stands for the New South, the New South with all the romance of music, beauty, poetry, idealism of a fading past." The Atlanta which local boosters celebrated was not a repository of antebellum culture, but "the wonder city of the South, youthful in years and energy."[35]

In Birmingham, the New South was the major temporal concept through which the city was related to the region. On one occasion, the editors of the *Age-Herald* protested a Mobile paper's designation of the "Magic City" as a "typical" southern urban area. "Birmingham is typical of the new industrial South," they claimed, "and perhaps the most cosmopolitan of all southern cities. . . There is nothing here of the easy-going complacency that characterizes so many towns and cities in the south, where much of the ante-bellum spirit survives." The city tended to boast, in fact, of its lack of tradition. "Birmingham lives in the present, not the past, and builds for the future. It has a different atmosphere from most of the southern cities that date back to the Civil War, or an earlier period. With all due respect for the fine old customs of the past, they lacked some of the progressiveness that is indispensable nowadays for the south's proper development." Though the New South owed much to the Old South, it was "a gentle debt to be paid only in kind." While some features of an older culture deserved admiration, the central fact was, "The Old South is but a fragrant memory; the New South is a mighty, pulsating force in American life." A cartoon in the *Age-Herald*, announcing the 1920 census returns, pictured three men representing different southern cities standing before a bar, each with a "jug" symbolizing that particular city's population increase. The figure representing Birming-

35 Nashville *Tennessean*, February 13, 1925; Atlanta *Constitution*, July 2, 1923; quoted in Garrett, *Atlanta and Environs*, II, 805; Dudley Glass (ed.), *Men of Atlanta* (Atlanta, 1924).

ham was drinking from the largest container and was pictured as young, clean-shaven, and clad in a modern business suit. The figures symbolizing Atlanta and New Orleans were older, bearded, and dressed very much like antebellum planters.[36]

By 1900 the "cohesive group" that had originally formulated and espoused the New South creed was gone, though their vision continued. Indeed, as Gaston concluded, there was no need for such a group "so long as the mythology created by the first one endured."[37] But the idea of a New South did not simply dissipate into the ideological atmosphere. Rather, it passed into the keeping of a larger and less cohesive, but perhaps more influential, group—the urban commercial-civic elite—and its social and economic views were embodied fully in the urban ethos of the 1920s. In some respects, it was stated even more forcefully in the twentieth century than it had been in the nineteenth.

The New South ideal was the principal conception with which many commercial-civic spokesmen linked the urban ethos with regional history and tradition. They also employed it as a device for promoting the virtues of progress, expansion, stability, civic loyalty, and urban unity behind commercial-civic leadership. Commercial-civic spokesmen were both threatened and buoyed-up by local history, and their dilemma was especially acute in those cities where "progress" was not accepted as the only conceivable policy. But this additional ambiguity of the decade was resolved as so many other ambiguities were—by ordering the facts and perceptions in such a way as to bolster prevailing social thought and conceptions of the urban community. The progressive-evolutionary interpretation provided a meaningful context for an urban ethos of expansion, and the firm connections established between past, present, and future (accomplished with considerable wrenching of the facts) gave a comforting sense of continuity and strength to contemporary policies. The result was that the New South ideal extended well into the twentieth century.

36 Birmingham *Age-Herald*, September 11, 1922, May 18, 1926, October 17, 1926, June 30, 1920. It is interesting to compare this cartoon with C. Vann Woodward's statement in *Origins of the New South*, 161: "When the New South was personified by the cartoonist it was, significantly, in the garb of the ante-bellum planter."
37 Gaston, *The New South Creed*, 221.

Epilogue

"The urban mind in America has actually been like the eye of the fly under a microscope, composed of thousands of glittering faces."

—Michael Kammen, *People of Paradox* (1972)

THE ORIGINS of the southern urban ethos are so diffuse, the threads so intertwined from so many different sources, that they can probably never be completely unraveled or precisely sorted. As with the eye of the fly, closer examination reveals myriad detail. But a pattern did exist, sketched out in hundreds of various publications and rooted in the major concerns of the southern urban commercial-civic elite during the period. This ethos—with the concept of the corporate-expansive city at its core—was surely not unique to this region or to this period. It may well have been advanced throughout American history by urban elites when they desired urban growth at the same time that they feared actual or suspected changes attendant to growth. But one does not have to look far for the particular complex of social realities that provided the context for the urban ethos in the South. For this context was the emergence of the twentieth-century metropolis in the nation's least urban region.

The commercial-civic elite was a dynamic group which played a crucial role in changing the face of the southern city, and its considerable impact

217

should not be obscured by the exaggerations of booster rhetoric. Its members were neither planters disguised as businessmen nor established merchant princes—but business and civic leaders primarily engaged in increasing their influence and control over a growing, shifting urban domain. They encountered an urban world in the 1920s that was different in many ways from that of the late nineteenth century. It was larger, more heterogeneous and complex, and less susceptible to elite direction. Growth, expansion, and development were still siren calls of opportunity, and the Old South was a heritage to be dutifully worshipped—though by this time mostly in museums. But the accumulated problems of large population growth and geographical expansion placed a higher premium on urban order. The boom town had become by the 1920s a term of opprobrium, and "responsible citizenship"—defined, of course, in characteristic commercial-civic terms—seemed a crucial component of the desirable modern city. At the same time, technological innovations like the automobile heralded a new urban era of unprecedented promise and potential fragmentation. Altogether, the major southern cities of this period bore a striking resemblance to their counterparts in other sections of the country—especially when it came to the demands and challenges posed by growth and change.

The southern urban ethos of the 1920s was an attempt by the commercial-civic elite to comprehend the city and to resolve a variety of conceptual dilemmas; and it was also—though perhaps secondarily—a guide for the shaping of the city. At the very least, it delimited a particular range of alternatives and channeled the thinking of its adherents in certain directions. It was also, significantly, a *rationale for metropolis* inspired by the desire to unite the various parts of the expanding city in a large, synergic landscape and to resolve, or at least meliorate, the tension between centrifugal and centripetal forces. Thus the metropolis—characterized by a discernible and vital center or core, a variety of specialized activities and land uses, a large population, and a huge territory—was conceptually fashioned into a positive goal.

One is impressed by the degree to which the urban ethos coincided with reality—especially certain economic trends. But as the basis of municipal policy its flaws and inconsistencies seem, in retrospect, all too apparent. The notions that all classes and groups shared the same basic interests and goals, that they could be effectively united purely on the basis of greater prosperity and civic loyalty, that they could be content with commercial-civic leadership, had enough measure of truth to sustain them in the 1920s perhaps—but they were demonstrably false, especially in a metropolitan milieu. Class and ethnic differences were very real and could hardly be confronted when their significance and reality were ignored or denied. The belief that expansion would reinforce social stability and civic unity was, no doubt, a comforting thought; but such a framework precluded any genuine understanding of the realities and problems of both growth and community. The misconceptions which underlay the concept of the corporate-expansive city served, ironically, to cripple any chances American cities may have had of becoming the "ideal" metropolises envisioned by the commercial-civic elite. And the urban ethos was further weakened because it was both an abstract goal and a means of social control, a means of retaining the existing order within a dynamic framework.

Advocates of the urban ethos attempted to create an organic urban community on the basis of voluntarism, without any basic revision of the prevailing system of social and economic inequity and social injustice that festered in the urban body. It was a community fashioned more out of wishful thinking than out of reality, more out of will than out of experience. Like the concept of community which Richard Sennett detected in modern affluent suburbs, this type of common identity "is a counterfeit of experience. People talk about their understanding of each other and of the common ties that bind them, but the images are not true to their actual relations. But the lie they have formed as their common image is a usable falsehood—a myth—for the group. Its use is that it makes a coherent image of the community as a whole: people draw a picture of who they are that binds them together as one being, with a definite set of desires, dislikes, and goals. The image of community is purified of all that might convey a feeling of difference, let alone conflict, in who 'we' are. In this way the myth of community solidarity is a purification ritual."[1] In short, policies wrought on assumptions of social unity or the wish for social solidarity, while they might serve to unite elements of the commercial-civic elite behind certain common values and goals, could not deal adequately with conditions of variety and diversity. And the cities of the South—like those elsewhere in America—would not be molded in the image of elite groups.

1 Richard Sennett, *The Uses of Disorder: Personal Identity and City Life* (New York, 1970), 33, 36.

The urban ethos, enunciated by the southern white commercial-civic elite, rooted by its proponents in local and regional history, and shaped by the awareness of urban problems and by comparisons of the large city with rural areas, small towns, and other urban areas—was calculated to meet immediate needs, maintain the existing social order, insure urban expansion, and justify social conformity to commercial-civic values and goals. It failed, of course, to generate a metropolitan sense of community; indeed, it made such a thing even more difficult to achieve. Its psychological prescriptions simply could not be sustained without some solid foundation of social and economic reality. But since it was the general conceptual context within which the commercial-civic elite interpreted and influenced urban policy, the ragged outlines of its imprint can be seen in the appearance, structure, and problems of southern cities for at least several decades after the 1920s.

Bibliographical Essay

THE RANGE of materials in southern urban history is enormous and barely manageable even for a single decade. Some kinds of sources, especially manuscripts and city documents, are not available for many cities in anywhere near the extent or variety that we would like; but the main problem has been that, until relatively recent times, few serious scholars have taken advantage of them. Detailed references in the footnotes are the reader's best guide to the sources, but specialists may be interested in a further discussion of the principal materials consulted in the writing of this book.

I have relied primarily on a variety of newspapers and periodicals. The most important of these are listed below, with the dates for which they were examined:

Alabama Baptist (Birmingham, 1920–30)
Atlanta *Christian Index* (Baptist, 1922–29)
Atlanta *City Builder* (Atlanta Chamber of Commerce, 1920–30)
Atlanta *Constitution* (1920–30)
Atlanta *Independent* (1920–30)
Atlanta Life (1926–30)
Birmingham (Birmingham Chamber of Commerce, 1926–30)
Birmingham *Age-Herald* (1920–30)
Birmingham *Labor Advocate* (1920–30)

Charleston *News and Courier* (1920–30)

The Circuit Rider (First Methodist Episcopal Church, South, Birmingham, 1926–29)

The City Club of Memphis Bulletin (1919–22)

Knoxville *Journal and Tribune* (1920–23)

Memphis Chamber of Commerce Journal (1918–30)

Memphis *Commercial-Appeal* (1920–29)

Memphis *Labor Review* (1922–30)

Memphis *Tattler* (May 4–June 22, 1929)

Memphis *World* (1931–32)

Nashville *Banner* (1920–30)

Nashville *Christian Advocate* (Methodist, 1920–30)

Nashville *Globe* (1907–13, 1933–35)

Nashville *Review* (1920–30)

Nashville *Tennessean* (1920–30)

Nashville This Week (1925–30)

National Municipal Review (1920–30)

New Orleans Association of Commerce News Bulletin (1920–30)

New Orleans *Times-Picayune* (1920–29)

Norfolk *Journal and Guide* (1920–30)

Richmond *Planet* (1920–30)

Southern Labor Review (Birmingham, 1922–30)

Southern Literary Magazine (1923–26; became the *Southern Magazine* when it moved from Atlanta to Nashville in 1924)

Additional newspapers were consulted on a less comprehensive basis for particular information on events and personalities or to check the continuity and consistency of response to specific municipal policies. These included the Atlanta *Journal*, the Atlanta *Tribune*, the Birmingham *News*, the Birmingham *Post*, and the New Orleans *Item*.

Manuscript collections did not prove very useful in the research for this book, though the following were of some value: the papers and memoirs of Lee I. Blum, Jacob McGavock Dickinson, and Archibald Trawick ("Things Remembered, 1872–1935") in the Tennessee State Library and Archives, Nashville; the papers of William Edward Burghardt Du Bois, Charles S. Johnson, and James Carroll Napier in the Special Collections at Fisk University, Nashville; and Robert R. Otis' mimeographed diary, "Atlanta's Plan, 1909–1932," in the Georgia State Library, Atlanta.

The various reports of the United States Census provided crucial population data for the cities under consideration, and a number of letters, reports, minutes, ordinances, regulations, and other documents were examined in each of the five major cities (the most significant of these materials are indicated in the footnotes).

A large body of literary works was consulted, primarily for conceptions of southern cities and urban life. Many of them, of course, are hardly memorable either for their substance or their literary skill, and have been deservedly ignored by those interested in the finer achievements of southern letters. But they can provide valuable, even if sometimes peripheral, comments on the city in general and the urban South in particular. Ellen Glasgow's work, much of it dealing with her native Richmond, stands out as the most sensitive and perceptive literary appraisal of the region during the 1920s, especially *One Man in His Time* (Garden City, 1922) and *Barren Ground* (New York, 1925). The *Letters of Ellen Glasgow*, edited by Blair Rouse (New York, 1958) are an additional source of her views during the period. Other literary works which treat specific cities or urban life in general that have been of some value to this study include: Sherwood Anderson, "A Meeting South" in Etolia S. Basso, ed., *The World from Jackson Square: A New Orleans Reader* (New York, 1948), 343–53, and *Dark Laughter* (New York, 1925); Hamilton Basso (New Orleans), *Cinnamon Seed* (New York, 1934), *In Their Own Image* (New York, 1935), and *Courthouse Square* (New York, 1936); Jack Bethea (Birmingham), *Cotton: A Novel* (Boston, 1928); William Faulkner, *New Orleans Sketches*, edited by Carvel Collins (New York, 1958), and *Mosquitoes* (New York, 1927); Gloria Goddard (Birmingham), *A Breadline for Souls* (New York, 1938); Ward Greene (Atlanta), *Ride the Nightmare* (New York, 1930); DuBose Heyward (Charleston), *Skylines and Horizons* (New York, 1924); *Porgy* (New York, 1925), and *Mamba's Daughters* (Garden City, 1929); Oliver La Farge (New Orleans), "Completely New" in Basso, ed., *The World from Jackson Square*, 361–77; Clara Elizabeth Mabry (Birmingham), *Afterglow* (Birmingham, 1939); W. R. Manlove (Nashville), *Kunjur Tales and Oddments* (Nashville, 1930); Louise Crenshaw Ray (Birmingham), *Color of Steel* (Chapel Hill, 1932); Katherine Ball Ripley (Charleston), *Sand Dollars* (New York, 1933); Fred Short (Birmingham), *Hilltops* (Birmingham, 1926); T. S. Stribling, *Unfinished Cathedral* (Garden City, 1934); Charles Walt [Albert Bein], *Love in Chicago* (New York, 1929); and Clement Wood (Birmingham), *Nigger: A Novel* (New York, 1922).

The most useful travel accounts of the urban South were: Jennie Margerie Bly, *Adventures of a Book Agent* (Boston, 1925); Mildred Cram, *Old Seaport Towns of the South* (New York, 1917); and Edward Hungerford, *The Personality of American Cities* (New York, 1913).

A comprehensive history of southern cities has been needed for some time, though the pathbreaking study edited by Rupert B. Vance and Nicholas J. Demerath, *The Urban South* (Chapel Hill, 1954), has admirably, even if partially, filled this void for the past two decades. The most useful essays in this collection are those by Rudolf Heberle, "The Mainsprings of Southern Urbanization," and T. Lynn Smith, "The Emergence of Cities." *The City in Southern History: The Development of Urban Civilization in the South*, edited by Blaine A. Brownell and David R. Goldfield, to be published by Kennikat Press in 1976, is a collection of original essays intended to provide a relatively comprehensive survey and set forth some of the major conceptual problems involved. A very brief essay on the recent South is B. A. Brownell, *The Urban South in the Twentieth Century* (Saint Charles, Mo., 1974).

Southern historians are fortunate, of course, to have an exceptional array of secondary works available on this single region. Two of the best of these are Volumes IX and X of the magisterial series, A *History of the South:* C. Vann Woodward, *Origins of the New South, 1877–1913* (Baton Rouge, 1951), and George Brown Tindall, *The Emergence of the New South, 1913–1945* (Baton Rouge, 1967). These superb works are models of graceful style, richness of detail, and interpretive strength.

Wilbur Joseph Cash's *The Mind of the South* (New York, 1941), though marked by a decided Piedmont bias and flawed in its coverage of the urban South, remains one of the best, and most provocative, assessments of regional ideology and values. Paul M. Gaston's *The New South Creed: A Study in Southern Mythmaking* (New York, 1970), while by no means a replacement of Cash, is a more fruitful examination of the ideology and values that permeated southern urban leadership in the late nineteenth century. Anne Firor Scott was one of the first recent scholars to consider the challenges and opportunities of southern urban history in "The Study of Southern Urbanization," *Urban Affairs Quarterly,* I (March, 1966), 5–14. Howard W. Odum's *Southern Regions of the United States* (Chapel Hill, 1936), is a monument to the regionalists at the University of North Carolina and an important collection of data on virtually every aspect of southern life; and the various essays in William T. Couch, ed., *Culture in the South* (Chapel Hill, 1934), especially those by Edd Winfield Parks and Josephine Pinckney, provide a valuable contemporary look at southern cities.

Other useful sources on aspects of southern urbanization include: Richard J. Hopkins, "Are Southern Cities Unique? Persistence as a Clue," *Mississippi Quarterly,* XXVI (Spring, 1973), 121–41; Robert Earl Garren, "Urbanism: A New Way of Life for the South," *ibid.,* X (Spring, 1957), 65–72; Gerald M. Capers, "The Rural Lag on Southern Cities," *ibid.,* XXI (Fall, 1968), 253–61; William D. Miller, "Myth and New South City Murder Rates," *ibid.,* XXVI (Spring, 1973), 143–53; Rudolf Heberle, "Social Consequences of Industrialization of Southern Cities," *Social Forces,* XXVII (October, 1948), 30–34; Walter J. Matherly, "The Emergence of the Metropolitan Community in the South," *ibid.,* XIV (March, 1936), 311–25; Kenneth T. Jackson, *The Ku Klux Klan in the City, 1915–1930* (New York, 1967); George B. Tindall, "Business Progressivism: Southern Politics in the Twenties," *South Atlantic Quarterly,* XLII (Winter, 1963), 92–106; Lyndon E. Abbott and Lee G. Greene, *Municipal Government and Administration in Tennessee* (Knoxville, 1939); Blaine A. Brownell, "Southern Urbanization: A Unique Experience?" *Mississippi Quarterly,* XXVI (Spring, 1973), 105–20; and Brownell, "A Symbol of Modernity: Attitudes Toward the Automobile in Southern Cities in the 1920s," *American Quarterly,* XXIV (March, 1972), 20–44.

In the study of urban imagery, two works are particularly prominent: Anselm L. Strauss, *Images of the American City* (1961), and Kevin Lynch, *The Image of the City* (Cambridge, 1960). While rather inadequate in their historical evaluations, both of these volumes are invaluable in suggesting the importance of views of the city and in positing productive lines of future investigation. Other works on this subject include: John K. Bettersworth, "The Urbane Bourbon," *Mississippi Quarterly,* X (Spring,

1957), 79–87; Charles N. Glaab, "Visions of Metropolis: William Gilpin and Theories of City Growth in the American West," *Wisconsin Magazine of History*, LXV (Autumn, 1961), 21–31; Anselm L. Strauss and R. Richard Wohl, "Symbolic Representation and the Urban Milieu," *American Journal of Sociology*, LXIII (March, 1958), 523–32; William Lloyd Warner, *The Living and the Dead: A Study of the Symbolic Life of Americans* (New Haven, 1959); Dana Francis White, "The Self-Conscious City: A Survey and Bibliographical Summary of Periodical Literature on American Urban Themes, 1865–1900" (Ph.D. dissertation, George Washington University, 1969); R. Richard Wohl and A. Theodore Brown, "The Usable Past: A Study of Historical Traditions in Kansas City," *Huntington Library Quarterly*, XXIII (May, 1960), 237–59; and Blaine A. Brownell, "The Agrarian and Urban Ideals: Environmental Images in Modern America," *Journal of Popular Culture*, V (Spring, 1972), 576–87.

Frank Freidel's essay, "Boosters, Intellectuals, and the American City" in Oscar Handlin and John Burchard, eds., *The Historian and the City* (Cambridge, 1966) is a brief, perceptive comment on the need to take booster rhetoric and ideology seriously. James Warren Prothro's *The Dollar Decade: Business Ideas in the 1920s* (Baton Rouge, 1954), and James Weinstein's *The Corporate Ideal in the Liberal State, 1900–1918* (Boston, 1968) provide suggestive, though very different, assessments of business thought in the period. August Meier's *Negro Thought in America, 1880–1915: Racial Ideologies in the Age of Booker T. Washington* (Ann Arbor, 1963) remains an invaluable survey and analysis of black opinion, and Thomas J. Woofter, Jr.'s *Negro Problems in Cities* (Garden City, 1928) contains much useful information on the condition of southern urban blacks in the early twentieth century. Robert King Merton's "Patterns of Influence: Local and Cosmopolitan Influentials," *Social Theory and Social Structure* (Rev. ed., Glencoe, 1949) presents an analysis of the relationship between socioeconomic status and various conceptions of the local community.

Though they represent but a small sample of the general works consulted on various aspects of southern and urban history, the following sources were particularly valuable: Robert S. and Helen M. Lynd, *Middletown in Transition: A Study in Cultural Conflicts* (New York, 1937); George E. Mowry, *Another Look at the Twentieth-Century South* (Baton Rouge, 1973); Mowry, *The Urban Nation, 1920–1960* (New York, 1965); Robert Moats Miller, *American Protestantism and Social Issues, 1919–1939* (Chapel Hill, 1958); and Sylvia L. Thrupp, "The City as the Idea of Social Order" in Handlin and Burchard, eds., *The Historian and the City*.

Southern cities vary, of course, in the quality and extent of their local records and historical materials. Some cities, like Memphis, have been the subjects of serious scholarly work while others, like Nashville, have primarily drawn the attention of local, amateur historians. Each individual city thus presents its own research challenges and opportunities; but every southern city contains sufficient historical sources to support the first-rate local studies that they deserve and that our understanding of southern history demands.

ATLANTA. There is as yet no published scholarly survey of the history of Atlanta, a deficiency which the ongoing multivolume Atlanta history project is designed to remedy. (See Dale A. Somers, Timothy J. Crimmins, and Merl E. Reed, "Surveying the Records of a City: The History of Atlanta Project," in the July, 1973 volume of *American Archivist*, 353–59. The first volume scheduled for publication in the Project is "The Anatomy of Atlanta: Contours of Regional City Growth.") Two unpublished studies, however, have traced developments in the Georgia metropolis in the nineteenth century and in the first decades of the twentieth: James Michael Russell, "Atlanta, Gate City of the South, 1847 to 1885" (Ph.D. dissertation, Princeton University, 1972), and Thomas Mashburn Deaton, "Atlanta During the Progressive Era" (Ph.D. dissertation, University of Georgia, 1969). A study by Richard J. Hopkins, "Patterns of Persistence and Occupational Mobility in a Southern City: Atlanta, 1870–1920" (Ph.D. dissertation, Emory University, 1972) is excellent, and the best application of the methodology of the "New Urban History" to a Deep South urban area. Hopkins' researches are also presented in his "Status, Mobility, and the Dimensions of Change in a Southern City: Atlanta, 1870–1910" in Kenneth T. Jackson and Stanley K. Schultz, eds., *Cities in American History* (New York, 1972), 216–31; and "Occupational and Geographic Mobility in Atlanta, 1870–1896," *Journal of Southern History*, XXXIV (May, 1968), 200–13.

Of the published general histories, Franklin Garrett's multivolume *Atlanta and Environs: A Chronicle of Its People and Events* (New York, 1954), and Walter G. Cooper's *Official History of Fulton County* (Atlanta, 1934) are better than average local accounts that contain much valuable detail, and *Atlanta: Capital of the South* (New York, 1949), edited by Paul W. Miller in the American Guide Series, is of some interest. Cooper's work is particularly good on the area's commercial and civic leaders and groups, largely because he was secretary of the Atlanta Chamber of Commerce for over twenty years. John R. Hornady's *Atlanta: Yesterday, Today and Tomorrow* (New York, 1922), and Wilbur G. Kurtz's *Historic Atlanta: A Brief History of Atlanta and Its Landmarks* (Atlanta, 1929) are useful only for the contemporary conceptions of the city which they contain.

Major collections of material on local history are located in the Atlanta Public Library, which has a variety of chamber of commerce reports and publications; Emory University; the Atlanta Collection at the University of Georgia in Athens; the Georgia State Library; and the Atlanta Historical Society. The City Clerk's office has complete files of minutes for both the Board of Aldermen and the City Council during the 1920s.

Useful studies of Atlanta's Afro-Americans include August Meier and David Lewis, "History of the Negro Upper Class in Atlanta, Georgia, 1890–1958," *Journal of Negro Education*, XXVIII (Spring, 1959), 128–39; John Wiley Rozier, "A History of the Negro Press in Atlanta" (M.A. thesis, Emory University, 1947); Louis Delphia Davis Shivery, "History of Organized Social Work Among Atlanta Negroes, 1890–1935" (M.A. thesis, Atlanta University, 1936); and Dorothy Slade, "The Evolution of

Negro Areas in the City of Atlanta" (M.A. thesis, Atlanta University, 1946). Other works on related aspects of the city's history are Anne Lavinia Branch, "Atlanta and the American Settlement House Movement" (M.A. thesis, Emory University, 1966), and Solomon Sutker, "The Jews of Atlanta: Their Social Structure and Leadership Patterns" (Ph.D. dissertation, University of North Carolina, 1950). Charles Paul Garofalo traces the major themes of business thought in "Business Ideas in Atlanta, 1916–1935" (Ph.D. dissertation, Emory University, 1972). Elizabeth Anne Mack Lyon's profusely illustrated "Business Buildings in Atlanta: A Study in Urban Growth and Form" (Ph.D. dissertation, Emory University, 1971) is a very useful analysis of the city's central business district, and Howard Lawrence Preston's "A New Kind of Horizontal City: Automobility in Atlanta, 1900–1930" (Ph.D. dissertation, Emory University, 1974) is an innovative effort to assess the impact of the automobile on the urban structure of Atlanta and the first full-length study of its kind for a single major city in this period.

Some of the more interesting of the contemporary materials on the Gate City are: Ivan Allen, *Atlanta from the Ashes* (Atlanta, 1928); *Atlanta Centennial Year Book, 1837–1937* (Atlanta, 1937); Atlanta Public Schools, *City of Atlanta by Seventh Grade Pupils of the Atlanta Public Schools* (Atlanta, 1921); Edna Baker, *My City: A Workbook for Geography of Atlanta* (Atlanta, 1932); John A. Beeler, *Report to the City of Atlanta on a Plan for Local Transportation, December, 1924* (Atlanta, 1924); Forward Atlanta Commission, *Report of the Forward Atlanta Commission* (Atlanta, 1930); Dudley Glass, ed., *Men of Atlanta* (Atlanta, 1924); and Sarah Huff, *My 80 Years in Atlanta* (Atlanta, 1937).

BIRMINGHAM. No historical survey of Birmingham exists, though the city has been the focus of a limited number of published and unpublished scholary studies. Martha C. Mitchell's valuable thesis, "Birmingham: Biography of a City of the New South" (Ph.D. dissertation, University of Chicago, 1946), concentrates on the city's history prior to 1900, and Carl Vernon Harris' perceptive "Economic Power and Politics: A Study of Birmingham, Alabama, 1890–1920" (Ph.D. dissertation, University of Wisconsin, 1970) deals with local affairs in terms of patterns of social and economic leadership and decision-making. A revised version of his dissertation will be published by the University of Tennessee Press in 1976. For a general survey of the city during the 1920s, see Blaine A. Brownell, "Birmingham, Alabama: New South City in the 1920s," *Journal of Southern History*, XXXVIII (February, 1972), 21–48.

Birmingham has also been the subject of some excellent specialized works, including Paul B. Worthman, "Working Class Mobility in Birmingham, Alabama, 1880–1914" in Tamara K. Hareven, ed., *Anonymous Americans: Explorations in Nineteenth-Century Social History* (Englewood Cliffs, N.J., 1971), 172–213; Worthman, "Black Workers and Labor Unions in Birmingham, Alabama, 1897–1904," *Labor History*, X (Summer, 1969), 375–407; William Robert Snell, "The Ku Klux Klan in Jefferson County, Alabama, 1916–1930" (M.A. thesis, Samford University,

1967); Carl V. Harris, "Reforms in Government Control of Negroes in Birmingham, Alabama, 1890–1920," *Journal of Southern History,* XXXVIII (November, 1972), 567–600; Edward S. LaMonte, *George B. Ward: Birmingham's Urban Statesman: An Essay in Honor of Mervyn H. Sterne* (Birmingham, 1974).

Irving Beiman's "Birmingham: Steel Giant with a Glass Jaw" in Robert S. Allen, ed., *Our Fair City* (New York, 1947), 99–122, and George Ross Leighton's account of the city in his *Five Cities: The Story of Their Youth and Old Age* (New York, 1936) are heavily influenced by Birmingham's economic collapse during the Depression. John C. Henley, Jr.'s *This is Birmingham: The Story of the Founding and Growth of an American City* (Birmingham, 1960), and James F. Sulzby, Jr.'s *Birmingham Sketches, from 1871 through 1921* (Birmingham, 1945) are books written by long-time residents of the city.

The Department of Southern History of the Birmingham Public Library is the best single source for materials on the city's history, including scrapbooks of newspaper clippings concerning the mayoral administrations of David E. McKlendon (1921–25) and James M. Jones, Jr. (1925–40), and Jones's papers are available at the Alabama Department of Archives and History in Montgomery. The city commission minutes and a relatively small collection of official reports and documents are located in the offices of the City Clerk. There are no known extant copies of black newspapers during the 1920s, such as the now-defunct Birmingham *Reporter;* and no files of the Birmingham *World* (which began publication in 1931) are available prior to 1941.

A number of historical works are useful principally as primary sources, such as George M. Cruikshank's multivolume *A History of Birmingham and Its Environs: A Narrative Account of Their Historical Progress, Their People, and Their Principal Interests* (Chicago and New York, 1920), and also Mary Powell Crane, *The Life of James R. Powell and Early History of Alabama and Birmingham (1860–1930)* (New York, 1930); John R. Hornady, *The Book of Birmingham* (New York, 1921); Florence Hawkins Wood Moss, *Building Birmingham and Jefferson County* (Birmingham, 1947); and Elberta Taylor, *Birmingham Is My Home* (Birmingham, 1940).

Bessie A. Brooks's *A Half-Century of Progress in Family Welfare Work in Jefferson County* (Birmingham, 1936), and E. M. Henderson, Sr.'s "Relief in Jefferson County: A Brief Survey" (MS in Birmingham Public Library, 1934) are moderately useful on aspects of public assistance in Birmingham.

Among those contemporary materials which proved of greatest interest were: Birmingham Civic Association, *Birmingham Year Book, 1920: An Epitome of the Achievements and Resources, Civic, Commercial and Industrial, of the Birmingham Mineral District* (Birmingham, 1920); *1921 Fiftieth Anniversary Announcement* (Birmingham, 1921); *Forty Years of Birmingham and the Birmingham Trust & Savings Company, 1887–1927* (Birmingham, 1927); Ross W. Harris, "Traffic Survey on the Vehicular and Street Railway Traffic Situation of Birmingham" (Madison, Wis., 1927); Warren H. Manning, *Warren H. Manning's City Plan of Birmingham* (Birmingham, 1919); Pioneers Club, *Early Days in Birmingham* (Birmingham, 1937); and Wallace Rice, *The Pageant of Birmingham . . .* (Birmingham, 1921).

MEMPHIS. There are, fortunately, several recent scholarly works on Memphis in the early twentieth century. William D. Miller's *Memphis During the Progressive Era, 1900–1917* (Memphis, 1957) is one of the finest studies of a single southern city, and his *Mr. Crump of Memphis* (Baton Rouge, 1964), though criticized by some as too praiseworthy of its subject, remains essential to the literature on Memphis and the best extant work on the city's leading political figure. Other studies of the city include: Gerald M. Capers, "Memphis: Satrapy of a Benevolent Despot" in Robert S. Allen, ed., *Our Fair City*, 211–34; Miller, "Rural Values and Urban Progress: Memphis, 1900–1917," *Mississippi Quarterly*, XXI (Fall, 1968), 263–74; Virginia Phillips, "Rowlett Paine, Mayor of Memphis, 1920–1924," *West Tennessee Historical Society Papers*, XIII (1959), 95–116; and James H. Robinson, "A Social History of the Negro in Memphis and in Shelby County" (Ph.D. dissertation, Yale University, 1934). Shields McIlwaine's *Memphis Down in Dixie* (New York, 1948) is of limited value, and a doctoral thesis by Clayton Reynolds Robinson, "The Impact of the City on Rural Immigrants to Memphis, 1880–1940" (Ph.D. dissertation, University of Minnesota, 1967), is a disappointing work which lacks focus, authority, precise terminology, and a clear conclusion.

The Memphis Public Library's Memphis Room is the recommended location for local historical materials, including many municipal reports and documents, chamber of commerce publications, and an excellent clippings file. The Memphis and Shelby County Archives have been recently established, though their collections are short on materials dealing with the 1920s. The two-volume *Memphis Digest: 1931* is a good source of information on municipal government, and the Board of Commissioners Minute Books are available at the City Hall.

Contemporary sources include Harland Bartholomew, *A Comprehensive City Plan: Memphis, Tennessee* (Memphis, 1924); Andrew A. Bruce and Thomas S. Fitzgerald, "A Study of Crime in the City of Memphis, Tennessee," *Journal of the American Institute of Criminal Law and Criminology*, XIX (August, 1928), 3–124; Boyce House, "Memphis Memories of 50 Years Ago," *West Tennessee Historical Society Papers*, XIV (1960), 103–12; The Inter Racial League, Memphis and Shelby County Division, *The Inter Racial Blue Book* (Memphis, 1926); Memphis Chamber of Commerce, "Memphis Industrial Survey" (Typescript in Memphis Public Library, 1929); *Special Meeting of the Board of Commissioners of the City of Memphis, December 9, 1926, in Commemoration of Hundredth Anniversary of the Incorporation of the City* (Memphis, 1926); and Annah Robinson Watson, *The Blossoming of the Century Plant: Memphis Centennial Celebration, 1819–1919* (Memphis, 1919).

NASHVILLE. Secondary works on this important central southern city are largely antiquarian and unanalytical and therefore of limited use to the professional historian, though they contain interesting detail. A recent volume edited by William Waller, *Nashville in the 1890s* (Nashville, 1970), fits this description, as do Jesse Clifton Burt's *Nashville: Its Life and Times* (Nashville, 1959); Alfred Leland Crabb's *Nashville: Personality of a City* (Indianapolis, 1960); and William Henry McRaven's *Nashville:*

Athens of the South (Chapel Hill, 1949). Contemporary historical accounts include: William E. Beard, *Nashville: The Home of History Makers* (Nashville, 1929); William E. Beard, *Red Letter Days in Nashville* (Nashville, 1925); and Maude Weidner, *Nashville Then and Now, 1780–1930* (Nashville, 1930).

Historians of Nashville are fortunate, however, to have several serious examinations of the city's population and urban problems written during the period: Harlan Welch Gilmore, *Racial Disorganization in a Southern City* (Nashville, 1931); J. Paul McConnell, "Population Problems in Nashville, Tennessee, Based on United States Census Reports for 1920 and 1930 and other related local data" (unpublished manuscript, Y.M.C.A. Graduate School, Nashville, 1933), a copy of which is available in the Tennessee State Library and Archives; and W. D. Weatherford, *A Survey of the Negro Boy in Nashville, Tennessee* (New York, 1932).

The Nashville Public Library maintains a special collection on local history, containing the reports of city departments for most of the years between 1880 and 1912, reports of the Board of Education through the 1920s, and various chamber of commerce publications. The Metropolitan Clerk's Office contains minutes of the City Commission (1920–21) and City Council (1921 and after), as well as municipal resolutions, ordinances, charters, and codes for the period. There are also useful materials in the Tennessee State Library and Archives and at Vanderbilt University.

A variety of contemporary sources are also of interest: General Outdoor Advertising Company, *Nashville: Metropolis of Central Tennessee* (Nashville, 1930), and Nashville Chamber of Commerce, "Statistical Record: Nashville, Tennessee, December 31, 1930" (Typescript in the Nashville Public Library). Edwin Mims, a professor at Vanderbilt, included some observations on the city in his *Adventurous America: A Study of Contemporary Life and Thought* (New York, 1929).

NEW ORLEANS. For the South's largest city during the late nineteenth and early twentieth centuries, New Orleans is notably lacking in general, scholarly historical accounts which cover the 1920s. The late nineteenth century period is covered fairly well by Joy J. Jackson's *New Orleans and the Gilded Age: Politics and Urban Progress, 1880–1896* (Baton Rouge, 1969), and by Dale A. Somers' very good book, *The Rise of Sports in New Orleans, 1850–1900* (Baton Rouge, 1972). Harlan W. Gilmore's essay, "The Old New Orleans and the New: A Case for Ecology," *American Sociological Review*, IX (August, 1944), 385–94, is an interesting analysis of urban growth patterns in the Crescent City, and George M. McReynold's *Machine Politics in New Orleans, 1897–1926* (New York, 1936) sets the backdrop for the city's politics in the 1920s. A more flamboyant treatment is Hermann B. Deutsch, "New Orleans Politics—The Greatest Free Show on Earth" in Hodding Carter *et al.*, eds., *The Past as Prelude: New Orleans, 1718–1968* (New Orleans, 1968). Recent Crescent City politics are examined in Edward F. Haas, *DeLesseps S. Morrison and the Image of Reform: New Orleans Politics, 1946–1961* (Baton Rouge, 1974).

New Orleans has, however, produced more than its share of contemporary accounts, historical and otherwise, that are particularly notable for their images of the city and conceptions of its past. See especially Thomas Ewing Dabney, *The Indestructible City...* (New Orleans, 1929); John Smith Kendall, *History of New Orleans* (2 vols.; Chicago and New York, 1922); Carmelite Janvier, *Whimsical Madam New Orleans* (2nd ed., New Orleans, 1928); Edward Alexander Parsons, *The Latin City: A Plea for Its Monuments* (New Orleans, 1925); and Lyle Saxon, *Fabulous New Orleans* (New York, 1928).

The New Orleans Association of Commerce was particularly active, and published a number of materials during the decade that furnish valuable (though not wholly reliable) statistics as well as conceptions of the urban community. These include *Red Book of New Orleans Commerce, 1928; Annual Report of the Association of Commerce* (New Orleans, 1929), and *A Survey of the New Orleans Industrial Zone* (New Orleans, 1929). A laudatory volume apparently published by the Choctaw Club, *Thirty-Five Years of Progress in New Orleans: "The City of the Future"* (New Orleans, 1931) is also of interest.

The City Archives, located in the New Orleans Public Library, contains an extensive collection of materials dating back to the earliest years of the city's history. Unfortunately, materials for the 1920s are comparatively sparse. Incoming correspondence of the mayor's office is currently being organized, but outgoing correspondence is available only for 1920. The reports of many city departments were apparently suspended in 1915, but the *Official Proceedings* of the Commission-Council are available after 1925 and Harland Bartholomew's extensive city plan for New Orleans has been preserved. Of particular interest is a "Report on Commercial Prostitution in the Vice and Gambling Investigation" (unpublished typescript, City Archives, 1927). Petitions, protests, and a complete set of resolutions and ordinances are available throughout the city's history, though no New Orleans black newspaper is apparently available before 1941.

CHARLESTON AND KNOXVILLE. Secondary materials on Charleston and Knoxville are especially rare. John Joseph Duffy's "Charleston Politics in the Progressive Era" (Ph.D. dissertation, University of South Carolina, 1963) is the best available study for the 1920s. Robert Molloy's *Charleston: A Gracious Heritage* (New York, 1947) and Herbert Ravenel Sass's *Charleston Grows: An Economic, Social and Cultural Portrait of an Old Community in the New South* (Charleston, 1949) are of limited value. Essays by William Watts Ball, *The Editor and the Republic: Papers and Addresses of Williams Watts Ball,* edited by Anthony Harrigan (Chapel Hill, 1954), and *The State That Forgot: South Carolina's Surrender to Democracy* (Indianapolis, 1932), are invariably articulate, and contain comments on the city and urban life by the editor of the *News and Courier.* Harriette Kershaw Leiding's *Charleston: Historic and Romantic* (Philadelphia, 1931) captures some contemporary views of the Palmetto City. The annual *Year Books* published by the city are available throughout the 1920s and provide both statistics and brief reports of various municipal officials and departments. For the purposes of this study, Betsey Beeler Creekmore's *Knoxville* (2nd ed.; Knoxville, 1967) was examined, though its genteel antiquarianism was far less valuable than the chapter on Knoxville in Kenneth T. Jackson, *The Ku Klux Klan in the City, 1915–1930.*

Index